Gennaro's
PASSIONE

Gennaro's
PASSIONE

THE CLASSIC ITALIAN COOKERY BOOK

Gennaro Contaldo

PAVILION

Contents

introduzione

introduction

I enjoyed the sort of unrestricted, free-range childhood that few children today can even dream of. The mountains were my back garden. The warm, turquoise sea was a perfect paddling pool just yards away from the house where I was born. The tiny village of Minori on the beautiful Amalfi Coast of southern Italy was my heaven.

School didn't feature much in my life. I played truant constantly, and my days were spent outdoors, fishing with the local fishermen, hunting with my father, gathering herbs from the mountains for my mother and exploring the countryside. It was the perfect apprenticeship for a chef, and I was already becoming passionate about food.

As soon as I could talk, my large family and our community of neighbours taught me to love and understand the food we ate. Cooking and eating were pleasures entwined in every thread of local life. Good food was central to every family and community occasion.

The excitement I felt as a child, discovering the possibilities of taste and texture and the sheer pleasure of mealtimes, has never faded. My father, Francesco, was the first to inspire me. He was a linen dealer by trade, but was also a great cook. Unusually for an Italian man, he took on the role of main cook in the family. He had a gift for combing flavours and could create an amazing dish from practically nothing. From my father, I learned the importance of using the best and freshest ingredients. He knew which farms had the finest produce and where to catch the best fish, and he taught me to hunt for game.

On Sundays he was in his element. It was a feast day for every family, and he made ours extra special. When the church bell struck midday, all the children knew it was time to run home. I would drop whatever I was doing and hurry through the village to my grandfather's house. What a way to work up an appetite! Glorious cooking smells wafted from every house on the way, and I could detect what each family was going to be eating that day. By the time I reached home, my mouth would be watering.

There were always at least 25 people around my grandfather's big table – aunts, uncles and cousins, as well as my four sisters, our parents and me. The dogs and cats waited under the table for us to throw scraps, which flew more generously as the wine flowed freely. The huge kitchen would be filled with the wonderful aroma of smoke from the wood-burning oven. My father was always at the centre, holding court and, more often than not, arguing with my grandad about the right combination of ingredients – a matter they both took very seriously.

My father was also serious about wanting me to attend school. It wasn't enough that I shared his passion for food; he wanted me to have an education, too. But I angered him by repeatedly playing truant. There seemed to be so many better things to do than go to school. I liked to go down to the sea armed with a hook and spend the day fishing and swimming. On cooler days, I would set off for the mountains to wander through the forests and talk to the farmers.

My mother, Eufemia, didn't mind my playing truant. In fact, she positively encouraged it. She knew she couldn't make me go to school, so she put my time to good use. She sent me to collect salt from the rocks by the sea, and herbs and mushrooms from the mountains. And she loved it when I went down to the sea and brought home fish. As an ex-dancer, she was a natural performer, and quite a character. Many village people believed she was a white witch. They turned to her for advice with their problems and swore by her herbal remedies. Fortune-telling was another of her talents. She was respected but people were also rather afraid of her powers.

I adored her. Vivacious and exuberant, always great fun to be with, she was a wonderful mother, and I think she understood me very well. She let me have my freedom but all the while she was teaching me about wild herbs and plants as I gathered them for her remedies. We were very close, and I feel proud that people often say I am like her.

When I was eleven, my father decided on a radical solution to my lack of interest in school. One morning, without warning, he dropped me off at his friend's new restaurant to work in the kitchen. I worked from seven in the morning until eleven at night all through the summer. Looking back, it was child slavery. It might have been intended to send me scuttling back to the classroom but I loved it. Fascinated by every detail, I was prepared to do anything. Although the chef was strict, he taught me a great deal about food. Much to my family's irritation, I began to think I was an authority and started criticising the way they cooked at home.

Living in a small fishing village, you can't help but be aware of nature and the seasons changing around you. You can watch the weather transform in the distance over the sea. You can smell the changes in the earth and sea with each new season. I love the different seasons. The sense of anticipation as you wait for the cherries to ripen on the trees, for instance. You think you can remember the taste but when you actually eat them after an eight-month wait, the flavour is sensational. Today it feels as if there are no seasons. You can buy any food you want at any time of year. But it all tastes the same. I can't believe it when I go into a supermarket at Christmas and find cherries there. Real cherries are ready in April, May and June. To me, there is no such thing as a cherry at Christmas.

September has always been my favourite month. The smell of autumn is fantastic. With the first drop of rain, the scent of the dry earth, leaves and herbs come alive. The wind is fresher and the sea is rougher and colder. In Minori, all the tourists would disappear and the village became mine once again. I would watch the swallows, which had been with us all summer, forming groups high in the sky, ready to emigrate for the winter. The bats and lizards gradually disappeared and the fishermen brought home a different sort of catch.

Officially, it was time for me to go back to school. My teacher paid personal visits to encourage it, but to no avail. I stopped going down to the sea every day but I started going up to the mountains. The game season was beginning. The fruit was ripe on the trees, wild berries were appearing on the bushes and there was an abundance of mushrooms. Autumn is the time for finding and preserving food to enjoy in the cold winter months. The mountain farmers were curious to know why I was always wandering around on my own. But they were hospitable and kind. I wanted to watch how they lived, what they cooked and ate, and how they preserved food. I was learning all the time.

The village priests knew all about food, too. They used to eat with all the families in their flock but some households – noticeably the ones with good wine to offer – were visited more frequently than others. They would often move on to enjoy pudding with a different family, this time choosing one renowned for its baking. I was a favourite of Padre Mateo, a very tall priest who looked after the church. He loved children, and used to tell us stories and give us sweets and leftover communion bread. In return, we would do the work around the church for him. He always called on me to carry the cross at the benediction when someone in the village had died. It was a privilege, but I hated the job. I didn't like being in a room with a dead person. It was only made bearable because the grieving families tipped us generously and offered us lots of good food.

I came to England in 1969 at the age of 20. It sounded so beautiful. Every young man I knew wanted to go there. England was cool – it had the Beatles – and I had always been fascinated by damp weather. Perfect. The reality, though, was not the glamorous life I had dreamed of. I found myself working as a kitchen porter at Putney General Hospital. It was the only way I could get a work permit. I was appalled by the terrible meals produced there. The kitchen had beautiful equipment and many varieties of fresh meat and vegetables were delivered. But once the food had been cooked, the result was disgusting. They cooked a dish they called 'Italian'. I had never heard of it and I certainly couldn't eat it. The pasta was cooked days in advance and then reheated. Vegetables were boiled to within an inch of their lives.

Eventually, the chef grew tired of my constant complaints and told me I could do breakfast – 400 boiled eggs and toast. With my poor grasp of English, I set out and, instead of boiling, I poached 400 eggs. No mean feat, I was exhausted, but I think the chef was impressed. After that, I was always allowed to help and, if there was a party on, the hospital would ask me to cook.

By day I was a porter at the hospital but by night I worked as a chef in Prego, an Italian restaurant in Soho. It was one of the best Italian restaurants of its day. The head chef was Antonio Ruocco, a very talented chef from the same part of Italy as me. I learned a lot from him before moving on to work in two other London restaurants: a private club for City bankers, under a French chef, and Meridiana in Chelsea, where I was trained by Angelo Cavaliere. When I was just 22, I was appointed head chef at the Talbot Inn, a restaurant in the Midlands. From the Midlands, I moved to Scotland, where I trained in English cuisine – and also learned the Scottish way to cook. I loved the Highlands, and went hunting and fishing at every opportunity, until I finally decided to return to London. This time I worked in a fashionable spot in St John's Wood for a couple of years. But at that time, Italian food was still considered a bit of a joke in England. The only Italian foods people knew were spaghetti bolognese and ice cream … and that upset me.

I decided to go back to Italy to learn as much as I could about the food of my childhood. I travelled all over Italy for a year, cooking as I went and learning all the time from the finest Italian chefs – famous ones in the big cities and unknown masters in the villages. It cemented my passion for cooking and reinforced my belief in the value of regional and seasonal foods.

I brought my rekindled passion for Italian food back to England and was employed in many Italian restaurants, culminating in Antonio Carluccio's, where I found myself cooking for the great and good, from royalty to football stars.

In 1999, together with my partner Liz, I opened up my own restaurant, passione, on London's Charlotte Street. We called it 'passione' because of my passion for creating beautiful food. It was a small, simple space with a small, uncomplicated menu, I baked fresh bread and focaccia each morning, made my own pasta, homemade preserves and cooked dishes with wild produce that we picked ourselves. The food was fresh, seasonal and I put my all into achieving perfection. The restaurant went from strength to strength and, after just a few years, won Best Italian Restaurant in London – one of my proudest moments.

Since then, I have been lucky to write cookbooks and appear on TV cookery shows, including my own series, filmed in Italy. All the while, I try to bring out the best of my homeland and, through the wonders of social media, I enjoy sharing my knowledge of Italian food and recipes with the world, bringing a taste of Italy to their homes.

For this, I thank my mother, my father, aunts, sisters and family friends who helped shape the foundations of my foodie life. At the time, it was normal to talk about food and where it came from and how to cook it – little did I know these mundane topics of conversation would become my life and career.

Whenever I return to Italy, I like to check out the local food. I visit markets for the freshest seasonal produce. I like to visit the family-run trattorie – the ones without a written menu are best! When I go to my home village, I visit my sister, who, at nearly 80 still enjoys cooking for the family on Sunday and when I'm there she cooks all my favourites. I love visiting the fishmonger, the butcher and the greengrocer and can feel my father's presence guiding me to the best choices. When I cook, I can feel my mother's presence so strongly that she might be standing beside me, watching.

I hope this book will bring you some of the joy of my childhood and teenage years. Many of the recipes and techniques I learned all those years ago are still my favourites and you will find them here. Happy reading, happy cooking and *Buon Appetito*, Gennaro. xx

ingredienti essenziali
essential ingredients

Anchovies
Preserved in either oil or salt, anchovies are a must in my store cupboard. I use them in many recipes – a couple of fillets gently 'dissolved' in olive oil before adding other ingredients enhances the flavour without giving an unpleasant fishy taste. Salted anchovies need washing under cold running water. The ones in olive oil need no preparation.

Chillies
I always keep a few fresh red chillies in the fridge, as well as a bunch of dried chillies hanging up in the kitchen. When I run out of fresh chillies I rely on the dried supply. Dried chillies are more concentrated, which means they taste hotter, so use them with caution.

Dried pasta
I keep at least one type of short dried pasta, such as penne, fusilli or farfalle, one type of long pasta, such as spaghetti or tagliatelle, and a small pasta shape for soups. This means I can prepare different dishes to suit a particular shape.

Dried porcini mushrooms
You can find dried porcini almost everywhere these days. I generally keep a packet in the cupboard to enhance my mushroom dishes, especially out of season, when I crave that 'wild forest fungi' taste. Before use, soak the mushrooms in warm water for 30 minutes and then drain.

Vegetables
I like to have onions, celery, a few carrots and some leeks in store. They form the basis of so many sauces and other dishes that they are known in Italy as *i sapori* – the flavours. They should be finely chopped and sweated gently in a little olive oil at the start of cooking a dish.

Garlic
I couldn't live without my beloved garlic! Look for bulbs with a pinkish-purple tinge to them, as this means they are very fresh. When garlic is fresh, the smell is strong but the flavour less intense. When it is dry, it tastes more pungent. Store garlic in an airtight container at room temperature.

When cooking, I like to crush the cloves roughly but leave them whole, sweat them gently in oil to infuse it, then remove them. I also like to slice the cloves very finely lengthways so they add just a subtle flavour to a dish. Be careful not to burn garlic, or it will taste bitter.

Herbs
Almost all my recipes include some fresh herbs to enhance the flavour. Supermarkets sell all sorts of herbs in packets but I suggest you buy them in pots and keep them on your windowsill, or grow them in your garden. My favourites are flat-leaf parsley, basil, rosemary, thyme, bay, mint and sage, and I always have at least one pot of each. Besides tasting delicious, they

look great in any kitchen and are easy to grow. Oregano is the only herb I keep dried in my store cupboard. Instead of chives, I often use the green part of spring onions.

Mozzarella cheese
For cooking, mozzarella cheese made from cow's milk (*fior di latte*) is fine, but be sure to buy an Italian make, packed in water. If you find *mozzarella di bufala* (mozzarella made from buffalo milk), then eat it fresh, simply served with a drizzle of good-quality extra virgin olive oil and some salt and black pepper. This is how they eat it in Campania, the home of this wonderful cheese. Or make a traditional *insalata di caprese*: roughly slice the mozzarella and arrange it on a plate with some sliced ripe tomatoes, then drizzle with extra virgin olive oil and sprinkle with salt and fresh basil leaves. Made with good ingredients, this is the king of salads and encapsulates the taste of summer and Italy.

Oils
Apart from Piedmont and Lombardy in the North, everywhere in Italy produces olive oil, so there is a wide variety available. In order for the oil to qualify as extra virgin, the production process has to meet several strict criteria – for example, the olives have to be hand-picked to avoid bruising and then taken to the mill immediately for pressing. Extra virgin olive oil is obtained from the first cold pressing of the olives.

I cannot stress the importance of investing in good-quality extra virgin olive oil. There are so many on the market these days that I suggest you spend a little time investigating which ones you prefer. My favourite is from Liguria. It is not too pungent, but light, delicate and easily digestible. I use it to dress salads, drizzle over grilled fish, meat and vegetables, and basically for any dishes in which the oil is to be eaten raw or hardly cooked.

The process for ordinary olive oil is less complicated, and although there are strict controls they are much fewer than for extra virgin. More abundant quantities are produced, so it is more economical to buy. I use olive oil from Liguria, Tuscany and Sicily. Olive oil is used for nearly all cooking purposes, as well as for marinades, deep-frying and preserving food.

Olives

Look for whole, firm olives and always buy unpitted ones. It may take a little time to remove the stones but they taste much better as they have been tampered with less. My favourite are Taggiasca olives – small, brownish ones from Liguria. I never buy flavoured olives, preferring to flavour them myself with some garlic, chilli and oregano, or pieces of lemon and orange.

Parmesan cheese

This is a cow's milk cheese from Emilia Romagna. I always keep a good hunk of Parmigiano Reggiano (the name for authentic Parmesan cheese) stored in the fridge wrapped in foil or clingfilm and then grate it as necessary for cooking purposes. Parmesan is also delicious to nibble as a snack when you are feeling peckish, or can be served as part of a cheese selection (see page 203).

Salt

I keep three varieties of salt in my store cupboard: fine sea salt for seasoning dishes, coarse sea salt for preserving food, and Maldon salt for topping focaccia.

Stock

When I don't have time to make my own stock, I use powder, of which I keep at least one vegetable and one meat variety in store. I find the powdered variety more versatile. It also dissolves much quicker in boiling water. I like the Swiss Marigold brand.

Vinegars

I use white and red wine vinegar as well as cider and balsamic vinegar. I usually make my own red wine vinegar from leftover bottles of wine. I pour all the leftovers into a large glass container, place a couple of bits of dried pasta in it, which speeds up the process, and leave it opened for about 20 days, shaking it gently each day. After this time, it should turn into vinegar – if not, leave it for longer. I then transfer the vinegar into smaller glass containers or bottles with corks and use it like any other wine vinegar. I find my home-made vinegar much stronger than the bought variety, and delicious on salads.

Balsamic vinegar is produced in Modena, in the Emilia Romagna region. Made from the must of local Trebbiano and Lambrusco grapes, it is cooked at high temperatures until it turns brown and syrupy, then transferred to wooden barrels and left to mature for anything from five to 50 years. This is known as *aceto balsamico tradizionale* and commands very high prices; the older it is, the more expensive it will be. You can buy a cheaper variety of inferior quality, which is matured for only a year and is known as *aceto balsamico di Modena*. This type will do for marinades, when you need a large amount. I suggest investing a little money and going for a five-year-old (or older, if you can afford it) *tradizionale*, to use sparingly in salad dressings, drizzled over boiled meats and poultry, and even over fresh strawberries. You will find that your bottle of balsamic vinegar lasts quite a while, as you need only a few drops at a time.

zuppe

soup

We make very fine soup in Italy. I remember having soup as a child and being able to pinpoint every single ingredient used. It tasted nothing like the bland liquid you find in a tin these days.

Every member of my family had a favourite soup. My uncle, the baker, who shared my passion for chestnuts, invented a chestnut soup. It was made from sun-dried chestnuts simmered in water with a single clove of garlic, olive oil, rosemary and lemon. Amazingly simple, yet so tasty.

My sister, Phelomena, ate soup because she believed it would help her keep her figure. She was fervent in her soup making, and was rewarded with a remarkable balance of flavours that I haven't tasted since. She made the most beautiful vegetable soup.

My mother loved soup because it was a good way of using up leftovers: cheese that was too hard to grate, scraps of meat and vegetables, even pasta. Despite this, her soups always tasted magnificent. My father liked to make game soup, using up all his hunting bounty.

We had soup all year round, including cold tomato soup in the hottest summer months. Over-ripe tomatoes were passed through a gadget to remove their skins, then oil, basil, lemon and cold vegetable stock were added to the pulp. The taste was phenomenal.

brodo di pollo
chicken broth

Ask your butcher for a boiling chicken, if he has one. If not, use a roasting chicken. The flavour of home-made chicken broth is wonderful, and it is very simple to make: just put everything in a pan and forget about it for an hour and a half. To make it into a soup, either add some pasta for a typical light Italian *brodino* or, for a more substantial soup, add shredded chicken, chopped vegetables and pasta.

You can use the broth as stock in other soups, risotto, etc. The chicken can be eaten hot or cold as a main course, together with the vegetables, livened up with a little Salsa Verde (see page 74). The chicken is also delicious served cold, drizzled with a little extra virgin olive oil and balsamic vinegar.

serves 6–8
1.75kg/4lb chicken
4 carrots, cut in half lengthways and
    then in half again
3 onions, peeled but left whole
6 celery stalks, including lots of leaves,
    squashed and roughly chopped
6 cherry tomatoes, squashed
a bunch of parsley stalks,
    roughly chopped
4 litres/7 pints water
salt

Place all the ingredients in a large saucepan and bring just to the boil. Reduce the heat, cover with a lid and simmer very gently for 1½ hours.

Remove the chicken and vegetables from the pan and strain the liquid through a fine sieve to give a clear broth. Alternatively, if you prefer, you can leave the little bits of vegetables and herbs floating in the broth. The broth will keep in the fridge for 5 days.

Variation To make an Italian *brodino*, place some of the liquid in a smaller saucepan and bring to the boil, then add small dried pasta or small meat-filled agnolotti (see page 34). Reduce the heat slightly and simmer until the pasta is *al dente*. Serve immediately in individual soup bowls with some freshly grated Parmesan.

zuppa di piselli e menta fresca
pea and fresh mint soup

As soon as spring arrived, we loved to make dishes with the season's new produce, such as fresh peas and herbs. Although the days were hotter, the evenings were still cool, so to keep warm but still have that fresh spring flavour, we would often make a soup such as this one. Try to use fresh peas. It might be hard work to shell such a large quantity but it is well worth it in the end. If necessary you can use frozen peas, or a combination of both.

serves 4–6
2 tbsp extra virgin olive oil
2 shallots, finely sliced
50g/2oz pancetta, finely diced
½ celery stalk, finely chopped
500g/1lb 2oz fresh peas (shelled weight)
1 small iceberg lettuce, roughly chopped
1 large potato, peeled and cut into cubes
1 litre/1¾ pints vegetable stock
15 fresh mint leaves, finely chopped,
    plus a few sprigs of mint to serve
extra virgin olive oil, for drizzling
salt and freshly ground black pepper
for the crostini (optional):
a knob of butter
8–12 small slices of bread

Heat the olive oil in a saucepan, add the shallots, pancetta and celery and sweat gently for a few minutes. Add the peas and stir well, then add the lettuce, potato and stock. Stir well and season with salt and pepper (be careful when adding the salt, as pancetta is salty). Cover with a lid and simmer gently for 15 minutes, or until the peas are tender.

Remove from the heat and leave to cool slightly. Then pour into a blender or food processor and purée until smooth (in batches if necessary). Return the soup to the pan, add the chopped mint and heat through. Check the seasoning and adjust if necessary.

Meanwhile, make the crostini. Melt the butter in a frying pan, add the bread slices and fry until golden brown on each side.

Serve the soup drizzled with a little extra virgin olive oil, garnished with a sprig of mint and accompanied by the crostini.

zuppa di verdure invernali
mixed root vegetable soup

The combination of root vegetables here makes a very tasty soup that is simple and economical to prepare and a soothing winter warmer. Because of its cooler climate, root vegetables are more common in the north of Italy – especially *scorzonera* (or black salsify). This is a strange-looking vegetable, long and thin with a black skin, which needs to be washed well and peeled. The interior is white and has a very pleasant, nutty flavour. If you can't find scorzonera, replace it with salsify or extra quantities of any of the other root vegetables used. Parsnip is not an Italian vegetable, but I have included it in this recipe because it is readily available and I love the taste.

serves 6–8
6 tbsp olive oil
2 garlic cloves, squashed (optional)
1 small onion, roughly chopped
1 leek, roughly chopped
2 celery stalks, roughly chopped
3 scorzonera (or salsify),
   peeled and roughly chopped
1 large parsnip, roughly chopped
1 small celeriac, roughly chopped
1 large potato, roughly chopped
1 large carrot, roughly chopped
2 litres/3½ pints vegetable stock
salt and freshly ground black pepper
croûtons and/or chopped fresh chives,
   to serve (optional)

Heat the olive oil in a large saucepan, add the garlic, if using, and sweat for 1 minute. Add the onion, leek and celery and stir well. Sweat for a few minutes, then add all the root vegetables and cook, stirring well, for a couple of minutes. Pour in the stock and bring to the boil, then reduce the heat, cover and simmer gently for 30 minutes, until the vegetables are tender.

Remove from the heat, cool slightly and then pour into a blender or food processor and purée until smooth (do this in batches if necessary). Return the soup to the saucepan and heat through. Check the seasoning and adjust if necessary. Serve immediately, garnished with some croûtons and/or chopped chives, if desired.

Nearly all our soups contained a base of pulses, such as chickpeas or beans as these ingredients could be very cheaply bought from the local grocer's. I remember sacks full of dried beans lined up against the wall of the shop. But these weren't good enough for my mother. She didn't trust their quality because she didn't know where they came from. Instead, we bought fresh beans from local farmers in the summer and dried them in the sun. They were so delicious, I always thought they tasted as if the sun had kissed them. My mother used to store them in jars ready for winter use. I really looked forward to autumn and winter, just so I could open the jars and taste the beans again.

Everyone used pulses. In the alleyways of my village, you would invariably see people who looked as if they were panning for gold. In fact, they were sifting through dried beans to pick out any stones that had got mixed up with them in the drying process. You always knew they were going to have soup the next day.

When we wanted to use the dried beans, my mother would soak them overnight. The next day, she added fresh vegetables and maybe some dried meat and cooked them slowly in plenty of water. The taste was out of this world. Bean soup is still one of my favourites.

*Mamma at our table
in the garden*

zuppa di borlotti
fresh borlotti bean soup

If you can find fresh borlotti beans at the market or your greengrocer's in spring, buy them; they taste delicious. The pod is the same shape as a broad bean but the colour is a pretty cream and mottled reddish purple.

If you can't get fresh borlotti, soak the dried variety in water overnight, then drain them and follow the recipe below. Bear in mind you will need to double the cooking time.

serves 4–6

100 ml/3½fl oz/7 tbsp olive oil
1 onion, finely chopped
1 carrot, finely chopped
1 celery stalk, finely chopped
¼ leek, finely chopped
400g/14oz fresh borlotti beans
   (shelled weight)
   or 130g/4½oz dried
a handful of parsley stalks,
   finely chopped
3 ripe cherry tomatoes, quartered
1 garlic clove, crushed
1.5 litres/2½ pints vegetable stock
a handful of celery leaves
salt and freshly ground black pepper
crostini (see page 155) and extra virgin
   olive oil, to serve (optional)

Heat the olive oil in a large saucepan, add the onion, carrot, celery and leek and sweat until softened. Stir in the borlotti beans and parsley stalks, then add the tomatoes, garlic and stock and bring to the boil. Reduce the heat, cover the pan and simmer for 50 minutes, until the beans are tender.

Stir in the celery leaves, then taste and adjust the seasoning. Serve with crostini and a drizzle of extra virgin olive oil, if desired.

zuppa di lenticchie
lentil soup

When I was growing up, we had a wonderful array of pulses to choose from and lentils were a family favourite. We would often make this soup during autumn and winter – it was a tasty way of keeping warm as well as being a good source of protein. Served with some good bread, it is extremely filling and satisfying.

Lentils were sold from huge sacks and the shopkeeper would scoop out the amount you required. Later, at home, we had to sift through them as there were many small stones and impurities. I still sift through my lentils today (old habits die hard), although there is no need, as all shop-bought pulses are now carefully controlled.

If you keep this soup in the fridge for a day or two it will thicken. Either serve it as a stew or thin it down with a little stock.

serves 4

4 tbsp extra-virgin olive oil, plus a little
   extra to serve
1 small red onion, finely chopped
1 carrot, finely chopped
1 celery stalk, finely chopped
¼ leek, finely chopped
4 cherry tomatoes, quartered
   and squashed
1 garlic clove, crushed
200g/7oz green or brown lentils
1 medium-sized potato, peeled and cut
   into cubes
1 litre/1¾ pints vegetable stock
a few celery leaves, finely chopped,
   to serve
salt and freshly ground black pepper

Heat the olive oil in a large saucepan and sweat the onion until softened. Then add the carrot, celery and leek and cook, stirring, for 1 minute. Add the tomatoes and garlic, followed by the lentils and potato. Pour in the stock and bring to the boil. Reduce the heat, cover and simmer gently for 35 minutes, until the lentils are tender. Taste and adjust the seasoning if necessary. Serve garnished with the celery leaves and a drizzle of extra virgin olive oil.

stracciatella al pomodoro
tomato soup with whisked egg whites

Stracciatella is usually a vegetable or chicken broth with a couple of eggs beaten in just before serving to make it more nourishing. In this recipe I have combined a simple tomato soup with whisked egg whites. Make sure you use good ripe tomatoes. To give it colour and body, I have also included some tomato passata. If you prefer not to use the egg whites, you can omit them and you will still have a delicious tomato soup.

serves 4–6

600g/1lb 5oz ripe tomatoes
250g/9oz tomato passata
6 tbsp extra virgin olive oil
750ml/1¼ pints vegetable stock
a handful of fresh basil, plus a few leaves
 to garnish
2 garlic cloves, finely chopped
4 egg whites
1 tbsp fresh breadcrumbs
4 tbsp freshly grated Parmesan cheese
salt and freshly ground black pepper

Skin the tomatoes (see page 139), then cut them into quarters and remove the seeds. Strain the seeds and pulp through a fine sieve over a saucepan to extract as much juice as possible. Add the tomato quarters to the juice in the pan, together with the tomato passata, olive oil, stock, basil and garlic. Season with pepper and bring to the boil, then reduce the heat and simmer for 10 minutes.

Remove from the heat, allow to cool slightly and then pour into a blender or food processor. Purée until smooth (in batches if necessary), then return the soup to the pan, check the seasoning and adjust if necessary. Keep warm.

Whisk the egg whites until stiff, then fold in the breadcrumbs and Parmesan. Fold this mixture into the tomato soup and heat through for about 5 minutes, stirring all the time. Serve immediately, garnished with a few basil leaves.

pasta

pasta

Pasta is an essential part of all Italian families' diets and mine was no exception. My mother made fresh eggless pasta at least once a week, usually on a Sunday. The process was a magical and exact performance from beginning to end. First, I would be sent up to the mountains to collect the jars of spring water needed for making the best pasta. I would get into such trouble if I used one of the jars to bring down the newts or frogs I caught up there. Spring water creates the most wonderful, tasty, shiny pasta with the right firm texture.

The area around us was so mountainous that it was useless for growing wheat, so my father would bring back great sacks of the best wheat from his travels around the region. Much to my mother's frustration, he would insist on grinding it himself. The first press was done with a pestle and mortar, then the rough mixture was put between two massive grinding stones, which he turned slowly. When I was good, my father would let me have a go. It was all very primitive but I loved it; I thought it was real man's work. My mother, on the other hand, hated it. It would drive her crazy. Bits would fly off from the machine and make the most terrible mess, and in any case the resulting flour was too coarse to make good pasta. She went along with it, though, for tradition and to keep my father happy. But when he wasn't looking, she would send me off to the village mill with a sack of wheat to have it ground to the perfect texture – neither too fine nor too coarse. It was a small, incredibly noisy place. They would take your sack of wheat and grind it for you for virtually no charge.

Making pasta was second nature to my mother. She knew instinctively how much water to add, how thick the flour and semolina mixture should be and how it should be kneaded. She was the keeper of the secret of pasta in my family. She always made the pasta in the evening. It was a relaxing family time and we would gather around the big table and chat while she worked away. She used a rolling pin to roll out the dough and she stuck to three different shapes. The one I most liked watching her make was fusilli.

I collected the long, thick canes she needed to shape it (I found these were also good for making kites, although my mother was never too happy when I poached her pasta-making equipment for kite making!). She would roll the dough out into a long sausage shape, then roll this around the stick – it looked such fun to do. She would also make maccheroni and orecchiette using these sticks. On Sundays we had fusilli, but not the short type, a long shape which was handmade. We ate it with a ragu (see page 100), which would take about two hours to cook.

I love dried pasta as well as fresh, and there are some recipes for which only dried pasta will do. It supplies a good, *al dente* texture that is impossible to achieve with fresh pasta. When buying dried pasta, always choose one from a traditional Italian manufacturer.

An unofficial but considerable pasta trade went on between families in my village. Certain individuals became renowned for their pasta-making abilities and their services were always in demand. When my mother was too busy to make her own pasta, rather than go to the shop to buy some I was sent around the village to barter for it. It has to be said that this was a job I enjoyed. One of the families that made great pasta also had a number of very pretty daughters. Needless to say, I was a very willing errand boy to this house.

My family used to turn up their noses at commercially made pasta but I was strangely drawn to the village's pasta factory. I was fascinated by the massive machines and the dusty bags of flour that were scattered around the floor. The pasta made there seemed to taste better than other commercial pasta. I think it was the combination of fresh sea air, sunshine, spring water and the care put into making it. The factory was right on the sea front, with big doors that opened out to overlook the beach. I used to hover in the entrance and watch the

teams of men and women at work. Despite the machines, it was still a manual job. The pasta was pushed through the machines by hand and people waited underneath them to catch the pasta as it came out.

After shaping, the pasta was strung across long canes and hung from the ceiling to dry. It was amazing to see so much pasta in one place, all hanging down from the ceiling with people working below. Once it had dried, it was put outside in the sun to harden off. It's unbelievable now to think that the pasta was put on an area outside the factory that was really just part of the pavement, but people accepted it as part of life then.

Left: Pasta hung out to dry in the streets outside the factory. Below: Making filled pasta with my sister Adriana.

pasta fresca
basic pasta dough

Making fresh pasta is not as difficult as it may seem. I make it twice a day at the restaurant, in the morning for lunch and in the afternoon for dinner. I am well equipped there with electric pasta machines and large work surfaces, so it is obviously much easier to make large quantities twice a day. At home I still enjoy making pasta and I do it the traditional way, by hand, then use a small Imperia pasta machine to roll it out. I recommend you purchase one of these before making your own pasta, as it will make life much easier. They are not very expensive and are widely available these days – although when I first came to England, I had to bring my own from Italy. A small pasta machine is compact enough for the tiniest of kitchens and easy to store when not in use.

Makes about 300g/11oz
150g/5oz Italian '00' pasta flour
50g/2oz semolina
2 medium eggs

Mix the flour and semolina together on a clean work surface or in a large bowl. Make a well in the centre and break in the eggs. With a fork or with your hands, gradually mix the flour with the eggs, then knead with your hands for about 5 minutes, until you get a smooth dough; it should be pliable but not sticky. Shape the dough into a ball, wrap in clingfilm and leave for about 30 minutes or until you are ready to use.

Divide the pasta dough into 4 portions and put each one through your pasta machine, starting at the highest setting. As the pasta gets thinner, turn down the settings until you get to number 1 and the dough is almost wafer thin.

Place the sheet of pasta on a lightly floured work surface and use according to your recipe.

Eggless fresh pasta This is invaluable for vegans or anyone who cannot eat eggs. Simply substitute 120ml/4fl oz warm (not boiling) water for the eggs and make as above.

agnolotti ripieni di carne macinata
agnolotti filled with meat

In Italy this is traditionally made from leftover roast meat mixed with chopped herbs and grated Parmesan. If you want to make meat ravioli but don't have any leftover roast meat, follow this simple recipe using minced beef and pork. Serve with melted butter and fresh sage leaves, or with a tomato sauce of your choice (see pages 142–143).

serves 4
1 quantity of Basic Pasta Dough
   (see page 30)
for the filling:
3 tbsp olive oil
1 small onion, finely chopped
1 garlic clove, crushed but left whole
100g/4oz minced beef
100g/4oz minced pork
1 tbsp fresh thyme leaves
a handful of fresh parsley,
   finely chopped
4 tbsp white wine
2 tbsp freshly grated Parmesan cheese
salt and freshly ground black pepper

To make the filling, heat the olive oil in a small pan, add the onion and garlic and cook until softened. Add the meat and cook until well browned all over. Then add the thyme and parsley and season with salt and pepper. Raise the heat, pour in the wine and let it bubble until completely evaporated. Remove from the heat, discard the garlic and allow the mixture to cool a little. Place in a food processor with the Parmesan and whiz for about 30 seconds, until finely chopped. Transfer to a bowl and check the seasoning.

Divide the pasta dough into quarters and use one portion at a time, keeping the rest wrapped in clingfilm so it doesn't dry out.

Roll the pasta out in a pasta machine, or roll it out with a rolling pin on a lightly floured work surface until it is so thin you can almost see through it. Cut it into rounds with a 3cm/1¼in cutter and put a small amount of the filling on each one. Fold each circle in half to make a pasty shape and press the edges with your fingertips to seal. Press the filling down a little with your finger, roll it gently over in half and then fold back the corners (see page 32).

Bring a large saucepan of lightly salted water to the boil, drop in the agnolotti and cook for about 3 minutes, until *al dente*. Drain and serve with a sauce of your choice.

Alternative meat fillings You could use minced lamb and follow the above recipe, omitting the thyme, or use leftover roast meat with a flavouring, for example, roast lamb and mint, roast duck and chestnuts, or roast beef with thyme. Simply shred the leftover meat and chop it very finely in a food processor. Add the appropriate flavouring, plus some grated Parmesan cheese. Bind the filling ingredients together with an egg.

conchiglioni ripieni al forno
baked pasta shells filled with cheese

Baked pasta (*pasta al forno*) is very common throughout Italy and includes the popular lasagne and cannelloni. In southern Italy there is a baked pasta dish made for special occasions that is based mainly on rigatoni, with a variety of other ingredients including meatballs and boiled eggs. It is very rich, as most baked pasta dishes tend to be, but I would like to share my lighter version of *pasta al forno*, which is simply based on cheese and tomato sauce. Here I have filled large pasta shells with cheese and fresh basil. You could also fill them with leftover roast meat (see page 34), as an alternative to agnolotti (this way you don't have to make the pasta dough).

If you don't want the hassle of filling shells, you can make baked pasta with any cooked short dried pasta mixed with tomato sauce and topped with cheese. It is also a good way of using up leftover pasta – again, just mix with a little sauce and cheese and bake.

serves 4
16 conchiglioni rigati (large pasta shells)
1 quantity of Salsa di Pomodoro Leggara
  (see page 142)
3 tbsp freshly grated Parmesan cheese
1 ball of mozzarella cheese, sliced
for the filling:
150g/5oz ricotta cheese
1 ball of mozzarella cheese,
  very finely diced
2 tbsp freshly grated Parmesan cheese
16 large fresh basil leaves
salt and freshly ground black pepper

Preheat the oven to 200°C/400°F/Gas Mark 6. Cook the pasta shells in plenty of lightly salted boiling water until *al dente*. Drain well, making sure you empty the shells of water, and leave to cool.

To make the filling, mash the ricotta with a fork, stir in the diced mozzarella, Parmesan and some salt and pepper to taste and mix well. Shape the mixture into 16 balls, wrap each ball in a basil leaf and place in a cooled pasta shell.

Pour a layer of the tomato sauce over the bottom of an ovenproof dish and place the filled shells on top. Pour over the remaining tomato sauce, sprinkle over the Parmesan and top with slices of mozzarella. Cover with aluminium foil and bake for 35 minutes. After this time, remove the foil and bake, uncovered, for a further 5 minutes. Serve immediately.

ravioli ripieni di ricotta e limone con salsa di burro e menta

ravioli filled with ricotta and lemon, served with butter and mint

This recipe comes from Minori, my home village, and was given to me by Antonio, the local pasta maker. Lemon and pasta may seem a strange combination but it is actually very good, and dishes like spaghetti and lemon and black pepper are quite common. When I tried this recipe in England, I found that I had to keep adding more lemon zest and juice. The lemons in Italy are much more pungent, so less is needed. When you make the filling, taste it and, if necessary, add more lemon – the zest only, otherwise it might become mushy.

serves 4
1 quantity of Basic Pasta Dough
  (see page 30)
for the filling:
225g/8oz ricotta cheese
4 tbsp finely grated lemon zest, plus a
  little extra to garnish
2 tsp lemon juice
2 tbsp freshly grated Parmesan cheese
salt
for the sauce:
100g/4oz butter
30 fresh mint leaves, plus a few sprigs to
  garnish
4 tsp lemon juice
4 tbsp freshly grated Parmesan cheese

To make the filling, place the ricotta in a bowl and crush it with a fork, then mix in the lemon zest and juice, Parmesan and some salt to taste. With the help of 2 tablespoons, form the mixture into balls about 2cm/¾in in diameter and set aside.

Divide the pasta dough into quarters and use one portion at a time, keeping the rest wrapped in clingfilm so it doesn't dry out. Roll the pasta out in a pasta machine, or roll it out with a rolling pin on a lightly floured work surface into a paper-thin rectangle. Lay the pasta sheet on the work surface with a short edge nearest to you. Put balls of the filling in a line down the pasta sheet about three-quarters of the way in from one side, spacing them about 2.5cm/1in apart. Fold the sheet lengthways in half and press with your fingertips between the balls of filling to seal. Cut round the filling with a ravioli wheel or a sharp knife. Gather up all the trimmings, re-roll and repeat. (It's important to work quite quickly, so the pasta doesn't dry out.) When you have finished, repeat with the remaining pieces of dough.

Bring a large saucepan of lightly salted water to the boil, drop in the ravioli and cook for about 3 minutes, until *al dente*.

Meanwhile, make the sauce. Put the butter in a large frying pan with the mint leaves. Add the lemon juice and cook on a gentle heat until the butter begins to bubble.

Quickly drain the pasta, reserving a couple of tablespoons of the cooking water. Add the pasta to the frying pan, together with the reserved cooking water to help give the sauce a little more moisture. Mix in the Parmesan and serve immediately, garnishing each portion with some grated lemon zest and a sprig of mint.

Alternative potato, cheese and mint filling This filling is traditionally used in a Sardinian speciality known as *culurzones*. They are quite a complicated shape but the filling is delicious, and perfect for simple ravioli. As a sauce to accompany this pasta, I would choose either Pomodori in Bottiglie (see page 143) or simply melted butter and sage topped with freshly grated Parmesan cheese. Mix 2 large boiled and mashed potatoes with 1 egg, 50g/2oz each of provolone, Pecorino and Parmesan cheeses and a handful of finely chopped fresh mint leaves. Use to fill ravioli, following the instructions above.

spaghetti con fave, pomodorini e caprino
spaghetti with broad beans, cherry tomatoes and goat's cheese

This is a light, spring/summer dish that is extremely simple to prepare and looks lovely and colourful. Without meaning to, it has the colours of the Italian flag – green, red and white. For maximum flavour, do use fresh broad beans if possible. However, if they are out of season, you can use frozen broad beans. I use soft Italian caprino cheese, which you can find in good Italian delicatessens. Alternatively, you can use any soft, mild Welsh or French goat's cheese but avoid strong goat's cheeses, as they will overpower the delicate flavours of the other ingredients.

serves 4
300g/11oz fresh broad beans
   (shelled weight)
300g/11oz cherry tomatoes, quartered
   and deseeded
100ml/3½fl oz/7 tbsp extra virgin olive
   oil, plus a little extra to serve
2 garlic cloves, finely chopped
20 fresh basil leaves, plus a few
   extra to garnish
½ red chilli, finely chopped (optional)
300g/11oz spaghetti
100g/4oz mild goat's cheese, diced
salt and freshly ground black pepper

Blanch the broad beans in a large saucepan of lightly salted boiling water for 1 minute, drain, rinse in cold water and drain again. Slip the skins off the broad beans and set aside.

Put the tomatoes, olive oil, garlic, basil, chilli (if using) and some salt and pepper in a large bowl and mix well. Then stir in the broad beans and leave to marinate while you cook the pasta.

Bring a large pan of lightly salted water to the boil and cook the spaghetti until *al dente*. Drain and add to the tomato and broad bean mixture, together with the goat's cheese. Mix well and serve immediately, sprinkling some freshly ground black pepper, a drizzle of olive oil and a few basil leaves on top of each portion.

linguine al granchio
linguine with crab

I used to fish for crabs quite a lot as a child but the crabs found on my shore were very small, so to get a meal out of them you had to catch plenty and spend many hours cleaning them.
It was not until I came to England that I discovered the large, meaty crabs on the shores of Cromer in Norfolk.
I believe England's crabs are excellent quality and what better way to enjoy them than with pasta?

serves 4
2 medium-sized fresh crabs
   (ask your fishmonger to prepare them
   for you and reserve the shells)
350g/12½oz linguine
for the base sauce:
6 tbsp olive oil
1 large onion, finely chopped
1 small leek, finely chopped
2 carrots, finely chopped
2 garlic cloves, squashed and
   finely chopped
a handful of parsley stalks,
   finely chopped
150ml/¼ pint white wine
12 cherry tomatoes, squashed
500ml/17fl oz vegetable stock
to finish the sauce:
4 tbsp olive oil
2 garlic cloves, finely sliced lengthways
1 red chilli, finely chopped
the leaves from the parsley stalks (above)
120ml/4fl oz white wine
salt and freshly ground black pepper

To make the base sauce, heat the olive oil in a large saucepan, add the onion, leek, carrots, garlic and parsley stalks and cook gently until soft. Stir in the crab shells and sauté for a minute. Then add the wine and allow it to evaporate, then add the tomatoes and cook for a further 2 minutes. Pour in any juices from the crab meat and the stock, bring to the boil and simmer for 10 minutes. Remove from the heat, take out all the crab shells and place them in a bowl. Pour a little hot water over the shells, as if rinsing them, and then add the water only to the sauce. Place the sauce back on the heat, bring to the boil and simmer for 3 minutes. Strain through a fine sieve into a bowl, pressing down on the vegetables with a wooden spoon to obtain as much liquid from them as possible. Discard the vegetables and crab shells.

Bring a large saucepan of lightly salted water to the boil and cook the linguine until almost *al dente*.

Meanwhile, to finish the sauce, heat the olive oil in a large frying pan, add the garlic and chilli and sweat until softened. Add the parsley leaves and crab meat and season with salt and pepper. Pour in the wine and allow it to evaporate, then add the base sauce and simmer for 2 minutes. Taste and adjust the seasoning. Drain the linguine about a minute before it is done and add to the sauce. Continue to cook for 1 minute in the sauce, then serve.

One of the greatest adventures I ever had was while I was trying to catch a tuna fish. I was 15 years old and had gone out with two friends for a day's fishing. We set out to sea in a tiny boat with a box of sardines. It was a lazy, sunny day and we were all just taking it easy when, out of the blue, the thick, brown line we had hanging off the side of the boat started to pull. I took hold of it and realised the enormity of the situation. Whatever was on the other end of the line was huge. The three of us tried to pull it in, but it started dragging the boat down. It was terrifying but exciting. We fought with the fish for about three hours, until it was too exhausted to fight any more.

Together, we tried to pull the 95-kilo tuna on to the boat but it was just too big. So we finished it off and dragged it in behind the boat on a hook. I felt sad for this amazing old fish but very proud of myself. I had always wanted to catch a really big fish.

Some fishermen on a motorboat had stopped and made fun of us when we were struggling with the tuna, but I think they were just jealous of our gigantic catch. By the time we got back to shore, word had spread that we had caught an enormous fish and a big crowd had gathered on the beach to witness our return. We were heroes. My mother and father were at the front of the crowd. I jumped on to the beach, my head held high, and my mother stepped forward and gave me a clout round the head, then launched into a public tirade about how stupid I had been. She had been worried sick about me and my father just thought it was funny. Still, it was the biggest fish I'd ever caught and it made me a hero in the village. **,**

Old friends Gianni, Rino, Alfredo and Guido on the beach in Amalfi.

penne con funghi, gamberi e zafferano
penne with mushrooms, prawns and saffron

Mushrooms and prawns may seem an unusual combination but they are quite delicious together and remind me of my hunting days in the autumn. I would pick mushrooms, go fishing and take it all home where my father would make a similar pasta dish to this one. The base sauce can be prepared a day or two in advance and kept in the fridge. Don't be alarmed about using the prawn heads and shells – this is what gives the sauce so much flavour.

serves 4
200g/7oz fresh raw tiger prawns
   or other large prawns
350g/12½oz penne
for the base sauce:
100 ml/3½fl oz/7 tbsp olive oil
1 onion, roughly chopped
1 leek, roughly chopped
2 small carrots, roughly chopped
8 cherry tomatoes, halved and
   slightly squashed
120ml/4fl oz white wine
120ml/4fl oz water
to finish the sauce:
100 ml/3½fl oz/7 tbsp extra-virgin
   olive oil
2 garlic cloves, finely chopped
½ red chilli, finely chopped
100g/4oz button mushrooms,
   finely sliced
a handful of fresh parsley, roughly
   chopped
120ml/4fl oz white wine
a pinch of saffron
salt and freshly ground black pepper

Twist off the heads from the prawns and peel off the shells. Remove the black line and discard. Roughly chop the heads and shells and set aside. Slice the prawns lengthways into strips and set aside.

To make the base sauce, heat the olive oil in a large pan, add the onion, leek, carrots and tomatoes and sweat for a couple of minutes. Add the prawn heads and shells and season with salt and pepper. Pour in the wine, allow it to evaporate, then add the water. Cover the pan and simmer gently for 4–5 minutes, until the vegetables are tender, then remove from the heat and leave to cool. Put the contents of the pan into a food processor and whiz to a fairly smooth consistency. Strain into a bowl through a fine sieve, pressing the mixture with a spatula to extract as much juice as possible. You should get about 140ml/4½fl oz of fairly thick sauce.

Bring a large saucepan of lightly salted water to the boil and cook the penne until *al dente*.

Meanwhile, to finish the sauce, heat the extra virgin olive oil in a large pan, add the garlic and chilli and sweat until softened. Add the mushrooms and parsley and stir-fry for a minute. Then add the strips of prawn, season and stir-fry for another minute. Add the wine and simmer until it has reduced by half, then add the base sauce and simmer for a couple of minutes. Drain the pasta and add to the sauce, still on the heat. Stir well and cook for about 1 minute. Remove from the heat, stir in the saffron and serve immediately.

trofie con pesto, fagiolini e patate

trofie with pesto, green beans and potatoes

I came across this dish when I was in Liguria a few years ago. Trofie pasta is made with durum wheat flour and water (no eggs are used), then shaped by hand into small spirals that have pointy ends and are thicker in the middle. This type of pasta takes longer to cook than most; check the instructions on the packet but you will find it usually takes 15–20 minutes. The thicker middle bit always remains *al dente*.

Pesto also comes from Liguria, where delicate olive oil is produced and lovely sweet basil grows in abundance. You can find ready-made pesto everywhere these days but it really is worth making your own. You could use a food processor but when the sauce is made by hand with a pestle and mortar it is slightly crunchier, and you can taste all the ingredients much more. Fresh pesto keeps in the fridge for about a week.

serves 4

350g/12½oz trofie
4 small new potatoes, scrubbed and cut into quarters
20 green beans, trimmed and cut in half
freshly grated Parmesan cheese, to serve (optional)

for the pesto:

50g/2oz fresh basil
2 tbsp pine nuts
1 garlic clove
½ tsp coarse sea salt
100 ml/3½fl oz/7 tbsp olive oil (Ligurian, if you can get it)
50g/2oz freshly grated Parmesan cheese, plus extra for sprinkling
30g/1oz freshly grated Pecorino cheese

First make the pesto. Remove and discard the stalks from the basil and set the leaves aside. Place the pine nuts, garlic and salt in a mortar and grind to a paste with a pestle. Add a few basil leaves and some of the olive oil and grind and stir with the pestle. Continue like this until you have used up all the basil leaves and about half the olive oil – the sauce should become silky in consistency. Then add the remaining oil and the cheeses and mix well together.

Bring a large saucepan of lightly salted water to the boil and add the pasta, potatoes and green beans. Cook until the pasta is *al dente* and the vegetables are tender. In a large bowl, combine the pesto, drained vegetables and trofie and a couple of tablespoons of the pasta cooking water. Serve immediately with some grated Parmesan, if desired.

tagliatelle con tonno, limone e rucola

tagliatelle with tuna, lemon and rocket

This needs hardly any cooking and tastes delicious. When I was growing up in Italy, we didn't have tinned tuna but in late spring/early summer my mother would buy fresh tuna from local fishermen and preserve it in oil, so we could have it all year round. Tinned tuna in extra-virgin olive oil has the best flavour; don't buy it in brine or spring water.

serves 4

350g/12½oz tagliatelle
4 tbsp extra virgin olive oil
1 garlic clove, finely chopped
½ red chilli, finely chopped
2 x 160g/6oz tins of tuna in extra virgin
  olive oil, drained and lightly mashed
  with a fork
a handful of rocket, plus a little
  extra to serve
grated zest and juice of 1 lemon
salt and freshly ground black pepper

Bring a large saucepan of salted water to the boil and cook the pasta until *al dente*.

Meanwhile, heat the olive oil in a large frying pan, add the garlic and chilli and sweat for 1 minute. Drain the pasta, add to the pan along with the tuna and half of the rocket and toss together well.

Remove from the heat, stir in the lemon zest and juice. Serve immediately with the remaining rocket scattered over the top.

tagliolini al tartufo nero
tagliolini with black truffle

A truffle is a fungus, found underneath the ground, which can be detected only by specially trained dogs. There are three types of truffle in Italy: the very expensive white truffle from the Alba region in Piedmont (*Tuber magnatum*), the black winter truffle from Umbria (*Tuber melanosporum*), and the black summer truffle (*Tuber aestivum*), again mainly from Umbria. They are quite ugly to look at and resemble small potatoes, with a hard, black skin. For a special occasion, do splash out on a small fresh truffle and try this recipe.

I dedicate this recipe to my eldest son Michael, who appreciated the subtle but sophisticated taste of this fungus from an early age.

serves 4
400g/14oz fresh or dried tagliolini
   (or tagliatelle)
400ml/14fl oz vegetable stock
40g/1½oz black truffle, shaved on
   a small mandoline or with a very
   sharp knife
40g/1½oz/3 tbsp butter
2 tsp truffle oil
grated Parmesan cheese to serve
   (optional)

Bring a large saucepan of lightly salted water to the boil and cook the pasta until almost *al dente*.

Meanwhile, put the stock in a large frying pan with a few shavings of truffle and bring to a gentle simmer, just to infuse the stock with the truffle. Drain the pasta and add to the stock. Turn up the heat and continue to cook the pasta for 1 minute, until about three-quarters of the stock has evaporated. Stir in the butter and truffle oil and mix in about half the truffle shavings. Remove from the heat and serve immediately, with the remaining truffle shavings on top. Serve with freshly grated Parmesan, if desired.

pennette con fiori di zucchina
pennette with courgette flowers

I find courgette flowers a real treat. When I first came to England, I discovered that the flowers were destroyed here so the courgettes would grow bigger. I was distraught! I remember asking an old neighbour if he wouldn't mind giving me the flowers from his courgette plants. He looked at me suspiciously and I told him they were to decorate the kitchen. I think he would have thought I was mad if he knew I ate them. Fortunately, you can now find courgette flowers during the early summer in some good greengrocer's, or you could grow your own courgettes. Picking the flowers regularly will help the plants to grow. *Pictured on pages 48–49.*

serves 4 as a starter
100 ml/3½fl oz/7 tbsp olive oil
2 garlic cloves, crushed but left whole
2 anchovy fillets
2 small onions, finely chopped
2 small courgettes, finely
   sliced lengthways
200ml/7fl oz vegetable stock
20 courgette flowers, torn in half
20 fresh basil leaves
350g/12½oz pennette (or another type
   of short pasta)
20g/¾oz Parmesan cheese, freshly grated
extra virgin olive oil, for drizzling
salt and freshly ground black pepper

Heat the olive oil in a large pan, add the garlic and cook gently until golden. Remove the garlic from the pan and add the anchovy fillets. Stir with a wooden spoon until the anchovies have almost dissolved into the oil, then add the onions and cook gently until softened. Add the courgettes and stock. Bring to a gentle simmer and cook, stirring, over a medium heat for 2 minutes until courgettes have softened, then add courgettes flowers, basil and season with salt and pepper to taste.

Meanwhile, cook the pasta in a large saucepan of lightly salted boiling water until *al dente*, then drain. Add the pasta to the sauce, mix well and stir in the Parmesan. Serve immediately, drizzled with some extra virgin olive oil.

farfalle con piselli, pancetta e ricotta

farfalle with peas, pancetta and ricotta

This quick and simple pasta dish is very nutritious and a great family favourite. You could use other pasta shapes, such as fusilli, spirali or penne.

serves 4

350g/12½oz farfalle
3 tbsp olive oil
50g/2oz pancetta, cut into thin strips
1 small onion, finely sliced
100g/4oz fresh or frozen* peas
    120g/4½oz ricotta cheese
salt and freshly ground black pepper
freshly grated Parmesan cheese, to serve
    (optional)

Bring a large saucepan of lightly salted water to the boil and cook the pasta until *al dente*.

Meanwhile, make the sauce. Heat the olive oil in a large pan, add the pancetta and cook until browned. Add the onion and cook for a few minutes, until softened and translucent. Stir in the peas and about 4 tablespoons of the pasta cooking water*, season with black pepper and cook for 2–3 minutes, until the peas are tender. Remove from the heat, stir in the ricotta and mix well.

Drain the pasta, reserving 1–2 tablespoons of the cooking water. Add the pasta and reserved cooking water to the sauce. Mix well and allow the moisture to be absorbed slightly. Check the seasoning, then serve immediately with a little Parmesan, if desired.

*Please note if using frozen peas you may need less water and if using fresh peas, you may need a little more, as well as a little more cooking time.

Papá, on the right, with his
friends Constatino and Mino
at the local bar.

polenta, risotto, gnocchi

As alternatives to pasta, Italians enjoy polenta, risotto and gnocchi. Polenta is usually served as a main course or a side dish. Gnocchi and risotto, however, are served as the primo course, which comes between the antipasto and the main course. These three dishes are mainly northern Italian in character and were not very common in our household when I was growing up, although we did have our own versions of risotto and gnocchi.

polenta

Polenta mixed with hot milk was traditionally the staple diet of the poor in the North. This is why we southerners called the people from the North *polentoni* (polenta eaters). When I was young, I thought polenta looked disgusting, and found it hard to believe that northerners ate it daily. I remember my mother occasionally making it for breakfast, but more often than not she used it to feed the chickens and pigs. I now know what a mistake that was, and over time I have come to consider polenta a delicacy. It is delicious accompanied by a heavy meat or mushroom ragu, or simply served with a slice of gorgonzola gently melting over the top.

Cooking traditional polenta well takes a long, long time. Even in restaurants we only cooked it on special occasions, mainly because you have to tend to it for over an hour. The end result is worth it, though. The taste is magnificent after you have added flavour in the form of cheese or vegetables.

polenta concia
basic polenta with cheese

Polenta is ground maize flour, which is cooked with water until it turns into a soft, creamy mass. Once cooked, it is flavoured with lots of butter and cheese and can be served with tomato-based ragu and stews. It can also be left to cool and set, then sliced and grilled to serve as an accompaniment to meat and game dishes. Polenta flour makes an interesting addition to cakes and biscuits instead of ordinary flour and I use it to sprinkle on baking trays when making bread.

To make the very best polenta, you should use the traditional variety that needs stirring continuously for about 40 minutes. The alternative is quick polenta (*polenta svelta*), which takes only a few minutes to cook. It doesn't have quite the same taste as traditional polenta but it makes a very acceptable substitute if you don't want to stand over the stove for ages.

This recipe is known as *polenta concia*, and is flavoured with butter and cheese. You can omit these for a lighter version.

serves 4
1 litre/1¾ pints water
salt
200g/7oz polenta
40g/1½oz/3 tbsp butter
75g/3oz Parmesan cheese, freshly grated
100g/4oz Fontina cheese, cut into
   small cubes

Put the water and some salt in a medium saucepan and bring to the boil. Gradually add the polenta, stirring all the time until it has all been amalgamated. Reduce the heat, as polenta does tend to bubble quite a bit. Beware of any lumps forming and, if they do, just beat very energetically until the lumps have dissolved. Stir the polenta with a wooden spoon for 30–40 minutes, until it starts to come away from the side of the pan. If you are using quick polenta, follow the instructions on the packet. Then add the butter, Parmesan and Fontina, and mix well. Serve immediately, with a tomato ragu (see page 100) if desired.

polenta alla griglia
grilled polenta

Grilled polenta makes a tasty accompaniment to meat and game dishes. It can be made in advance, stored in the fridge for a couple of days and then grilled when necessary. Topped with some preserved vegetables (see page 138), it makes a wonderful antipasto or snack.

serves 4
1 quantity of Polenta Concia, made
   without the cheese (see above)
a little olive oil

As soon as the polenta is cooked, pour it into a lightly oiled baking tray. Leave to cool, then cut into slices or use a pastry cutter to cut into rounds.

Heat a charcoal grill or ridged grill pan until very hot, add the polenta and cook on both sides until crisp.

Alternatively, fry the polenta. Heat a non-stick frying pan until very hot, then brush with olive oil. Add the polenta and fry on both sides until crisp. The pan should be very hot before you add the polenta slices, otherwise they will stick.

gnocchi di polenta con sugo ai peperoni

polenta gnocchi with a red and yellow pepper sauce

This is a different and more interesting way of using polenta by making the mixture into quenelles and serving them in a sauce, like pasta or gnocchi. You could make the sauce and quenelles the day before, store them in the fridge and just reheat the sauce when ready, adding the quenelles and heating through.

serves 4–6
500ml/17fl oz water
2 tsp salt
25g/1oz/2 tbsp butter
120g/4½oz quick-cook polenta
25g/1oz Fontina cheese, diced
25g/1oz Parmesan cheese, freshly grated
for the sauce:
3 tbsp extra virgin olive oil
2 anchovy fillets
1 garlic cloves, squashed but left whole
1 small red chilli, left whole
1 red and 1 yellow pepper, roasted,
   skinned and sliced into thin strips
   (see page 139)
50ml/2fl oz/4 tbsp white wine
50ml/2fl oz/4 tbsp vegetable stock
scattering of fresh basil leaves, to garnish

First make the sauce. Heat the olive oil in a large frying pan, add the anchovy fillets and cook, stirring, over a low heat until they have almost dissolved into the oil. Add the garlic and chilli and fry until the garlic becomes golden brown, then remove and discard the garlic and chilli. Add the strips of pepper and sauté for a few minutes. Pour in the wine and let it bubble until it evaporates slightly, then add the stock and simmer for 5 minutes. Remove from the heat and set aside.

To make the polenta gnocchi, put the water in a large saucepan with the salt and butter. Bring to the boil, stirring all the time until the butter melts. Reduce the heat and gradually add the polenta, stirring constantly with a wooden spoon. Cook according to the directions on the packet until you obtain a medium-thick consistency. Mix in the Fontina and Parmesan and remove from the heat.

Make quenelles with the polenta mixture by taking a tablespoonful of it, scooping it off the spoon with another tablespoon and then scooping it back again until it is a neat oval shape, turning the spoons against each other. Have a bowl of cold water ready by your side so that the tablespoons can be dipped in the water after each quenelle is made – this makes it easier for the quenelle to slide off the spoon.

Put the pepper sauce back over a medium heat. Place the quenelles in the pepper sauce and heat through. Serve immediately, scattered with a few basil leaves.

risotto

I mastered the art of making good risotto in my years travelling around Italy as a chef. After I left home, I sometimes went back to visit my family and cooked them risotto. They just couldn't understand why you should have to spend half an hour standing by a pot, constantly stirring and adding stock. One of the reasons risotto never really took off in southern Italy was that the climate is so warm that it really isn't comfortable to stand at a hot stove for long.

risotto

basic risotto

The first rule when making risotto is to use the correct Italian rice, such as Arborio, Carnaroli or Vialone Nano, because they can absorb a huge amount of liquid without breaking up. Next, use good stock and the risotto will taste wonderful. Home-made stock is ideal but a good-quality cube or powder will suffice. Your stock can be any type, depending on the flavours you are adding. For a basic risotto, use vegetable or chicken stock. Cook the risotto at a gentle simmer and stir constantly to make sure it absorbs the liquid evenly and doesn't stick to the pan. Add stock a little at a time, making sure that each batch has been absorbed by the rice before adding more. The stock must be hot, otherwise the risotto will stop cooking when it is added and the dish will be ruined, so keep it simmering in a separate pan. You may find you need a little more or less stock than the amount specified in the recipe, so always have a little extra ready. If you follow these few simple rules then there is no reason why you shouldn't make successful risotto. Just like pasta, it can be a homely, comforting dish using vegetables, or a chic dinner-party affair with wild mushrooms, seafood or even truffles.

serves 4

1.5 litres/2½ pints vegetable or chicken stock
3 tbsp olive oil
1 medium onion, finely chopped
375g/13oz Arborio or other Italian risotto rice
50g/2oz/4 tbsp butter
40g/1½oz Parmesan cheese, freshly grated
salt and freshly ground black pepper

Put the stock in a saucepan and bring to a gentle simmer. Leave over a low heat. In a medium-sized heavy-based saucepan, heat the olive oil and sweat the onion until soft. Add the rice and stir until each grain is coated with oil. You will notice the rice becoming shiny. At this stage, add a couple of ladlefuls of the hot stock and cook, stirring all the time, until it has been absorbed. Repeat with more stock. Continue adding the stock in this way until the rice is cooked, which usually takes about 20 minutes. To check if it is done, taste the rice – it should be soft on the outside but *al dente* inside.

Remove from the heat, add the butter and Parmesan and beat well with a wooden spoon to obtain a creamy consistency. In Italy, this procedure is known as *mantecare*. Taste and adjust the seasoning. Leave to rest for 1 minute, then serve.

risotto con piselli, fave e zucchini
risotto with fresh peas, broad beans and courgettes

All the flavours of spring in one dish! Obviously, if you can't find fresh produce you could use frozen peas and beans. However, do try it with fresh ones, if possible. They are easily available in the spring, and it really does make a difference to the taste – and the texture, since fresh peas and beans are crunchier. This makes an excellent vegetarian main course.

serves 4
2 courgettes
1.2 litres/2 pints vegetable stock
4 tbsp olive oil
½ celery stalk, very finely chopped
½ leek, very finely chopped
350g/12oz Arborio or other Italian
   risotto rice
120ml/4fl oz white wine
100g/4oz fresh peas (shelled weight)
100g/4oz fresh broad beans
   (shelled weight)
50g/2oz/4 tbsp butter
40g/1½oz Parmesan cheese,
   freshly grated
salt and freshly ground black pepper

First of all prepare the courgettes. Trim off the ends, then cut off the skin in thick strips (a good 5mm/¼in thick) and discard the white flesh, which tends to be mushy (you could save it to add to vegetable stocks). Chop the green part of the courgettes very finely and set aside.

Put the stock in a saucepan and bring to a gentle simmer. Leave over a low heat.

Heat the olive oil in a medium-sized heavy-based saucepan. Add the celery and leek and sweat until softened. Add the rice and stir until each grain is coated with the oil. You will notice the rice becoming shiny. At this stage, add the wine and keep stirring, until it evaporates. Then add the peas, beans and courgettes and mix well, making sure that the vegetables do not stick to the pan. Add a couple of ladlefuls of the hot stock and cook, stirring all the time, until it has been absorbed. Repeat with more stock. Continue adding the stock in this way until the rice is cooked, which usually takes about 20 minutes. To check if it is done, taste the rice – it should be soft on the outside but *al dente* inside.

Remove from the heat and beat in the butter and Parmesan with a wooden spoon to obtain a creamy consistency. Taste and adjust the seasoning. Leave to rest for 1 minute, then serve.

risotto all'acetosella

risotto with sorrel

Sorrel has a lemony flavour and grows wild but you can also buy a cultivated variety. It's an easy plant to grow in your garden. Usually, sorrel is added to enhance sauces that accompany fish, but its citrus tang also works extremely well with Parmesan cheese.

When we opened my restaurant Passione, I put this dish on the very first menu and it became one of the restaurant's signature dishes.

serves 4

1.5 litres/2½ pints good vegetable stock
3 tbsp olive oil
1 small onion, finely chopped
1 celery stalk, finely chopped
375g/13oz Arborio or other Italian
    risotto rice
150g/5oz sorrel
50g/2oz/4 tbsp butter
40g/1½oz Parmesan cheese,
    freshly grated
salt and freshly ground black pepper

Put the stock in a saucepan and bring to a gentle simmer. Leave over a low heat.

Heat the olive oil in a medium-sized heavy-based saucepan. Add the onion and celery and sweat until soft. Add the rice and stir until each grain is coated with oil. You will notice the rice becoming shiny. At this stage, add a couple of ladlefuls of the hot stock and cook, stirring all the time, until it has been absorbed. Repeat with more stock. Continue adding the stock in this way until the rice is cooked, which usually takes about 20 minutes. To check if it is done, taste the rice – it should be soft on the outside but *al dente* inside.

Remove from the heat, add the sorrel, butter and Parmesan and beat well with a wooden spoon to obtain a creamy consistency. Taste and adjust the seasoning. Leave to rest for 1 minute, then serve.

risotto 'terrone'

southern Italian risotto with vegetables

This is the way I remember most people in the south making risotto and how my mother would make it for us.

It does not include butter and Parmesan and you do not follow the usual risotto method. However, it is much easier to make. The end result is similar but without the creaminess you get with the northern risotto. If you like risotto but don't have the patience to stir it for 20 minutes, then try this alternative.

serves 4

1 small onion, sliced
1 small leek, sliced
2 carrots, chopped
1 medium potato, peeled and cut into large chunks
2 Jerusalem artichokes, peeled and cut into small chunks
300g/11oz Arborio or other Italian risotto rice
4 tbsp extra virgin olive oil, plus extra for drizzling (optional)
750ml/1¼ pints vegetable stock
salt and freshly ground black pepper
freshly grated Pecorino cheese, to serve

Place all the vegetables in a large saucepan with the rice, olive oil and stock. Cover with a lid and bring to the boil. Then reduce the heat to very low (the contents should not even be simmering) and cook, covered, for 25 minutes. Do check the risotto from time to time to ensure that the rice is not sticking to the pan – if it does, give it a quick stir and add a little more liquid. After 25 minutes, the rice will have absorbed all the liquid and the risotto is ready to serve. Check the seasoning, sprinkle with the Pecorino and drizzle with some extra virgin olive oil, if desired.

gnocchi

We love gnocchi in the south of Italy. You will find them
in restaurants all year round, served plain or with tomato
sauce, game or cheese. I could happily eat them every day.

My father knew how to make remarkably fine, soft gnocchi.
You could taste the delicate flavour of the potato through
the sauce as the gnocchi melted in your mouth. His secret
was his rather dubious source of very tasty potatoes. They
were grown by his friend high up on the hill under the
cemetery wall in Minori. Every time we ate gnocchi my
father would mention this. He said they tasted so good
because the potatoes he used were full of fertiliser from the
dead bodies in the cemetery. I knew it wasn't true but was
still disgusted at the thought. My father would just sit there
and chuckle but my mother would get upset and say that he
was being blasphemous.

When I came to England, there were many varieties
of potato and I was confused as to which one to use.
I experimented with several until I came across the
King Edward and bingo! Perfect.

Gnocchi are usually made with mashed potatoes but can
also be made with ricotta, pumpkin or even bread. As they
tend to be quite heavy, they are best with simple sauces, such
as tomato and basil, butter and sage, or pesto.

gnocchi di patate ripiene di asparagi con salsa al balsamico

potato gnocchi filled with asparagus with a butter and balsamic sauce

If you like potato gnocchi, these are a real treat. I have used asparagus as my filling, because I find it fresh and light, but you could use a variety of ingredients – peas, broad beans, mixed vegetables, meat, mushrooms... As long as the ingredients are very finely chopped, cooked and mixed with a little grated Parmesan, you have a filling.

The sauce I have chosen is a classic butter and sage one, but I have added a few drops of balsamic vinegar to finish. I find the balsamic cuts the richness of the gnocchi and imparts a characteristic tangy flavour.

serves 4
250g/9oz floury potatoes, such as King Edward
150g/5oz plain flour, plus extra for dusting
20g/¾oz cornflour
2 eggs
salt
for the filling:
1 courgette
3 tbsp extra virgin olive oil
1 large spring onion, finely chopped
4 large asparagus spears, peeled and finely chopped (tough ends discarded)
4 tbsp water
4 tbsp freshly grated Parmesan cheese

salt and freshly ground black pepper
for the sauce:
50g/2oz/4 tbsp butter
a handful of fresh sage leaves
2 tbsp freshly grated Parmesan cheese
a drizzle of balsamic vinegar

Place the unpeeled potatoes in a saucepan of lightly salted water, bring to the boil and simmer until tender. Keeping the potatoes whole like this means they don't absorb water; if you prefer, you can bake them in the oven.

While the potatoes are cooking, make the filling. Prepare the courgette (see page 60) and then chop the green part very finely. Heat the olive oil in a small pan, add the spring onion and sweat until softened. Then add the asparagus and courgette, and sauté over a medium heat for 1 minute. Season with salt and pepper, add the water and simmer for a few minutes, until the vegetables are tender but still a little crunchy. Place the filling mixture in a bowl, leave to cool and then stir in the Parmesan.

Once the potatoes are cooked, drain and leave to cool. Peel and discard the skin and mash the potatoes (preferably using a potato ricer, or 'Italian masher', as this gives a much smoother mash).

Place the mashed potato in a large bowl with the flour and cornflour. Add the eggs and some salt and mix well until you get a smooth but slightly sticky dough. Place on a floured work surface and use a rolling pin to roll out the dough into a thin sheet about 3mm/⅛in thick. Cut into rounds with a 5cm/2in pastry cutter. Place a teaspoon of the filling in the centre of half the rounds. Cover with the remaining rounds and press down the edges with your fingers to seal. Re-roll the trimmings to make more gnocchi.

Bring a large saucepan of lightly salted water to the boil and drop in the gnocchi. At first they will sink; as they come up to the surface, cook for a further 2 minutes (remember these are filled gnocchi and much thicker than normal ones, so they need a little longer to cook through).

Meanwhile, make the sauce. In a large saucepan, melt the butter over a medium heat, add the sage leaves and mix in the Parmesan. As the gnocchi are done, drain and place in the butter sauce. Mix together well. Drizzle some balsamic vinegar over the top and serve.

gnocchi di pomodori secchi con salsa alle olive nere

sun-dried tomato gnocchi with black olive sauce

If you like sun-dried tomatoes, you will love this recipe. Very finely chopped sun-dried tomatoes are added to a basic potato gnocchi mixture, worked into a dough, then shaped and cooked in boiling water until they come up to the surface.

serves 4
500g/1lb 2oz floury potatoes, such as
    King Edward
150g/5¼oz plain flour
2 egg yolks
12 whole sun-dried tomatoes preserved
    in oil, drained and dried on
    kitchen paper
salt and freshly ground black pepper
for the sauce:
4 tbsp olive oil
1 small onion, finely chopped
2 garlic cloves, squashed but left whole
120g/4½oz black olives, pitted and
    roughly chopped
a few sprigs of fresh thyme
120ml/4fl oz red wine

Place the unpeeled potatoes in a saucepan of lightly salted water, bring to the boil and simmer until tender. Once the potatoes are cooked, drain and leave to cool. Peel and mash the potatoes, preferably with a potato ricer to give a really smooth mash.

In a large bowl, combine the mashed potatoes with the flour, egg yolks, salt and pepper. Chop the sun-dried tomatoes very finely, almost to a pulp – if necessary, once chopped, blitz in a blender or food processor. Add the tomatoes to the potato mixture and mix well to form a soft dough. Take large pieces of the dough and roll them into sausage shapes, then slice into 2cm/¾in squares. Roll each one over the back of the tines of a fork to mark it slightly and give a traditional gnocchi shape.

Bring a large saucepan of salted water to the boil. Meanwhile, make the sauce. Heat the olive oil in a large frying pan, add the onion and garlic and cook gently until the onion is softened. Add the olives, thyme and wine and simmer until the wine has evaporated. Season with salt and pepper.

Drop the gnocchi into the pan of boiling water and simmer until they rise back up to the top. As they float to the surface, lift them out of the water with a slotted spoon, drain well and add to the olive sauce. Mix well and serve immediately.

gnocchi di zucca gratinati
pumpkin gnocchi baked with butter and sage

This makes a tasty alternative to traditional potato gnocchi, especially in the autumn when pumpkins are plentiful. Pumpkin gnocchi are quite common in northern Italy, and the idea was given to me by Mario, my sous-chef at Passione, whose aunt and mother often make them during the pumpkin season.

serves 6
a knob of butter
400g/14oz pumpkin (peeled weight), cut into small cubes
225g/8oz ricotta cheese
175g/6oz Italian '00' pasta flour
50g/2oz ground almonds
50g/2oz Parmesan cheese, freshly grated
25g/1oz provolone cheese, grated (if you can't get provolone, a mature Cheddar makes an excellent substitute)
2 egg yolks plus extra if needed
a pinch of ground cinnamon
salt and freshly ground black pepper
for the sauce:
175g/6oz butter
12 fresh sage leaves, plus a few extra to garnish
40g/1½oz Parmesan cheese, freshly grated
a few flaked almonds (optional)

Melt the butter in a saucepan over a medium heat, add the pumpkin and stir well. Reduce the heat, cover and cook until tender, stirring from time to time and adding 2–3 tablespoons of water if necessary to prevent sticking. When soft, remove the pan from the heat and tip the pumpkin into a piece of muslin. Squeeze well with your hands to extract excess liquid. Unwrap the pumpkin and whiz through a mouli-légumes, or mash with a fork or potato masher. Leave to cool.

Preheat the oven to 220°C/425°F/Gas Mark 7. Put the cooled pumpkin purée in a large bowl with all the remaining ingredients and mix well to a creamy but firm consistency. If it is too runny, add a little more flour; if it is too stiff, add another egg yolk. Put the mixture in a piping bag. The opening should be wide enough for the mixture to come out in finger-thick lengths.

Bring a large saucepan of water to the boil. Pipe the pumpkin mixture into 4cm/1½in long sausage shapes and drop into the boiling water. (Be careful not to burn your fingers with the steam.) When the gnocchi float up to the surface of the water, drain with a slotted spoon and place in a greased ovenproof dish.

To make the sauce, gently heat the butter and sage leaves in a small frying pan until the butter melts. Pour the butter and sage over the gnocchi and sprinkle with the Parmesan, together with the flaked almonds if using. Place in the oven and bake for 12 minutes or until golden brown. Garnish with extra sage leaves and serve immediately.

ndundari con salsa di pomodoro e basilico
pasta dumplings served with tomato and basil sauce

Here is a dish that comes from my home village and is made each year to celebrate the feast of the patron saint, Santa Trofimena, on 13 July. It is said to be an old Roman recipe, and is made in the same way as potato gnocchi but uses ricotta cheese instead of potatoes, making the dumplings much lighter. Each family has its own way of making them but the basic ingredients are always ricotta, flour and eggs, while the sauce varies depending on what you like. I enjoy these dumplings with a simple tomato sauce (see page 142) but they are equally good with pesto (see page 44).

serves 4
200g/7oz Italian '00' pasta flour
225g/8oz ricotta cheese, well drained
3 egg yolks
20g/¾oz Parmesan cheese, freshly grated
a pinch of ground nutmeg
freshly ground black pepper
for the tomato and basil sauce:
2 x 400g/14oz tins of plum tomatoes,
    drained and chopped in half
12 large fresh basil leaves
6 tbsp olive oil
3 garlic cloves, thickly sliced
salt and freshly ground black pepper

In a large bowl, mix the flour, ricotta, egg yolks, Parmesan, nutmeg and black pepper together to form a soft, moist dough. Place on a floured work surface and knead for 3–5 minutes, until smooth. With your hands, roll the dough into a large sausage shape and then use a knife to cut it at right angles into rectangular shapes about 2cm/¾in long.

Bring a large saucepan of salted water to the boil and add the dumplings. Wait until they rise to the surface, then simmer for a further 2 minutes.

Meanwhile, make the sauce. Place the tomatoes and their juice in a bowl with half the basil, add some salt and pepper and mix well. Heat the olive oil in a large pan and add the garlic. When the garlic begins to change colour, remove the pan from the heat and add the tomato mixture. Replace on the heat and cook gently for 4 minutes, until the mixture is bubbling. Stir in the remaining basil leaves.

Lift the dumplings out with a slotted spoon and add to the sauce. Mix thoroughly and serve immediately.

pesce

fish and shellfish

Our house was set on a cliff edge, 30 metres above the sea. I was born there on a stormy night to the sound of crashing waves battering the windows. The sea was the first thing I ever heard and I fell in love with it there and then.

I don't remember learning to swim, it was just something I could always do. I used to swim in the sea every day as a child. I liked to pretend I was all alone on a desert island, running along the shore and screeching like Tarzan, or leaping through the waves like a dolphin and swimming around the bottom of the cliffs with the fish. I would have such arguments with the fish, diving under the water and chasing them around the rocks.

The sea used to come alive with fish in the summer months. Octopus, red and grey mullet, sea bass, bream, groupers, scorpion fish – you name it. I went after them on boats, from the rocks, off the beach. I fished at night and during the day. I was encrusted with sea salt. Even now, if I put my tongue against my arm I can taste the salt.

The sea was part of me and I mastered the art of reading it. It told me what the weather was going to be like, the best time to go fishing and where to find the finest fish. The secret nooks and crannies of the rocks were my private hunting ground. I improvised with my equipment: fashioning together a hook and line, making my own harpoons, or gathering up cast-off pieces of net from the fishermen. The route to the prime fishing spots was not easy, as the rocks were sharp and dangerous. I learned to scramble across craggy cliff faces and swim through underwater arches to get to my special fishing spots. When I caught some fish, I often built a small fire and cooked them there and then. My favourite was sardines cooked on a stick.

Sometimes I would collect mussels, limpets and sea urchins. The mussels were small but full of the tastiest meat imaginable, and delicious eaten raw with just a squeeze of lemon. The oysters were even better. To get to the best oysters I had to dive down about four or five metres. I learned to take a big breath and pinpoint exactly where they were, then dart through the water like a torpedo and snatch them off the seabed. I ate them straight away, fresh from the sea.

I always took a lemon on my fishing excursions and it served many purposes apart from flavouring the fish I caught. It quenched my thirst when I was far away from fresh water and acted as a disinfectant if I scraped myself on the rocks. To this day, I always carry a lemon with me. My mother used to tell me that every slice of lemon would give you an extra year of life.

The sea was crystal clear in those coves, and you could see hundreds of small, colourful shrimps darting through the shallow water. These couldn't be caught with a simple hook or net. Instead, I had to make a special trap from very fine net and a ring of metal. It was hard work lying on my front and scooping the tiny shrimps out of the water, but it was worth it because they were extraordinarily sweet to eat and people paid good money for them.

Back from a fishing trip with Gianni (left).

insalata di merluzzo con fagiolini e salsa verde
hake salad with green beans and salsa verde

A wonderfully delicate fish, hake tends to be undervalued in the UK, although I believe it has experienced a revival lately. It is eaten a lot in Italy, especially in the South, and in other Mediterranean countries. If you can't find hake, you could replace it with cod. The combination of delicate fish, crunchy vegetables and tangy salsa verde is really delicious. *Salsa verde* is Italian for 'green sauce', and traditionally used to flavour steamed fish or boiled meats and sausages. If you double or triple the quantities, you can store it in the fridge for up to seven days and use it to liven up meals during the week.

serves 4

2 turnips, cut in half and sliced
4 large, flat green beans (such as runner beans or mangetout), sliced on the diagonal into 2cm/¾in lengths
100g/4oz fine green beans, trimmed
1 fennel bulb, outer layers removed, heart thinly sliced
500g/1lb 2oz whole hake or 400g/14oz hake fillet
lemon wedges, to serve (optional)

for the salsa verde:

a bunch of fresh parsley
25 fresh mint leaves
3 anchovy fillets
1 tbsp capers
1 garlic clove, peeled
3 cocktail gherkins (cornichons)
6 tbsp extra virgin olive oil
1 tbsp lemon juice
1 small tsp English mustard

Cook the turnips, large beans and fine beans in a large saucepan of boiling water until tender. Lift out with a slotted spoon and set aside to cool. Blanch the fennel in the same water for 1 minute, then lift out and set aside to cool. Cook the hake in the same water as the vegetables. If you are using a whole piece of hake, this will take 10 minutes; if you are using hake fillet, this will take 5 minutes. Drain the fish and leave to cool, then remove and discard all the bones and the skin. Break the fish into large chunks and set aside.

To make the salsa verde, chop the parsley and mint very finely on a chopping board with a mezzaluna, if you have one. On the same board, chop the anchovy fillets, capers, garlic and gherkins, gradually mixing and chopping all the ingredients together very finely. You could do this in a food processor but I prefer to do it by hand, as you get more texture. Place in a bowl, add the olive oil, lemon juice and mustard and mix well.

Arrange the fish chunks and vegetables on a large serving dish or individual plates and drizzle the salsa verde over the top. Serve with lemon wedges, if desired.

carpaccio di trota

raw marinated trout

England and the English were romantic visions of my childhood. I used to dream of dressing as an elegant English gentleman – and fishing for trout in my elegant clothes amid the glorious English countryside. I had heard many stories about fly-fishing and, desperate to try it out, I once spent a whole afternoon catching flies and sticking them on to my hook and line. I don't need to tell you that it was a complete failure.

When I moved to England, I was introduced to the secrets of real fly-fishing. I fulfilled my childhood dream and became a master trout fisherman. Winning the prize for the biggest trout in Walthamstow may not sound very romantic but it was one of my proudest moments.

serves 4
2 very fresh trout fillets,
   cleaned and scaled
juice of 2 large lemons or 4 small ones
2 fennel bulbs, very finely sliced
baby salad leaves, to serve
for the dressing:
120ml/4fl oz extra virgin olive oil
4 tbsp lemon juice
salt and freshly ground black pepper

Put the trout fillets in a dish, pour over the lemon juice and leave to marinate for about 15 minutes.

To make the dressing, place the olive oil, lemon juice and some salt and pepper in a small bowl and beat well until slightly thickened.

Remove the trout fillets from the lemon marinade and place on a chopping board. With a very sharp knife, cut wafer-thin slivers of trout and arrange evenly on a large plate, discarding the skin. Spoon some of the dressing over and leave for a couple of minutes.

Arrange a few baby salad leaves on 4 serving plates, followed by some fennel, and top with the marinated trout. Beat the leftover dressing and drizzle over the top. Serve immediately.

ippoglosso con capperi e aneto
halibut with caper and dill sauce

I discovered halibut when I came to England. I loved its light, delicate flavour immediately and it has become one of my favourite fish. I have included two recipes for it in this book: here it is served with a simple green sauce, which gives it a Mediterranean flavour. Serve with boiled new potatoes.

serves 4
4 pieces of halibut fillet, weighing about 200g/7oz each
juice of 2 lemons
4 tbsp olive oil
salt
for the sauce:
6 tbsp capers
1 garlic clove, peeled
4 anchovy fillets
a handful of fresh parsley
a large bunch of fresh dill
2 tbsp finely grated lemon zest
120ml/4fl oz extra virgin olive oil

Score the halibut skin with a sharp knife, then place the fillets in a bowl and pour over the lemon juice. Leave to marinate for about 15 minutes.

Make the sauce. Place the capers on a chopping board and squash them slightly with the flat of a knife blade. Place the garlic, anchovy fillets, parsley and dill on the same board and chop all the ingredients very finely, mixing together as you do so. Place in a bowl and mix with the lemon zest and extra virgin olive oil. Set aside.

Remove the halibut from the marinade, pat dry with kitchen paper and season with a little salt. Heat the olive oil in a large frying pan and cook the fish skin-side down for 3–4 minutes, covering it with a lid to prevent the oil splashing everywhere. Turn the fish over and cook the other side, covered, for 3 minutes. About a minute before the end of the cooking time, uncover the pan and spread a little of the sauce over the top of the halibut.

Place a spoonful of the remaining sauce on each serving plate, place the fish on top and serve immediately.

ippoglosso con burro e limone
halibut with lemon and butter

This is an even simpler way of serving really good, fresh halibut. Serve with boiled new potatoes and green beans.

serves 4
4 pieces of halibut fillet, weighing about 200g/7oz each
juice of 2 lemons
100g/4oz butter
salt

Score the halibut skin with a sharp knife, then place the fillets in a bowl and pour over the lemon juice. Leave to marinate for about 15 minutes. Drain, reserving the lemon juice, and pat dry with kitchen paper.

Melt 75g/3oz of the butter in a large frying pan (keep the heat gentle, as it is easy to burn butter), add the halibut and cook for 3–4 minutes on each side. Then increase the heat, pour in the lemon juice from the marinade and allow to bubble and evaporate slightly. Add the remaining butter; the sauce will thicken. Serve immediately.

orata in aqua pazza
whole sea bream cooked with cherry tomatoes

This dish is very typical of all southern Italian coastal regions. Freshly caught sea bream, fresh tomatoes, basil, extra virgin olive oil and garlic – it encompasses the taste of the sea and the flavours of the South. It is an extremely simple dish to prepare and, provided you have the freshest ingredients and good-quality extra virgin olive oil, you can't go wrong. Even if you live in the city and make this dish on a grey miserable day, it will give you the feeling of being by the sea in the warm southern sunshine.

serves 4
175ml/6fl oz extra virgin olive oil
2 sea bream, weighing about
   500g/1lb 2oz each, cleaned and scaled
4 garlic cloves, roughly chopped
20 cherry tomatoes, quartered
a handful of fresh basil leaves,
   plus extra to garnish
1 small red chilli, finely chopped
salt, to taste
400ml/14fl oz water

Heat the olive oil in a large, heavy-based frying pan over a fairly high heat. Add the bream, followed by the garlic, tomatoes, basil, chilli and some salt. Pour in the water, turn the heat down slightly and cook the fish for 7 minutes on each side. When you flip the fish over, you will know that it is done if the eye has turned white.

Remove the fish from the pan and place on a large serving dish. Turn up the heat, cook the sauce for 30 seconds to concentrate the flavours slightly, and then pour it over the fish. Serve immediately, garnished with basil leaves and with lots of good bread to mop up the delicious sauce.

orata all'agrodolce
sea bream fillets in a honey and white wine vinegar sauce

Sea bream is one of my favourite fish and I used to catch lots of them in Italy. The sweet and sour combination of the honey and wine vinegar works extremely well with the chicory and delicate flavour sea bream. Just make sure you have three pans – one for the chicory, one for the sauce and one for the fish. Try this dish for a dinner party; it's bound to impress your guests!

serves 4

4 sea bream fillets
6 heads of chicory
120ml/4fl oz olive oil
120ml/4fl oz water
4 tbsp honey
200g/7oz butter
220ml/7½fl oz white wine vinegar
salt and freshly ground black pepper

Score the skin of each sea bream fillet 3 or 4 times with a sharp knife. Season the flesh side with salt and pepper, then set aside.

Cut each chicory head in half lengthways, discard the small, hard central piece, then cut the chicory into cubes. Heat half the olive oil in a frying pan, add the chicory and sauté over a medium heat for 1 minute. Season with salt and pepper, add the water and cook until the liquid evaporates and the chicory has softened but is still a little crunchy. Set aside and keep warm.

Put the honey, butter and vinegar in another pan over a gentle heat. When the butter has melted, gently simmer the sauce for about 10 minutes, until it thickens to a syrupy consistency and turns golden brown.

Meanwhile, heat the remaining olive oil in a large frying pan, add the sea bream fillets, skin-side down, and cook for about 3 minutes, pressing down on them with a wooden spatula so the fish doesn't curl up. Flip the fillets over and cook the flesh side for another 3 minutes.

Arrange the chicory on a large serving dish or 4 individual plates and place the fish on top. Pour the sauce over and serve immediately.

involtini di pesce spada con finocchio
rolled swordfish fillet with fennel

The filling in this recipe has quite a
strong flavour and I find it goes really
well with the meaty texture of swordfish.
Blanched fennel and onion give the dish
a freshness and crunchiness. It all takes
a little time to prepare but it is simple to
make and the results are stunning.
I would make it for a special dinner. Ask
your fishmonger for loin of swordfish,
which you can either take home and
slice yourself or get him to slice for you.

serves 4
500g/1lb 2oz swordfish loin,
    cut into 8 thin slices
6 tbsp olive oil
2 fennel bulbs, thinly sliced
2 onions, thinly sliced
extra virgin olive oil and
    lemon juice for drizzling
a little grated lemon zest to serve
salt and freshly ground black pepper
for the filling:
100g/4oz fresh breadcrumbs
2 tbsp extra virgin olive oil
20 large capers in brine, drained
4 anchovy fillets in olive oil, drained
1 small garlic clove
a handful of fresh parsley leaves
a handful of fresh mint leaves
4 tsp grated lemon zest
freshly ground black pepper

Place all the ingredients for the filling in
a food processor and whiz until mushy.
Take handfuls of the mixture and make
8 rough sausage shapes with it, then
set aside.

Place the swordfish slices in between
cling film and gently flatten with
a meat mallet or a rolling pin and
season with salt and pepper, if desired
(bearing in mind that the filling is quite
salty). Place a piece of filling on each
slice of swordfish; don't worry if the
filling comes apart slightly – just keep
gently pressing it together with your
fingers. Roll the fish up and secure with
toothpicks, ensuring the sides are closed.

Heat the olive oil in a large frying pan,
add the swordfish rolls, seam-side down,
and fry for about 1 minute, until golden
brown. Turn over and cook the other
side until golden brown.

Meanwhile, blanch the fennel and
onions for 30 seconds, drain well and
place on a large serving dish. Arrange
the cooked swordfish on top and drizzle
with some extra virgin olive oil and a
little lemon juice. Scatter over some
lemon zest and serve immediately.

branzino con salsa alla rucola
sea bass with rocket

Sea bass is another of my favourite fish and is very popular on the southern shores of my home in Italy – certainly a fish I would often catch. It has a lovely, delicate flavour and deserves a delicate sauce to go with it, such as this one made with rocket. Wild rocket has a much stronger flavour, so I leave it to you whether you prefer to use that or the milder, cultivated variety. If you have some sauce left over, or make extra, add a couple of tablespoons of extra virgin olive oil to it to make rocket pesto and use to flavour pasta as an alternative to the usual basil pesto.

serves 4
4 sea bass fillets
2 tbsp olive oil
25g/1oz butter
4 tbsp white wine
salt and freshly ground black pepper
for the sauce:
1 tbsp extra virgin olive oil
1 tbsp butter
3 anchovy fillets
2 shallots, finely chopped
1 medium courgette, finely chopped
300ml/½ pint vegetable stock
200g/7oz rocket, roughly chopped, plus
    a few handfuls of rocket to serve

First make the sauce. Heat the olive oil and butter in a pan, add the anchovy fillets and cook, stirring over a gentle heat, until they have almost dissolved into the oil. Add the shallots and courgette and cook until the shallots begin to soften, then add the stock, bring to the boil and simmer for 1 minute. Stir in the rocket, season with black pepper and simmer for 2 minutes. Remove from the heat, allow to cool slightly, then whiz in a blender or food processor until smooth. Return to the pan and stir over a high seat with a wooden spoon until nearly all the liquid has evaporated and the sauce becomes creamy. Remove from the heat and set aside.

Season the sea bass with salt and pepper. Heat the olive oil and butter in a large frying pan, add the sea bass, flesh-side down, and cook over a medium heat for about 3 minutes, or until golden brown. Turn over and cook for another 3 minutes. Turn over again and gently peel off the skin. Add the wine, cover with a lid and cook for a few seconds. Uncover the pan, turn the fillets over, cover again and cook until the wine evaporates.

Meanwhile, reheat the sauce gently if necessary. Arrange some rocket on a plate, top with the sea bass fillets and pour the sauce either over the fish or on the side, as you wish.

polipo in umido

stewed octopus

I used to love catching octopus when I lived in Italy, and even more so taking it home for my father to cook. It's a shame they are not popular in Britain, as the sea here is full of them, but it seems they are caught and exported. A great pity, because they really are delicious, either stewed and served warm as in this recipe or dressed with olive oil and lemon to make a salad. I think a lot of people expect octopus to be chewy and tough, hence its unpopularity. The secret of tender octopus is to cook it without adding any liquid, as it exudes a lot of its own. (There is an Italian saying, 'You are like an octopus, go cook in your own juice.') The only liquid allowed is some olive oil to prevent it sticking to the pan. Follow this recipe and you will see how tender octopus can be – it should melt in your mouth.

serves 4

4 tbsp olive oil
3 garlic cloves, sliced
1 tsp capers
4 green olives, quartered
4 anchovy fillets
baby octopuses, weighing about
   800g/1 lb 12½oz, cleaned (ask your
   fishmonger to do this)
10 cherry tomatoes, squashed
a handful of fresh parsley, coarse stalks
   removed
salt

Heat the olive oil in a small saucepan (use one in which the octopus will fit tightly) and add the garlic, capers, olives and anchovies. Once the garlic begins to sweat, add the octopuses and a pinch of salt. Stir well, lower the heat, then add the tomatoes and parsley. Cover with a tight-fitting lid and cook over a low heat for 1 hour and 10 minutes, until the octopuses are very tender. During cooking they will shrink and exude quite a bit of liquid. Adjust the seasoning if necessary, then serve.

cozze 'scappate'
stuffed mussels with tomato sauce

Because I lived by the sea, mussels were part of my life, and as a child I would pick bucketfuls of them during the cooler autumn months. When we had larger mussels, my father would often make this dish by removing the mussels from their shells, mixing them with stale bread, garlic and parsley and then stuffing the shells with this mixture. Using mussels in this way made an unusual, tasty dish and also meant they would go further to feed a large family. If you like mussels, try this dish for an informal supper with friends; it's fun to eat, as you have to remove the raffia tied round each mussel.

serves 4
12 large mussels
4 tbsp extra virgin olive oil
4 anchovy fillets
1 garlic clove, thinly sliced lengthways
½ small red chilli, finely chopped
    (optional)
20 capers
3 tbsp white wine
a handful of fresh parsley, finely
    chopped, plus a few sprigs to garnish
100g/4oz stale bread, cut into small cubes

for the sauce:
2 tbsp extra virgin olive oil
½ small onion, very finely diced
½ tsp dried oregano
2 large green olives, pitted and sliced
400g/14oz tinned chopped tomatoes
salt and freshly ground black pepper

Clean the mussels in plenty of cold water, scrubbing them well and pulling off the beards. Place in a pan, cover and steam for 2–3 minutes until the shells open. Remove from the heat and discard any mussels that are still closed. Remove the flesh from the shells and any liquid and place in a bowl (if necessary, open up the shells a little more, taking care to keep the shells intact). Keep the empty shells for later.

Heat the olive oil in a pan, add the anchovies and stir with a wooden spoon until they have almost dissolved into the oil. Add the garlic, chilli if using, and capers. Once the garlic turns golden, stir in the mussels, reserving their liquid for later. Heat the mussels through, then add the wine and simmer gently for 1 minute. Pour in the liquid from the mussels and stir in the parsley. Remove from the heat, mix in the bread cubes, then leave to cool. When the mixture has cooled, place it on a chopping board and chop quite finely with a sharp knife. Transfer to a bowl and mix well until you get a mushy consistency.

Dry the mussel shells and generously fill one half of each shell with the mussel mixture. Close the shell, removing any excess filling that escapes, and wrap some raffia around the middle of the shell, tying it round a few times until nice and tight, so the shell cannot open (you could use string, but I think raffia looks much nicer). Trim off any excess raffia and put the filled shells to one side.

To make the sauce, heat the olive oil in a large pan, add the onion and, as soon as it begins to fry, add the oregano, olives and tomatoes. Season with salt and pepper and bring to a gentle simmer. Reduce the heat and simmer for 5 minutes. Add the mussels to the sauce, cover the pan and cook gently for 20 minutes, turning the mussels over halfway through the cooking time. Stir from time to time and, if necessary, add some water to prevent the sauce becoming too dry. Put the filled mussel shells on individual plates, pour a little sauce over and garnish with a sprig of parsley. Serve immediately and remember to provide finger bowls for your guests.

Variation: Baked Stuffed Mussels
This is an alternative recipe, in which the mussels are baked and the tomato sauce omitted. Remove the mussels from their shells and prepare the filling as for *Cozze 'Scappate'* (see above). Then fill both sides of each empty shell with the mussel mixture. Keep the shells open and place on a baking tray. Mix together a handful of breadcrumbs, a handful of parsley, finely chopped, and enough extra virgin olive oil just to moisten. Sprinkle this mixture over the open mussels. Place in an oven preheated to 200°C/400°F/Gas Mark 6 and bake for 15 minutes or until golden brown. Top each mussel with an anchovy fillet and a chopped green olive, drizzle over some extra virgin olive oil and serve with a few green salad leaves. This makes an excellent starter for a dinner party.

As with any love affair, I did have a few rough times with the sea. When I was about 13, I put to sea with a friend for an evening jaunt in my dinghy. We were having so much fun that we didn't notice the wind blowing us further and further from the safety of the shore. We tried to get back but the current was too strong. The people on the beach didn't take much notice of us. When we shouted, they thought we were just a pair of mischievous boys messing around. The truth was, we were stuck.

As it grew dark, we began to get really frightened. The sea was still and the lights of the town were visible for a long time, which kept us calm. But all too soon, they disappeared. I felt the bile of panic rising in my gullet. We imagined we were miles away, and talked about ending up in Africa and never seeing home again. Our young imaginations ran wild, turning the murmuring wind into the whisper of dead sailors, the booming of the ocean into sinister creatures trying to dash our flimsy vessel. We cried like babies as we bobbed around helplessly all night long.

The next morning a police boat found us. When we caught sight of it we started to scream with joy. It was part of a search party out looking for us. We were both severely reprimanded, then they took us home – it only took an hour to get back to shore, so we hadn't gone far at all. I was banned from going on a boat again for a very long time, and my dinghy was destroyed. To keep our dignity, we made up stories of our adventures for our friends – the giant fish we had seen and the dolphins that had saved us.

The coastline near Minori, Amalfi Coast.

gamberoni e granchio con aglio e peperoncino

king prawns and crab with garlic and chilli

Always use fresh seafood for this dish. Prawns and crab make a great combination but if you prefer not to use crab, just substitute extra prawns. If you find it difficult to extract the crab meat from its shell, ask your fishmonger to do it for you.

serves 4

meat from 2 large fresh crabs
175ml/6fl oz extra virgin olive oil
12 fresh raw king prawns, shell on
4 garlic cloves, sliced lengthways
2 red chillies, sliced lengthways
  into strips
2 handfuls of fresh parsley leaves
250ml/8fl oz white wine
1 lemon, cut into quarters, to serve
slices of bread, to serve
salt

Heat the olive oil in a large frying pan, add the prawns and cook for 1 minute over a high heat. Turn them over and cook the other side for another minute. Add the garlic, chillies and crab chunks, season with salt, then reduce the heat and cook for 2 minutes with the lid on. Add the parsley, increase the heat and pour in the wine and any reserved juices from the crab. Bubble until evaporated, then serve immediately, with lemon quarters and lots of bread to mop up the juices.

Minori was a fishing village. I used to hang around the fishermen when they came back with their catches, learning from them, teasing them and probably driving them crazy.

Every afternoon my friends and I waited on the beach for the fishermen to return from their trips. Quite often they would bring ashore a mighty turtle, which they had untangled from their nets. The poor creature would be half dead and brought back as a novelty. They may have caught it a few days earlier but they would have tied it to the back of the boat and dragged it to shore as a trophy. Sometimes the well-travelled sailors would take the turtles home to eat, and many people used their shells to decorate their houses. I never liked this. I knew instinctively that these beasts needed protecting.

One day I was alone on the beach when one of the fishing boats returned with a turtle in a poor state, but still alive. I asked the fishermen if I could have it and, using all my strength, I dragged the half-dead beast back into the sea and round to a small cove away from the main beach. I stayed with her all afternoon, willing her to recover her strength. At night I found a rope and tied her to a rock in the cover. The next morning, when I rushed down to check on her, I found to my joy that she was full of life and spirit, flapping around to try and free herself. I cut the rope and watched her swim away effortlessly.

After that, the turtles became my mission. Every time a fisherman brought one ashore, I would try to save it, though usually without as much success. To my relief, the fishermen soon began to understand that the turtles were special and stopped bringing them home.

pesce conservato
preserved fish

Preserving fish is an old tradition and, although its original purpose was to deal with a large catch, preserved fish is still eaten today as a delicacy rather than out of necessity. Here are some of the most popular preserved fish used in Italian cooking.

Acciughe
You can buy anchovies preserved in either oil or salt. For both types, fresh anchovies are gutted, layered with sea salt and left for about a month. They are then filleted and packed in jars or rinsed of the salt and placed in jars or tins with olive or vegetable oil. See page 12 for tips on using anchovies in cooking.

Baccalá
This is cod preserved in salt. It was traditionally known as 'poor food', and was eaten by people who lived inland and did not have access to the sea. Cod was the cheapest fish available and was preserved in large quantities, then kept in the store cupboard. However, it has become quite fashionable these days and commands a high price.

You can buy baccalá in pieces, which need to be soaked in several changes of fresh water for at least 24 hours before use, thereby removing the salt and softening the flesh. In some areas of Italy, such as Liguria, Venice and Naples, baccalá is very prominent on the menu. It is delicious steamed or boiled, then simply dressed with some extra virgin olive oil and lemon juice, eaten warm or cold as a salad, or cooked in a tomato sauce with black olives. It also makes delicious fish cakes and fritters.

Bottarga
This is cured roe of grey mullet and tuna, produced and consumed mainly in Sicily and Sardinia. It can be used like *mosciame* (see below), but is more commonly grated over seafood pasta dishes. You can find it in good Italian delicatessens.

Mosciame
This air-dried fillet of tuna has become quite a delicacy on many menus. It is available in Italian or Spanish delicatessens. Serve thinly sliced, drizzled with some extra virgin olive oil and lemon juice and accompanied by preserved vegetables (see page 138) as an alternate antipasto to cured meats.

Pesce affumicato
Smoked fish is becoming increasingly popular in Italy and swordfish, tuna, halibut and sturgeon are just some of the varieties available. Arrange an assortment of thinly sliced smoked fish on a large plate, drizzle with lemon juice and serve with mixed baby salad leaves and rocket for an antipasto or light lunch.

Stoccafisso
This is air-dried cod. It is sold whole and should be soaked in several changes of fresh water for about 24 hours before use. It also helps to tenderise it if you bash it with a mallet before soaking. Cook it in the same way as *baccalá* (see above).

carne

meat, game, poultry

The backyard of my childhood home was like a small farmyard. There were chickens scratching about in the dirt, lots of rabbits and guinea pigs, and we always had a pig. Every Sunday, we bought meat from one of the three village butchers. We only ate meat once or twice a week but it was truly fresh and we knew where it came from, whether it was the farm or our own back garden. Markets full of live animals – rabbits, chickens, lambs and cows – were part of our lives. We saw animals as a source of food, yet we cared for them and loved them as if they were our pets.

Every Thursday, a bullock was slaughtered in Minori. It was a fascinating event for the children. Great groups of us used to sit on the slaughterhouse wall to watch the gruesome spectacle. The butcher was a bull of a man himself, with a jutting chin. The killing was so cruel and brutal that to our childish eyes it looked like the crucifixion of Jesus. The butcher would tie the bullock's head to a post and bash it hard with a large mallet. Then he slit its throat and drained off all the blood. Finally the bullock was lifted up with large, heavy chains to be gutted and skinned.

People are so removed from the source of their meat these days. You go into a supermarket and see endless rows of pre-packaged poultry, meat and game. It's difficult to associate meat with live animals. For me, it was part of my culture. We respected animals because we knew they were our food. I never saw my mother buy a chicken or pigeon at the butcher's. She had a pigeon coop and she would take the birds out as she needed them.

By the time I was 11, my father was wise enough to see where my heart lay. During the summer holidays, he found me a job in a fine restaurant run by one of his friends – a great chef by the name of Alfonso. I adored the job, but I think I must have been rather a handful, if only because of my boundless enthusiasm.

As a very junior waiter, I was permitted to greet customers and tell them what was on the menu, but I was not yet entrusted with the important task of taking orders. However, I invented a special responsibility of my own. Almost immediately, I discovered that I could predict people's orders from their reaction when I recited the menu. I would run straight into the kitchen and prepare the ingredients necessary for those dishes, ready for the chef to cook them. Alfonso thought he was losing his mind when, time after time, he went to the preparation table only to find his work already done. He was afraid he had done it himself and then forgotten about it. Eventually he caught me in the act and, after much shouting and swearing, he banned me from the kitchen for the rest of the day. Later, he calmed down, and when he realised how keen I was to cook, he found me work in the kitchen.

Alfonso's restaurant had chickens, rabbits and sometimes even lambs in the backyard. We killed what we needed each day. If the chef ran out of chicken in the middle of a shift, I'd have to run out and prepare another. It might sound gruesome but it meant that all our meat was very fresh.

My time in the kitchen taught me about every sort of meat and every way to cook it. I learned not to waste anything; we used every last scrap.

Me, at 8 years old.

antipasto di pesche e prosciutto crudo di parma

antipasto of fresh peaches and Parma ham

Parma ham with melon, Parma ham with figs … both wonderful combinations, but in the middle of a warm summer why not with peaches? It makes a lovely and refreshing starter, but you must use ripe peaches. If you can find them, the small organic ones are out of this world. I dedicate this recipe to Dominique, who loves Parma ham so much she would have it at every meal.

serves 1
1 ripe peach
a few slices of Parma ham, very thinly and freshly cut
a handful of rocket
extra virgin olive oil
freshly ground black pepper

Remove the skin from the peach – this is made easier by immersing the peach in boiling water for a minute. Cut the peach in half and discard the stone. Arrange on a plate with the Parma ham and rocket. Drizzle with some extra virgin olive oil and grind over some black pepper.

polpette al vapore

steamed meatballs

This dish has great sentimental value for me, as my mother would cook it when I was recovering from an illness. Because the meatballs are steamed and not fried, they are gentle on the stomach and easy to digest. It's also a good way to enjoy meatballs without the added fat! Use the best lean minced beef you can find – minced steak is ideal.

serves 4–6
2 tbsp extra virgin olive oil
3 tbsp water
500g/1lb 2oz very lean minced beef
2 garlic cloves, very finely chopped
a handful of fresh parsley, very finely chopped
salt and freshly ground black pepper

Half fill a pan with water and bring to the boil. Cover with a plate roughly the same size as the pan, or just a little larger, and put half the olive oil and the 3 tablespoons of water on the plate.

Meanwhile, in a large bowl, mix together the mince, garlic, parsley, the remaining olive oil and some salt and pepper. It is much easier to do this with your hands. When all the ingredients are well combined, shape into about 25 small balls.

When the water begins to boil, turn down the heat to medium, so the water is gently simmering. Place the meatballs on the plate on top of the pan and cover with an upturned plate or, ideally, a glass bowl so that you can see through it.

Leave to steam for 30 minutes, turning the meatballs over halfway through. Serve immediately, as the meat tends to toughen slightly when cool. You can serve the meatballs with pasta or on their own, with some good bread to mop up the liquid.

vitello alla genovese
veal slow-cooked with onions

This is an old recipe from the Campania region, and not from Genoa as the name suggests. In the days of the old Italian maritime republics (Genoa, Amalfi, Venice and Pisa), this dish was made for Genoese sailors when they docked in Amalfi, hence the name. Although it takes three hours to cook, it is an extremely straightforward dish to make and you get two courses from just one pot. The onion sauce is used to flavour pasta as a starter, or primo, and the veal joint is served as a main course. Try it for a different Sunday lunch.

serves 4–6
1kg/2¼lb veal joint
3 garlic cloves, sliced
a handful of fresh parsley, roughly torn
150ml/¼ pint olive oil
2.5kg/5½lb large onions, sliced
1 celery stalk, diced
1 carrot, diced
1 bunch of rosemary sprigs, 2 bay leaves
    and 2 sage leaves, tied together to
    make a bouquet garni
200ml/7fl oz white wine
salt and freshly ground black pepper

Place the veal joint on a chopping board. With a sharp knife, unroll it until you obtain a long, flat piece, then put skin-side down. Season with salt and pepper, rubbing them well into the meat, followed by the garlic and parsley. Roll up again and tie together with 4 pieces of string, trimming off any excess.

Heat the olive oil in a large saucepan, add the veal and seal on all sides. Remove from the pan and set aside. Add the onions, celery and carrot to the pan, season with salt and pepper and stir well. Add the bouquet garni and cook until the onions begin to soften. Put the veal back in the pan, cover with a lid, then reduce the heat to low and cook for 3 hours, until very tender. Stir the onions and turn the meat from time to time to prevent sticking. After 3 hours, turn up the heat, add the wine and simmer for 5 minutes. Remove the meat from the pan and set aside. With a potato masher, mash the onions slightly. Taste and adjust the seasoning.

Serve the onion sauce with some cooked pennette pasta and freshly grated Parmesan. For the main course, slice the veal and serve with a little of the sauce and a green salad.

il ragu
stuffed beef rolls in tomato ragu

This recipe takes me back to my childhood Sunday lunches and, more recently, to family gatherings when I return to my home village. My Aunt Maria was the 'queen' of this dish and would spend the entire morning checking, stirring and making sure it was just right for all the family to enjoy. It is traditionally made every Sunday in all regions of southern Italy. It is a simple dish to prepare and takes about two hours to cook – some traditionalists will cook it for longer to get an even richer tomato sauce, but if you follow this recipe two hours will suffice. The tomato sauce is used to flavour pasta for the *primo* (pasta course) and the meat is eaten as a *secondo* (main course). Any leftover sauce can be used to flavour pasta dishes throughout the week.

serves 6
12 small thin sirloin steaks
25g/1oz Parmesan cheese, freshly grated
4 garlic cloves, finely chopped
a handful of fresh parsley, torn
salt and freshly ground black pepper
for the sauce:
6 tbsp olive oil
150ml/¼ pint red wine
1 onion, very finely chopped
1 celery stalk, very finely chopped
2 tbsp tomato concentrate or
    tomato purée, diluted in
    400ml/14fl oz lukewarm water
2 x 400g/14oz tins of chopped tomatoes
a handful of fresh basil leaves

Arrange the slices of meat on a chopping board or a clean work surface and flatten them with a meat tenderiser (if you don't have one, place a flat wooden spatula over the meat and bash with the palm of your hand). Season with salt and pepper, then sprinkle with the grated Parmesan, garlic and parsley. Roll each slice up tightly and secure well with toothpicks.

For the sauce, heat the olive oil in a large saucepan. When hot, lower the heat, add the meat rolls and seal well on all sides. Increase the heat again, add the wine and simmer until it has reduced by half. Remove the meat and set aside.

Add the onion and celery to the pan and stir well. Cook until the remainder of the wine has nearly evaporated, then put the meat back in the pan and pour over the diluted tomato concentrate and the chopped tomatoes. Season with salt and pepper and stir in the basil. Lower the heat and partially cover with a lid. Cook gently for 2 hours, stirring from time to time. Check the seasoning.

Serve the tomato sauce with some cooked pasta such as tagliatelle or large rigatoni. Then serve the meat rolls as a main course with a green salad.

cotolette di agnello alla griglia ripiene di prosciutto ed erbe

grilled lamb cutlets filled with Parma ham and herbs

You can make the filling in advance, or make lots of it and store some in the fridge or freezer for another time. When choosing lamb cutlets, go to a reliable butcher and ask for organic (if available) or the best-quality racks of lamb. Usually one rack of lamb contains approximately six cutlets.

serves 4
12 lamb cutlets
salt and freshly ground black pepper
for the filling:
10 fresh sage leaves
a handful of fresh rosemary needles
a handful of fresh parsley leaves
a handful of fresh basil leaves
1 garlic clove, finely chopped
6 tbsp freshly grated Parmesan cheese
100g/4oz butter, slightly softened
    (remove from the fridge about an
    hour before using)
6 slices of Parma ham

Place all the herbs on a chopping board and chop very finely together. Place them in a bowl with the garlic, Parmesan, butter and some salt and pepper and mix well until you get a smooth paste.

Arrange the Parma ham slices overlapping slightly on a piece of clingfilm and spread the paste evenly over them with a spatula. Then, with the help of the clingfilm, roll up the ham into a sausage shape, encased in the clingfilm, and tie the ends so the filling doesn't escape. Place in the fridge for at least an hour.

Slice each lamb cutlet horizontally through the centre, leaving it joined at one end, and open it up like a butterfly. With a meat tenderiser, flatten each piece. (You can ask your butcher to do this for you if you prefer.)

Remove the filling from the fridge and discard the clingfilm. Cut the filling into 2.5cm/1in slices, pressing slightly to flatten. Place on one side of each cutlet and fold the other side over the top. Press together well, making sure that none of the filling escapes. Transfer the cutlets to a baking tray lined with foil and season with salt and pepper.

Place under a hot grill and grill for about 2 minutes on each side for rare, 4 minutes for medium or, for well done, as long as you like! Serve immediately with Patate Saltate (see page 124).

I have always loved animals. My father kept cats and dogs and I grew up surrounded by a whole range of farmyard creatures, which became my playmates. But I soon learned not to become too attached to them.

Every Easter, my father would return from his travels laden with goodies for our traditional spring feast: the finest goat, chicken, capon and lamb, raised by his farmer friends. To make sure he was getting the freshest meat and the finest quality, he would make a point of seeing each animal alive before he bought it.

One year he made his mistake. A couple of weeks before Easter, he accepted a baby goat as payment for an old debt. It was just a few weeks old but he knew it would be perfect for our Easter lunch. He also thought it would be fun for me to have a baby goat to play with. To be fair to my father, he did tell me that it was our Easter lunch, but I was just a small child and really didn't want to believe such a brutal truth, so I pushed it to the back of my mind.

Looking after this hungry kid was a 24-hour-a-day job. I called him Bottiglia (Bottle) because I fed him milk from a bottle. He quickly became my whole life. My family and friends teased me mercilessly but I loved him. Bottiglia was my friend, constant companion and confidant. I created a wonderful adventure dream world in my head for the two of us. He came with me to the beach, trotted behind me on my jaunts to the mountains and wandered through the village streets with me. He was my little shadow, and I believe he loved me as much as I loved him. I was his surrogate mother and he was my pride and joy.

It came to school time and I kicked up a fuss. I didn't want to leave my new best friend at home but my parents threatened me, saying that if I didn't go to school they would take him away. For two weeks I went to school every day without fail and without complaint. I didn't want to lose Bottiglia.

The day before Easter, I ran home from school and straight through the house to find him. I had been thinking all day about Bottiglia and the adventures we could have. I was so looking forward to seeing him … and there he was, hanging by his back legs from the ceiling, his throat cut and blood still dripping from his neck. I couldn't believe the horror in front of my eyes. Even now, it still counts as the worst day of my life. I started to cry, and my mother shouted at my father, telling him he shouldn't have done it, knowing how much I loved the goat. My father would have none of it. As far as he was concerned, he had done nothing wrong. He walloped me for crying and said I was old enough to know better than to get attached to food.

The next day at lunch I felt sick. I couldn't eat my friend but I had to sit and watch everyone else tucking in. I'll never forget my little sister laughing at me, and the rest of the table joining in.

Although this might seem harsh, ultimately my father was right. The kid was always intended as our Easter meal. It was a valuable lesson. From that moment, I still loved animals but I also respected them as a source of food. ,

porchetta

stuffed rolled pork belly

Traditionally in Italy, porchetta is a whole piglet filled with lots of fresh herbs and slow-roasted either in a wood oven or outdoors on a spit. It is made at home or sold ready-made as a takeaway, and you can buy it whole, a few slices or just have a slice between bread as a sandwich. As whole piglets are not that easily obtainable, I use pork belly and the result is the same. It is simple to prepare and can be made in advance and eaten cold – a good idea for parties or to feed a large group of people for Sunday lunch.

serves 10–12

5kg/11lb piece of pork belly – ask the butcher to remove the ribs and trim off the excess fat
25g/1oz coarse salt
leaves from a large bunch of fresh thyme
needles from a large bunch of fresh rosemary, roughly chopped
a large bunch of fresh sage leaves, roughly chopped
1 tbsp fennel seeds (if you are lucky enough to find wild fennel, use it instead, finely chopped – its flavour is unique)
8 garlic cloves, finely chopped
2 tbsp olive oil
6 tbsp runny honey
coarsely ground black pepper

Preheat the oven to its highest setting. Lay the pork belly skin-side down. Sprinkle half the salt and lots of coarsely ground black pepper over it, rubbing them well into the meat with your fingers. Leave to rest for 10 minutes so the salt and pepper settle well into the meat. Then sprinkle the herbs, fennel seeds and garlic evenly all over it.

Next tie up the meat. You will need 10 pieces of string, each about 30cm/12in long. Carefully roll the meat up widthways and tie it very tightly with string in the middle of the joint. Then tie at either end about 1cm/½in from the edge and keep tying along the joint until you have used up all the string. The filling should be well wrapped – if any excess filling escapes from the sides, push it in. With your hands, massage 1 tablespoon of the olive oil all over the joint. Then rub the remaining salt with some more black pepper over it.

Grease a large roasting tin with the remaining olive oil and place the pork in it. Roast for 10 minutes, then turn it over. After 15 minutes, reduce the oven temperature to 150°C/300°F/Gas Mark 2 and cover the meat with aluminium foil. (If you like the crackling very crisp, don't bother with the foil, but remember that the porchetta needs to be sliced thinly and crispy crackling will make this difficult.) Roast for 3 hours.

Remove the joint from the oven and coat with the honey, drizzling some of the juices from the roasting tin all over it, too. Insert a fork in either side of the joint and lift it on to a wooden board. If you are serving the porchetta immediately, place the roasting tin on the hob and stir with a wooden spoon, scraping up all the caramelised bits from the base of the tin, until the juices from the meat reduce and thicken slightly. Slice the joint thinly and serve with the sauce. Alternatively, leave the meat to cool and slice when needed. It will keep for up to a week in the fridge.

polletto in agrodolce
baby chicken in a cider vinegar sauce

Baby chickens (poussins) are much more tender than a fully matured one. They also look more attractive when served. You can choose whether to serve a whole one or half per person, depending on people's appetite. If you are serving a starter and accompaniments, then one poussin between two people is sufficient.

serves 2–4
2 baby chickens (poussins), boned
  (ask your butcher to do this for you)
6 tbsp olive oil
salt and freshly ground black pepper

for the filling:
2 garlic cloves, peeled
2 tbsp capers
1 tsp sea salt
2 tsp extra virgin olive oil
needles from 2 sprigs of fresh rosemary
a handful of chopped fresh parsley
freshly ground black pepper

for the sauce:
2 garlic cloves, peeled
needles from 2 sprigs of fresh rosemary
120ml/4fl oz white wine
120ml/4fl oz cider vinegar
½ tbsp sugar
1 tbsp capers
scattering of fresh parsley,
  to serve (optional)

First make the filling by placing all the ingredients in a mortar and pounding them with a pestle until you obtain a pulp.

Open up each baby chicken like a butterfly and place skin-side down on a chopping board. Spread the filling evenly over the flesh side, then fold the poussin back over and secure the opening with wooden toothpicks, weaving them in and out. Season all over with salt and pepper. Heat the olive oil in a large frying pan, add the chickens, then reduce the heat slightly and cook until golden brown on all sides. Cover the pan and cook gently for about 20 minutes, until the chickens are cooked through.

Meanwhile, make the sauce. Place the garlic and rosemary in a mortar and pound with a pestle. Add the wine, vinegar, sugar and capers, and mix well.

Turn up the heat under the chickens, add the sauce and simmer until reduced by half, stirring all the time. Arrange on a plate and pour over the sauce. Serve immediately, scattered with parsley, if wished.

petti di pollo con limone e timo
chicken breasts with lemon and thyme

Oh, the taste of my childhood: chickens scratching in the backyard, lemons and thyme from the garden. A distant but very vivid memory. Try this recipe with free-range or corn-fed chicken breasts – the combination with lemon and fresh thyme is wonderful. Serve with boiled new potatoes and green beans.

serves 4
150ml/¼ pint white wine
juice of 1 lemon
4 boneless chicken breasts
plain flour, for dusting
120ml/4fl oz olive oil
2 small onions, finely sliced
1 lemon, zest and pith removed,
    thinly sliced, plus a few lemon slices
    to garnish
16 sprigs of fresh thyme, plus a few extra
    to garnish
salt and freshly ground black pepper

In a small bowl, mix together the wine and lemon juice, then set aside.

Season the chicken breasts with salt and pepper and rub in well. Lightly dust them with some flour, shaking off any excess. With the palm of your hand, flatten the breasts slightly. Heat the olive oil in a large pan. Add the chicken and seal on both sides (some chicken breasts contain water and may spit while cooking – to prevent this, cover the pan with a lid). Once they are well sealed and golden brown, remove the chicken breasts from the pan and set aside. Lower the heat, add the onions, season with salt and pepper and sweat until the onions are soft. Add the lemon slices, thyme mix well. Return the chicken to the pan, cover and cook over a gentle heat for 3 minutes.

Turn up the heat (but be careful not to burn the onions and lemon), add the wine and lemon juice mixture, then cover and cook for 10–15 seconds, until the mixture is bubbling. Remove the lid and simmer until the liquid has evaporated slightly – the sauce will begin to thicken. Taste and adjust the seasoning if necessary.

Arrange the chicken breasts on a large plate or on individual serving plates and pour the sauce over. Garnish with lemon slices and extra sprigs of thyme.

bocconcini di pollo con aceto alle mele

chicken bites wrapped in pancetta and sage with a cider vinegar dressing

This recipe came out of the blue when I was making a chicken dish for some guests at home. As usual, I had bought too much food and was left with a couple of chicken breasts. In the fridge I found pancetta and fresh sage, so I decided to put these ingredients together with a tangy cider vinegar dressing and made these delicious *bocconcini*, which I served with pre-dinner drinks. They make an excellent starter. Alternatively, you can make lots of them in advance for parties or as snacks with drinks. If you serve them cold like this, don't pour the dressing over as they will go soggy. Arrange the *bocconcini* on plates garnished with some salad leaves and put the dressing in small bowls for dipping.

serves 6
2 skinless, boneless chicken breasts
6 very thin slices of pancetta, cut in half
12 fresh sage leaves
2 tbsp olive oil
a few salad leaves, to serve
for the dressing:
120ml/4fl oz extra virgin olive oil
4 tbsp cider vinegar
1 tsp finely chopped fresh parsley
salt and freshly ground black pepper

Cut the chicken breasts lengthways in half and cut each half into 3 chunks. Lay the half slices of pancetta on a clean work surface, place a sage leaf on top of each one and wrap them around the chicken chunks.

Heat the olive oil in a frying pan over a medium heat, add the pancetta-wrapped chicken and seal all over, taking care not to burn the pancetta. Turn the heat down and, with the help of 2 forks, keep turning the *bocconcini* until the chicken has cooked through. This should take about 10 minutes.

Meanwhile, make the dressing. Place all the ingredients in a small bowl and whisk with a fork until it begins to thicken slightly.

Remove the *bocconcini* from the pan and drain on kitchen paper to remove excess oil. Arrange on a plate with some salad leaves and pour the dressing over. Serve immediately.

petti d'ánatra in limoncello
duck breasts in limoncello

Limoncello is a lemon liqueur made on the Amalfi Coast, near my home. When I was a child it used to be home-made only, but now it has become quite an industry and is sold worldwide. It is a very pure liqueur, made solely from lemons, sugar and alcohol. The citrus/sweet flavour goes very well with duck. Serve this dish with a purée of root vegetables such as carrot and celeriac.

serves 4
4 boneless duck breasts
2 large lemons
250ml/8fl oz limoncello liqueur
50g/2oz butter
2 tbsp olive oil
salt and freshly ground black pepper
To serve
400g/14oz celeriac, peeled weight
300g/10½oz carrots
large knob of butter

Pat the duck breasts dry and place them in a shallow dish. Peel the lemons with a potato peeler so you get ringlets of lemon zest, then squeeze the juice from them. Scatter the lemon ringlets over the duck, pour over the juice and limoncello and leave to marinate for about 30 minutes.

Remove the duck from the marinade, dry on kitchen paper and season well all over with salt and pepper. Do not discard the marinade.

Clarify the butter in a large frying pan by letting it melt, then when it begins to foam, carefully lifting off the foam with a tablespoon, leaving just the clear, golden liquid. Add the olive oil. When it is hot, place the duck breasts in the pan, skin-side down, and seal well on both sides. Reduce the heat and cook for about 12 minutes, turning the duck over from time to time. This will give you medium-cooked duck, which I think is ideal for this dish. Now turn the heat up to high, pour in the marinade and let it evaporate, turning the duck over and giving the pan a shake from time to time – this will help the sauce thicken.

Meanwhile, make the purée. Cook the root vegetables in boiling water for 20 minutes. Drain, then pass through a potato ricer, until smooth. Stir in the butter and season with salt and pepper to taste.

As soon as the sauce has thickened, remove the pan from the heat and place the duck breasts on a chopping board. Leave to rest for about 5 minutes, then cut them into slices, arrange on 4 plates or one serving dish and pour over the sauce. Serve immediately.

petto di faraona ripieno di erbe con salsa al balsamico

breast of guinea fowl stuffed with herbs and served with a balsamic sauce

This is an old recipe from the Naples region, traditionally made with pig's spleen. Spleen is no longer commonly available and probably a little off-putting to a lot of people, so I have used guinea fowl breasts instead. If you prefer, you can use chicken.

serves 4
4 boneless guinea fowl breasts
6 tbsp olive oil
150ml/¼ pint balsamic vinegar
150ml/¼ pint red wine vinegar
275ml/9fl oz red wine
salt and freshly ground black pepper
for the stuffing:
100g/4oz softened butter
4 garlic cloves, squashed and
    finely chopped
1 red chilli, finely chopped
50g/2oz fresh mint, finely chopped
50g/2oz fresh flat-leaf parsley,
    finely chopped

First make the stuffing. Put all the stuffing ingredients in a bowl and mix together until smooth, adding a little salt to taste. Shape into a ball, wrap in clingfilm and put in the fridge until ready to use.

Place the guinea fowl breasts on a chopping board, skin-side down. Make a small pocket in each one with a sharp knife and fill with the herb butter. Fold over the skin from both sides to cover the flesh and secure it with wooden toothpicks, weaving them in and out. Ensure that none of the filling comes out.

Heat the olive oil in a large saucepan, add the guinea fowl breasts and cook until sealed on all sides. Pour in the balsamic vinegar, red wine vinegar and wine, turn down the heat and cook for 20 minutes, turning the guinea fowl over halfway through the cooking time. Remove the guinea fowl from the pan and leave to cool. Take the saucepan off the heat and beat with a whisk until the sauce begins to thicken and has an almost creamy consistency. Taste and adjust the seasoning if necessary.

Remove the toothpicks from the guinea fowl and slice. Arrange the slices on a plate and pour the sauce over.

faraona con pancetta e uva passa
guinea fowl with pancetta and raisins

The sweetness of raisins goes well with guinea fowl – although you could substitute chicken if you prefer. You could also buy ready-cut guinea fowl pieces rather than jointing a whole bird, but I do recommend that you use the legs, as they enhance the flavour of the dish. Smoked streaky bacon can be substituted for the pancetta.

serves 4

1 x 1kg/2¼lb guinea fowl, jointed into 4 (you could ask your butcher to do this)
75g/3oz plain flour
4 tbsp olive oil
100g/4oz pancetta, cut into thin strips
10 garlic cloves, unpeeled
100g/4oz raisins
2 sprigs of fresh rosemary
1 glass of white wine
1 glass of chicken stock
salt and freshly ground black pepper

Preheat the oven to 150°C/300°F/Gas Mark 2. Coat the guinea fowl pieces in the flour, shaking off any excess. Heat the olive oil in a large, ovenproof heavy-based pan over medium heat, add the pancetta and fry until browned. Remove the pancetta from the pan and set aside.

Place the guinea fowl in the pan and cook until sealed on all sides. Add the garlic cloves, raisins, rosemary and wine. Simmer until the wine has reduced by half, then add the stock and return the pancetta to the pan. Cover tightly with a lid, transfer to the oven and cook for 30–40 minutes, until the guinea fowl is tender. Taste the sauce and adjust the seasoning, then serve.

coniglio con aglio e rosmarino servito con bruschetta
rabbit with garlic and rosemary served with bruschetta

Rabbit is cooked all over Italy in different ways and the method I have given here is the way we cook it at home. It was always my son Christopher's favourite dish at Sunday lunches and I dedicate this recipe to him. If you don't like rabbit, you can cook chicken, guinea fowl or turkey in exactly the same way. Use good extra virgin olive oil for this recipe, as you need quite a lot and the flavour really comes out.

serves 4

1 rabbit, weighing 1.5kg/3lb 5oz
   chopped into medium-sized chunks
   on the bone (including the liver,
   kidneys and ribs), or use ready-
   prepared boneless chunks of rabbit
plain flour for dusting
150ml/¼ pint extra virgin olive oil
cloves from 1 garlic head, kept whole
   with skins on
a large bunch of fresh rosemary,
   broken in half
150ml/¼ pint white wine
salt and freshly ground black pepper
for the bruschetta:
a few slices of slightly stale bread
a few garlic cloves, peeled but left whole

Season the rabbit with salt and pepper and dust with the flour. Heat the olive oil in a large, heavy-based frying pan. When hot, add the floured rabbit chunks and seal well on all sides until golden brown and quite crisp. Reduce the heat, add the garlic and rosemary, cover with a lid and cook gently for 30 minutes, turning the pieces of rabbit from time to time. Turn up the heat to high, remove the lid, pour in the wine and simmer until it has evaporated.

When the rabbit is ready, make the bruschetta. Toast the slices of bread, immediately rub them with the garlic and then drizzle with some of the olive oil that will have risen to the top of the rabbit sauce. Serve the rabbit accompanied by the bruschetta.

insaccati

preserved meats

Preserved meats are extremely popular throughout Italy, with each region having its own specialities. Although pig is the most common animal from which preserved meats are made, wild boar, goose and beef are also used.

Bresaola

Bresaola is air-dried beef. It is a popular antipasto on many Italian restaurant menus and can also be found ready-sliced in packets in most supermarkets, although this variety is very 'plastic' and tastes nothing like the original. My friend, Mauro Bregoli, who lives in the New Forest, is a master of curing and preserving meat, and his smoked bresaola is exceptional. Whenever I put bresaola on the menu at Passione, I ordered his. The best-quality bresaola can be found at good Italian delicatessens and you should ask for the *punta d'anca*, which is the fleshiest and most succulent part.

Bresaola should be served thinly sliced, drizzled with some extra virgin olive oil and lemon juice, and accompanied with some rocket and shavings of Parmesan cheese or with warm caprino (mild Italian goat's cheese).

Cotechino and zampone

These are both a type of huge sausage. Cotechino is a mixture of pork rind, fat and meat, all minced up and very finely seasoned with spices, then placed inside sausage skins and cooked for a long time. Zampone is pig's trotter minced up with pork rind, back fat, lean meat and some spices and seasoning. The mixture is then stuffed in sausage skin.

Both are now made commercially and sold in vacuum packs, making them easy to cook in boiling water at home. They are traditionally served at New Year with stewed lentils. The descriptions of both may sound a little off-putting, but I guarantee that if you like sausages, these are the best! They are easily obtainable at Italian delis. Serve with stewed lentils or mashed potatoes and braised cabbage for a filling winter meal.

Prosciutto crudo di Parma

Made from pigs raised in the Emilia Romagna region, this is probably Italy's most renowned cured ham. Other regions have their own versions – for example, San Daniele from Friuli and San Leo from Marche. The best-quality hams are cured on the bone for at least 18–24 months. Parma ham is traditionally served as part of an antipasto with other cured meats, pickles and preserved vegetables (see page 138). See also Antipasto di Pesche e Prosciutto Crudo di Parma on page 98.

Salami

Italy has a vast variety of salami, which are mostly commercially produced nowadays, although many farmers and local *salumerie* still make their own in the old-fashioned way.

Good salami is made with *suino* (pure lard), and the regional varieties have their own flavourings, such as black peppercorns, fennel seeds, chilli and red wine. Some of the most common varieties of salami found in delis in this country are Milano, Napoletano, Felino, Cacciatorino, Soppressata, Finocchiona and Calabrese, each of which has its own characteristics. I suggest you try a few slices of each before picking your favourite. Serve a selection of salami as part of an antipasto, with pickles and preserved vegetables (see page 138).

Sausages

There is a wide range of Italian sausages available in good delicatessens. Most are pork-based, with flavourings such as fennel seeds, rosemary, sage and chilli. They are usually short and fat, tied with string, and sold loosely from the cold counter. Italian sausages are delicious grilled or fried, as you would cook other sausages, or added to a thick tomato ragu (see page 100) to make a filling pasta sauce.

There is also the luganega sausage, which is a very long pork sausage, common in northern Italy, usually sold by the metre. Buy a long piece and wrap it round in a spiral shape (like the English Cumberland sausage), secure it with toothpicks and fry it, adding rosemary sprigs and finishing off with red wine. This is delicious eaten with polenta or mashed potatoes.

When I came to England at the end of the 1960s, there were two things I wanted: a pair of Levis and a gun. I had been out hunting with my father on Sunday mornings since I was tiny. Our family had hunted for at least two generations, so it was in my blood. When I was a small boy, I was effectively the dog! I would run through the undergrowth and frighten the birds out. When my father was about to shoot, he would shout, 'Hop!', which meant, 'Don't move!', and I would duck down. Then we would head back to the village to go to church. My father would leave his gun and pack of game outside. It would be full of blackbirds, wood pigeons, sparrows and quails.

I remember how strict my father was about his gun. I was never allowed to touch it. He always prepared and stored the cartridges at my grandfather's house and the gun at ours. He frightened me with stories of accidents and injuries, so I was always very careful. He usually let me have a couple of shots with his sixteen-bore at the end of a day's hunting, though.

I bought my gun and Levis almost as soon as I got to England. Then I found there was nowhere to shoot. I spent days going round the countryside asking farmers if I could shoot on their land. Eventually one took pity on me and allowed me on his property, as long as I stuck to wood pigeons and rabbits. There is quite a large hunting fraternity in England, which I was lucky enough to join, and I used to go hunting frequently. These days, if friends ask me to join them, I gladly go along.

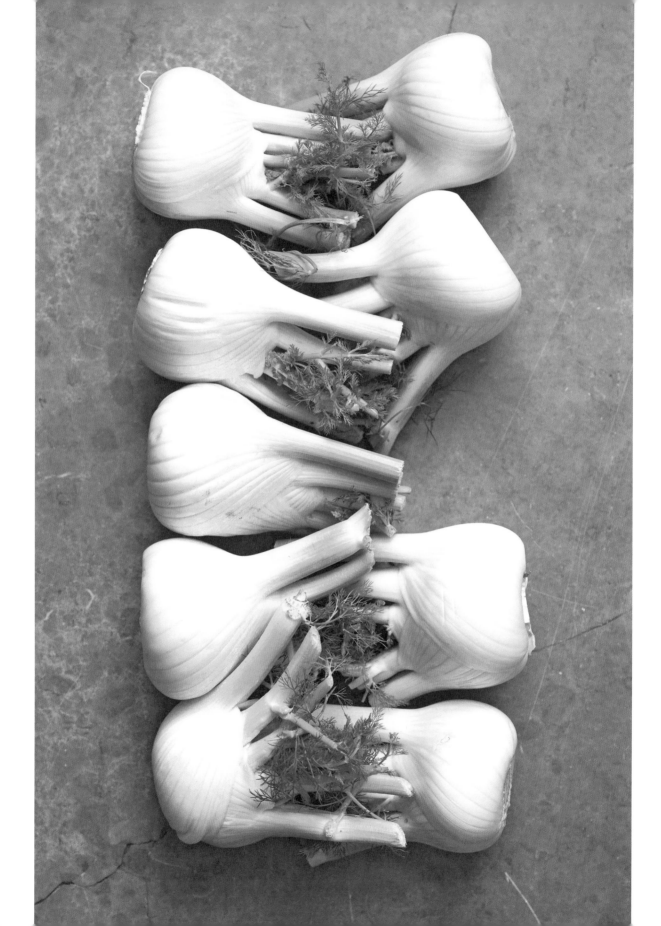

verdure

vegetables

Southern Italians love vegetables so much that Neapolitans used to be known as *mangiafoglie*, or leaf-eaters. To this day, Italians have a rich tradition of vegetable cookery and serve vegetables as main course dishes, not just starters and accompaniments.

When I was growing up, we usually ate meat only once or twice a week but we enjoyed an excellent, varied diet of seasonal vegetables. Nowadays, we can eat any vegetable all year round, but I miss the anticipation and excitement we felt at the beginning of each new season. We knew we couldn't rely on fresh veg all year round, so right from the very first crop of spring we would start preserving them for the winter months.

It was a joy eating the vegetables we had preserved from spring and summer – not just for the taste but also for the memories. Every time I opened a new jar, it reminded me of the day I had filled it. It may have been a feast day, or the first day of summer, or even a sad day, but the memories always came flooding back. The taste of those preserved vegetables was out of this world. Preserved aubergines, in particular, were so good that it was a miracle if they made it through to the winter months.

Winter was a joy for me in many ways. I loved the beautiful chestnuts, the dried figs and fruit, and the pungent flavours of preserved summer vegetables. But, after a long winter living on root vegetables and preserved vegetables, spring was really something to look forward to. It brought the first broad beans, peas, courgettes, chicory, cucumbers, onions, asparagus and endless salads.

The greengrocer shops gradually came alive with colour as they filled with new produce. As spring continued, more and more vegetables arrived – all kinds of cabbages, large aubergines and tomatoes. Then, with the summer, came an abundance of vegetables and the first fruit crops of the season. It was magnificent. Small pears and figs straight from the trees, herbs, chillies, peppers – everything was available and everything was delicious.

insalata di arancie e finocchio
orange and fennel salad

This salad is typical of Sicily, where oranges are grown in abundance. It is eaten all over the South as well, and I remember it was one of my father's favourite salads as a pre-lunch snack to refresh himself and stimulate his tastebuds – rather like an aperitif. The combination of sweet oranges, the aniseed flavour of the fennel and the saltiness of the anchovies makes this a very tasty salad indeed.

serves 4

4 oranges, peeled, zest and
   pith removed
8 black olives, sliced
1 large fennel bulb, finely sliced (reserve
   the feathery fronds)
8 anchovy fillets
4 tbsp extra virgin olive oil
2 tsp red wine vinegar
salt and freshly ground black pepper

Take an orange in the palm of your hand and with a small, very sharp knife cut out the segments from between the membranes, discarding the pips and any pith still attached. Repeat with the remaining oranges.

Place the orange segments and sliced olives in a bowl, then add the fennel and anchovy fillets. Season with salt and pepper (be careful with the salt as the anchovies are already quite salty). Mix in the olive oil and vinegar, leave to marinate for a minute or two and then serve. Decorate with the green feathery leaves from the fennel.

pure di ceci
chickpea purée

Try this purée as an alternative to potatoes or other root vegetables. It makes a wonderful accompaniment to meat dishes, such as Faraona con Pancetta e Uva Passa (see page 115).

serves 4–6

4 tbsp olive oil
1 celery stalk, finely chopped
½ leek, finely chopped
1 onion, finely chopped
2 small carrots, finely chopped
a few rosemary needles
250g/9oz dried chickpeas, soaked
   overnight in cold water and
   then drained
1 litre/1¾ pints vegetable stock
salt and freshly ground black pepper

Heat the olive oil in a large saucepan, add the vegetables and rosemary and sweat until softened. Stir in the chickpeas, then add the stock. Bring to the boil, reduce the heat, then cover the pan and simmer for about 1½ hours, until the chickpeas are tender and have absorbed almost all the liquid.

Remove from the heat, place in a food processor and whiz until smooth. Taste and adjust the seasoning. Serve immediately, or make in advance and then heat through gently just before serving.

patate saltate

sautéed potatoes

These are an essential accompaniment to all sorts of meat dishes and roasts. Leave the garlic cloves unpeeled and don't worry about the skin; it all adds to the flavour and appearance of the dish.

serves 4

400g (14oz) small new potatoes, scrubbed and cut in half

6 tbsp olive oil

3 garlic cloves, unpeeled and squashed with the back of a knife

4 sprigs of fresh rosemary

salt and freshly ground black pepper

Cook the potatoes in boiling salted water until tender, then drain.

Heat the olive oil in a frying pan and add the garlic and rosemary, followed by the potatoes. Allow the potatoes to colour on all sides over a fairly high heat, stirring now and again to prevent them sticking to the pan. Season with salt and pepper and serve immediately.

insalata di patate

warm potato salad

For maximum flavour, it is imperative that this dish is served when the potatoes are still warm, so make sure that all the other ingredients are ready as soon as the potatoes are cooked. It makes an ideal accompaniment to Involtini di Pesce Spada con Finocchio (see page 81) for a light al fresco lunch.

serves 4

8 medium new potatoes

2 medium red onions, very finely sliced

1 teaspoon dried oregano

120ml/4fl oz extra virgin olive oil

3 tbsp red wine vinegar

salt and freshly ground black pepper

Wash and scrub the potatoes well but don't peel them. Bring a saucepan of lightly salted water to the boil and cook the potatoes until tender. Drain and remove the skins, holding the potatoes in a cloth to avoid burning your fingers.

Cut the potatoes into quarters and place in a bowl with all the remaining ingredients. Mix well and serve warm.

tortino di patate e cavolo nero
potato and cavolo nero bake

Potatoes, cabbage and Taleggio cheese are a typically northern Italian combination. The climate is much cooler in the North and you would expect to eat such a dish there during winter. I have used cavolo nero in this recipe, as I find it much tastier, but you could use Savoy cabbage instead. Cavolo nero is grown mainly in Tuscany and has become widely available in supermarkets throughout the UK. Its name means 'black cabbage', referring to its long, thin leaves, which are so dark that they look almost black. It certainly stands out from the usual variety of cabbage found in greengrocer's.

Taleggio gives the dish a rich, creamy taste but if you can't find it, substitute Fontina or a mature Cheddar.

If you cook this in four individual terracotta dishes, it makes an ideal vegetarian main course, served with a simple green salad. Prepare it in advance and then bake once your guests have arrived.

serves 4

675g/1½lb cavolo nero
    (large leaves only)
8 medium potatoes, peeled and
    thinly sliced
150g/5oz butter
325g/11oz Taleggio cheese, thinly sliced
salt and freshly ground black pepper

Remove the stalks and hard central core from the cavolo nero leaves and cook in plenty of boiling salted water for 3–5 minutes, until just tender but still slightly crisp. Drain well, rinse in cold water and then drain again, squeezing out any excess water with your hands. Dry on a kitchen cloth. Cook the potato slices in a saucepan of lightly salted boiling water for 3 minutes, then drain, rinse in cold water, drain again and dry well on a kitchen cloth.

Preheat the oven to its highest setting. To make individual servings, you will need 4 terracotta dishes about 20cm/8in in diameter and 3cm/1¼in deep. Grease each dish generously with some of the butter. Arrange half the potato slices, slightly overlapping, over the bottom of the dishes, dot with some of the butter and season with salt and pepper. Arrange the cavolo nero leaves over the potatoes, with the larger part of the leaf hanging a quarter of the way over the edge of the dish. About 10 cabbage leaves should suffice for each dish. Arrange half the cheese on top of the cabbage and then season with salt and pepper. Top with the remaining potatoes, then with the remaining cheese. Place a cabbage leaf in the middle and fold over the excess leaves, pressing gently with your fingers so that none of the other ingredients are visible, then dot with butter. If you are making one large bake, grease a large baking tray with plenty of butter and then layer the ingredients as above.

Cover with aluminium foil, place in the oven and bake for 25 minutes. Remove from the oven and carefully lift off the foil, taking care not to burn yourself with the steam. Serve straight from the baking tray if you have made a large bake. If you have made individual portions, place a plate over each one and flip over. You should get a lovely layer of golden-brown potatoes on the top. Serve immediately.

paparoni ripiani
stuffed baby peppers

For this recipe, try to use small peppers or, if you prefer, the small, sweet long peppers. If you use the latter, slit them lengthways and remove the seeds, then make the filling as below, except for the provolone which you should slice in strips and place over the top of the peppers. Bake these long peppers for 20 minutes only. If you can't find either type of pepper, use ordinary peppers and serve one per person.

serves 4

8 red or yellow baby peppers
2 large potatoes, boiled and mashed
75g/3oz provolone cheese, cut into very small cubes
4 tbsp freshly grated Parmesan cheese
1 egg
3 tbsp finely chopped fresh chives
a little olive oil for drizzling
salt and freshly ground black pepper

Preheat the oven to 200°C/400°F/ Gas Mark 6. Remove the stalks from the peppers and set aside. With a small, sharp knife, remove the white membrane and seeds from inside the peppers, taking care not to tear the flesh.

Mix together the mashed potatoes, provolone, Parmesan, egg, chives and some salt and pepper. Using a teaspoon, fill the peppers three-quarters full with the mixture and then put the stalks back in place, like a stopper. Pack the peppers tightly into an ovenproof dish, drizzle with olive oil and bake for about 30 minutes, until tender. Serve immediately with a good green salad. They are also delicious eaten cold.

agrodolce di paparoni
sweet and sour peppers

Sweet and sour flavours go extremely well with peppers. This dish can be served as a starter with lots of bread to mop up the delicious olive oil, or as a side dish to accompany meat and game. It is ideal for making in large quantities for parties, as it can be eaten cold.

serves 2–4

6 tbsp extra virgin olive oil
1 large yellow pepper, deseeded and cut into thick strips
1 large red pepper, deseeded and cut into thick strips
3 anchovy fillets
2 garlic cloves, peeled but left whole
6 black olives
1 tbsp capers
1 tbsp sugar
4 tbsp white wine vinegar
salt and freshly ground black pepper

Heat the olive oil in a large frying pan, add the peppers and cook until the skins are golden brown. Then add the anchovy fillets, garlic, olives and capers. Stir in the sugar, then add the vinegar and allow to evaporate. Cook over a medium heat for about 5 minutes, or until the peppers are tender. Season to taste and serve either hot or cold.

carciofi ripieni
Stuffed globe artichokes

Artichokes are very popular in Italy, especially in the South where they grow in abundance. In fact, Italy is the largest producer of artichokes in the Mediterranean and a great number are exported as well as eaten locally. Just like chestnut sellers on street corners in England, we used to have artichoke vendors selling roasted artichokes. The smell was irresistible.

I love artichokes and cook them in a variety of ways – roasted, fried, steamed and in salads (see page 135). My favourite way of cooking the large globe artichokes is to stuff them and slow-cook them in a pot. Try this recipe; it's simple to prepare, makes a wonderful starter and looks very impressive when served – almost too lovely to eat! When serving, remember to provide finger bowls, spare plates to hold the discarded leaves, and plenty of good bread to soak up the sauce.

serves 4

4 handfuls of fresh parsley, roughly torn
4 garlic cloves, thinly sliced
8 anchovy fillets
16 cherry tomatoes, quartered
4 tsp capers
8 green olives, sliced
4 large globe artichokes
about 1.5 litres/2½ pints vegetable stock
8 tbsp extra-virgin olive oil, plus a little extra for drizzling
salt and freshly ground black pepper

Combine the parsley, garlic, anchovy fillets, tomatoes, capers and olives in a bowl and set aside.

With a small, sharp knife, remove the bottom outer leaves of each artichoke and cut off the stalk. Trim the base slightly so the bottom sits flat. With your fingers, gently open out the artichoke until you can see the hairy choke. With a small scoop or teaspoon, remove and discard the choke, which is inedible. Season the artichoke cavities with salt and pepper and fill each with the parsley mixture, gently pressing all the ingredients in.

Put the filled artichokes in a large saucepan, then pour in the stock. Pack them in tightly so they don't wobble during cooking. If your pan is too big and there is space between the artichokes, fill the gap with a large potato. The stock should come three-quarters of the way up the artichokes, so if necessary add some more.

Pour 2 tablespoons of olive oil into each stuffed artichoke. Bring to the boil, then reduce the heat, cover the pan and simmer for 1 hour or until the artichokes are tender; if you can pull out a central leaf easily, they are done.

Carefully lift out the artichokes with a large slotted spoon and place on individual serving plates, then gently open up the artichokes so the filling is exposed. Pour about half a ladleful of the stock over each artichoke and drizzle with some olive oil. Serve immediately, with lots of bread to dip into the sauce.

fagottini di zucchini
stuffed courgette parcels

This is a different and interesting way of using courgettes. They are simple enough to prepare, but allow yourself some time and you will find that once you get going they are fun to make. They look good, too, and make an ideal starter with some salad leaves or to serve with drinks. I am sure your guests will be intrigued to know how you got the filling in!

serves 6 as a starter

4 large courgettes
350g/12oz ricotta cheese
200g/7oz potatoes, boiled and mashed
5 tbsp freshly grated Parmesan cheese
8–12 fresh sage leaves
8–12 thin slices of Fontina cheese, about 4cm/1½in square (you could substitute mature Cheddar)
a little butter for greasing
salt and freshly ground black pepper

With a sharp knife, cut the courgettes lengthways into slices 5mm/¼in thick; you should get 4–6 slices from each courgette. Cook the courgette slices in plenty of lightly salted boiling water for about 2 minutes, until just tender, then remove and plunge into cold water. Drain and pat dry with kitchen paper.

Preheat the oven to 240°C/475°F/Gas Mark 9. In a large bowl, mix together the ricotta, mashed potatoes, Parmesan and some salt and pepper. Take 2 slices of courgette, place them on a clean, dry surface and shape them in a cross. Repeat with the rest of the courgette slices. With your fingers, shape the ricotta mixture into balls about the size of a pingpong ball (one for each courgette cross). Place a ball in the middle of each cross, place a sage leaf on top and then fold the strips of courgette over to make a parcel. Place a slice of Fontina on top and secure with a wooden toothpick.

Line a baking tray with aluminium foil or greaseproof paper and grease with some butter. Place the courgette parcels on the baking tray. (At this stage, you can also choose to refrigerate them and cook when needed.) Bake for 10–12 minutes, until golden. Remove the parcels from the oven, place on a serving dish and remove the toothpicks. Serve warm, with some salad leaves.

fette di melanzane con crosta di parmigiano e polenta
aubergine slices with a Parmesan and polenta crust

This idea was given to me by Liz while we were making Involtini di Melanzane alla Parmigiana (see page 134) together. It was her grandmother's version of 'vegetarian steak', which she would make for the family during wartime when meat was scarce. It can be served as a snack, side dish or, indeed, a vegetarian main course. The aubergine slices are delicious topped with Salsa alla Crudaiola (see page 142), a little garlic, basil, salt and pepper, or with preserved vegetables (see page 138).

serves 4–6

2 large eggs
25g/1oz Parmesan cheese, freshly grated
1 large aubergine, peeled and cut
    lengthways into slices 5mm/¼in thick
plain flour, seasoned with salt and
    pepper, for dusting
250g/9oz polenta
7 tbsp olive oil
salt and freshly ground black pepper

Break the eggs into a bowl, season with salt and pepper, then add the Parmesan and beat well. Dust the aubergine slices in seasoned flour, dip them into the egg mixture and then coat with the polenta.

Heat the olive oil in a large frying pan and, over a medium-high heat, fry the aubergine slices on both sides until golden brown. Remove, drain on kitchen paper and serve either hot or cold. When eaten hot, they are deliciously crunchy.

verdure alla griglia
grilled vegetables

There is nothing more visually appealing than a plate of mixed grilled vegetables. They can be eaten hot or cold, so can be prepared in advance if necessary. If you have a charcoal grill, then you will obviously get a better flavour. Ideal for barbecues for your vegetarian guests.

serves 4
1 yellow and 1 red pepper, roasted, skinned and sliced into strips 3–4cm/1¼–1½in wide (see page 139)
150ml/¼ pint olive oil
1 garlic clove, finely sliced
2 small courgettes
1 aubergine
1 Spanish onion
12 cherry tomatoes on the vine
a few fresh mint leaves, roughly chopped
a few fresh basil leaves, roughly chopped
balsamic vinegar for drizzling (optional)
salt and freshly ground black pepper

Place the roasted pepper slices on a plate and drizzle over a couple of tablespoons of the olive oil. Add the garlic and some salt and pepper and leave to marinate for 15 minutes.

Meanwhile, cut the courgettes and aubergine lengthways into slices about 5mm/¼in thick. Score each slice in a criss-cross fashion with a small, sharp knife. Peel the onion and cut it into 4 fairly thick slices. Put the vegetables on a lightly oiled ridged grill pan or under a hot grill for a couple of minutes on each side, until just tender. Grill the whole tomatoes, too, until soft.

Arrange the vegetable slices and tomatoes on a serving dish, drizzle the remaining olive oil over them and season with salt and pepper. Sprinkle the mint over the courgettes and the basil over the tomatoes. Arrange the marinated peppers on the dish. Scatter with the garlic, as you wish. You can leave it out, but I prefer it with!

If you like, you can drizzle some balsamic vinegar over the vegetables to give them extra zest.

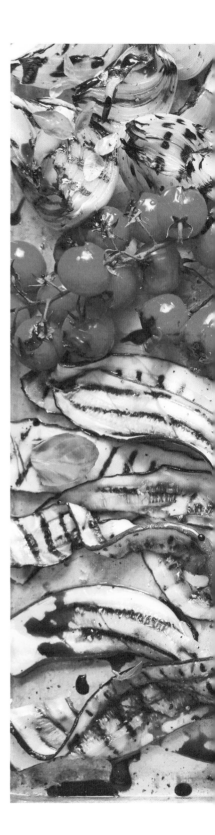

involtini di melanzane alla parmigiana
baked aubergine rolls filled with mozzarella

This is a speciality from southern Italy, where aubergines are found in abundance and are full of flavour. It makes a wonderful vegetarian main course.

I like making the aubergines into *involtini* (rolls), but if you prefer you can make layers of tomato sauce, aubergine slices, Parmesan cheese, mozzarella and basil, which is the traditional way of making this dish. Serve with a green salad for an informal mid-week supper.

serves 4–6

1 large aubergine, cut lengthways into
   6 slices about 5mm/¼in thick
2 tbsp plain flour
2 eggs, lightly beaten with some
   salt and pepper
olive oil for shallow-frying
40g/1½oz Parmesan cheese,
   freshly grated
18 large fresh basil leaves
300g/11oz mozzarella cheese,
   roughly sliced
salt and freshly ground black pepper
for the tomato sauce:
4 tbsp extra virgin olive oil
1 small onion, finely chopped
400g/14oz tin of plum tomatoes

To make the tomato sauce, heat the olive oil in a saucepan, add onion and sweat until softened. Stir in the tomatoes, season with salt and pepper, then cover the pan with a lid and simmer gently for 25 minutes.

Preheat the oven to 200°C/400°F/Gas Mark 6. Dust the aubergine slices in the flour, then dip them in the beaten egg. In a large frying pan, heat some olive oil to a depth of about 1cm/½in, add the aubergine slices and fry on both sides until golden. Remove and drain on kitchen paper. Line the aubergine slices up on a large chopping board, season with salt and pepper, then evenly sprinkle 25g/1oz of the Parmesan over the top. Place 3 basil leaves on each aubergine slice and top with a couple of slices of mozzarella, reserving half for the topping. Then carefully roll each slice up, making sure they sit seam-side down so they don't unravel.

Line a large ovenproof dish (or individual ones) with some of the tomato sauce and place the aubergine rolls on top, seam-side down. Spoon over the remaining tomato sauce and top with the remaining mozzarella slices and Parmesan. Place in the oven and bake for 15 minutes, until the top is very lightly coloured and beginning to bubble.

insalata di zucchine con menta fresca
courgette salad with fresh mint

Courgettes are delicious eaten raw, as long as they are firm and fresh and very thinly sliced. This quantity serves two people as a starter or four as a side dish. The longer you leave the courgette to marinate before serving, the better this salad will be. The secret of this dish is to use very fresh courgettes.

serves 2–4

120ml/4fl oz extra virgin olive oil
4 tbsp balsamic vinegar
1 garlic clove, finely chopped
a handful of fresh mint, finely chopped
4 small courgettes
salt and freshly ground black pepper

In a bowl, whisk the olive oil and vinegar together with the garlic, mint and some salt and pepper. Trim the ends of the courgettes and, with a potato peeler, slice them lengthways into wafer-thin ribbons. Add to the dressing, mix well and leave to marinate for 10 minutes or more before serving.

insalata di carciofi, asparagi e finocchio
salad of raw artichokes, asparagus and fennel

Raw artichokes are surprisingly delicious. They are usually served as a salad with shavings of fresh Parmesan, dressed with extra virgin olive oil and lemon juice. Here, I have omitted the Parmesan and added other crunchy, raw vegetables. If you don't like one of the vegetables, you could replace it with some raw carrots. This makes a lovely, healthy starter.

serves 4

4 small fresh artichoke hearts, cleaned (see page 139) and very finely chopped
4 small asparagus spears (use just the tips, about 5cm/2in), sliced lengthways in half
2 small fennel bulbs, finely chopped
8 chicory leaves, finely sliced in strips
2 small spring onions, finely chopped (optional)

for the dressing:

6 tbsp extra virgin olive oil
4 tbsp lemon juice
salt and freshly ground black pepper

When you have chopped all the vegetables, set them aside and make the dressing. Place all the dressing ingredients in a large bowl and mix well. Add the chopped vegetables and toss together. Serve immediately with some bread.

bietole rosse marinate
marinated beetroot

Fresh beetroot doesn't feature much on Italian menus but I remember it was one of my mother's favourite vegetables, and she would often preserve it. If you follow this recipe, the beetroot will keep for about two weeks in the oil; if you want it to last longer you will have to store it in sterilised jars. Once all the beetroot has been consumed, keep the oil and use it to flavour salads or pasta or to marinate some more beetroot. You need such a lot of olive oil for this recipe that it's a shame to throw it away.

Serve the marinated beetroot as you would pickles – perhaps as an antipasto with some salami or air-dried tuna (*mosciame*).

serves 6
650g/1½lb raw beetroot
500ml/17fl oz white or red wine vinegar
2 litres/3½ pints water
a pinch of salt
for the marinade:
2 garlic cloves, sliced
1 tbsp dried oregano
1 red chilli, finely chopped
500ml/17fl oz olive oil

Wash and scrub the beetroot under cold running water. Place them in a saucepan with the vinegar, water and salt and bring to the boil. Reduce the heat, cover the pan and simmer for about 1¼ hours, until the beetroot are tender.

Meanwhile, combine all the marinade ingredients in a bowl and set aside.

Once the beetroot are cooked, drain, place on a clean kitchen cloth or kitchen paper and pat dry. Remove the skins with the help of the cloth. Cut into slices, place in the marinade and mix well. Leave for a day before serving. The beetroot will keep for several days in a covered container in the fridge but should be brought to room temperature before serving.

verdure miste sott ólio

mixed preserved vegetables

Preserving vegetables was very common when I was a child. It was a means of enjoying certain vegetables all year round. Nowadays we can get all sorts of vegetables at any time of year but I still like to preserve them when they are in season. Not only is it an enjoyable task but preserving gives them a different flavour. Here I have chosen peppers and aubergines, which I have preserved raw so they remain nice and crunchy. Serve with a few slices of Parma ham and salami, plus lots of good bread for a delicious antipasto.

serves 8–10
600g/1lb 5oz red and yellow peppers
600g/1lb 5oz aubergines
150g/5oz salt
800ml/1¼ pints white wine vinegar
3 garlic cloves, thinly sliced lengthways
1 red chilli, thinly sliced
1 tbsp dried oregano
250ml/8fl oz olive oil

Cut the peppers in half and remove all the seeds and white membrane. Slice lengthways into very fine strips. Peel the aubergines, slice them lengthways and then cut finely lengthways into strips approximately the same size as the peppers.

Keep the vegetables separate. Take 2 plastic containers, one for the peppers and one for the aubergines. Line one container with the peppers, sprinkle with a good handful of the salt, then carry on with layers of peppers and salt, ending up with salt. Place a weight over the top and set aside. Take the other container and do the same with the aubergines. Leave the vegetables for 1½ hours, after which time they will have exuded a lot of liquid.

Take the vegetables in your hands and squeeze out the excess liquid. Place in separate containers, cover each with the vinegar and leave for 1½ hours again.

Drain the vegetables, squeezing out the excess liquid with your hands, and place together in a bowl with the garlic, chilli and oregano. Add the olive oil and mix well. Place in a jar, securing tightly with a lid, and leave for a couple of days before using.

consigli di gennaro sulla preparazione delle verdure
Gennaro's vegetable cooking tips

Artichokes

To prepare artichokes, remove the bottom outer leaves with a small, sharp knife and cut off the stalk. With your fingers, gently open up the artichoke until you can see the hairy choke. Remove it with a small scoop or teaspoon and discard. If you want to use just the hearts, then remove all the leaves except for a few tender inner ones. If your hands get black while cleaning the artichokes, wash them with lemon juice – the dark stains disappear quickly. Rub the artichokes with lemon juice too, to prevent discoloration and, if not cooking them immediately, keep them in a bowl of water acidulated with lemon juice.

You can cook artichokes in many ways, and even eat them raw when they are young and tender. Simply chop them finely, drizzle with some extra virgin olive oil and lemon juice, then season with salt and pepper. Place on a bed of rocket and top with Parmesan shavings.

Celery

To obtain maximum flavour, bash celery stalks with the flat of a knife blade before chopping them. Use the leaves as well. Added at the end of cooking, they give a wonderful fresh flavour to the dish.

Courgettes

Unless you are using very small, fresh courgettes, the white middle part does not really have much flavour. To make the most of courgettes, cut off the skin in long strips a good 5mm/¼in thick

and discard the white middle part (save it to add to vegetable stocks). Slice or chop the green strips according to your recipe.

Garlic

Before chopping garlic, squash the cloves whole, skin on, for the best flavour.

Mushrooms

Do not wash mushrooms, whether wild or cultivated. Use a soft brush or slightly damp cloth to clean them. Mushrooms are already full of water and immersing them in more destroys their flavour.

Onions

Soak whole onions in cold water for 30 minutes before peeling. You will find the skin comes off more easily and they will be less pungent when you chop them (so you will be less likely to cry!).

Parsley

Use the stalks, finely chopped, for stocks and soups. They are very flavoursome.

Peppers

To roast peppers, place them under a hot grill, turning several times, until the skin goes black. Remove and leave to cool. Peel off the skin, slice them in half and remove the white interior and seeds. Then slice according to your recipe.

For a delicious salad, slice roasted peppers into strips, sprinkle with extra virgin olive oil, chopped garlic, salt and

pepper and leave to marinate for 15 minutes. This makes a good antipasto with lots of bread. Alternatively, to make a sauce for pasta, place the skinned, deseeded roasted peppers in a food processor and whiz with enough extra-virgin olive oil to give a smooth sauce. Season, heat through gently and mix with some cooked penne or tagliatelle.

Potatoes

If you plan to mash your potatoes, don't peel them. Just wash them to get rid of any dirt, then boil them whole. Once tender, drain and remove the skin, which will peel off very easily. You will find that potatoes cooked this way make much better mash, as they are not so watery.

Salads

There are now so many different types of salad dressings from cuisines all over the world – all of them can be delicious, but for me the simple, classic Italian way to dress salads is the best. Place your salad leaves in a large bowl, then sprinkle them abundantly with salt and drizzle with two parts extra virgin olive oil to one part white or red wine vinegar. Mix well, using your hands – you will find that this way the dressing coats each leaf.

Tomatoes

To skin tomatoes, cut a tiny cross in the base of each with a sharp knife. Place them in a bowl of boiling water for no more than 30 seconds, then drain and place in cold water. Peel off the skins.

pomodori

tomatoes

The tomato played a very important role in our culinary life when I was growing up. It is integral to Italian cooking, the basis for so many sauces, and a delight to eat raw in salads.

I remember the anticipation I felt in late summer when I knew my favourite tomato, the San Marzano, was nearly ripe and ready to eat. This long plum tomato grows close to my home, in the Pompeii valley under the shadow of Mount Vesuvius. The fertile volcanic soil helps to produce what I think is the best-tasting tomato in Italy. These tomatoes were perfect in salads and delicious on their own, drizzled with olive oil and sprinkled with salt.

Because tomatoes were so important to our cuisine, we preserved them for use all year round. These days you can buy tinned tomatoes in every corner shop and supermarket, whole or chopped, plain or herb-flavoured. Tomato purée is readily available, and sun-dried tomatoes can be bought at most supermarkets and delicatessens. But when I was a child, we had to prepare the tomatoes ourselves. The hard work made us appreciate the food and brought the family together.

In my house, tomato preservation was a great ceremony and enormous fun. It was usually in September, when the San Marzano tomato was still available, that the family gathered together and the grand procedure began.

We preserved our tomatoes in small beer bottles made of thick, brown glass. The glass had to be thick to survive the pasteurisation process. A long wooden table was set out in the garden with lots of chairs arranged round it for all the family to sit at. On the table was a vast supply of freshly cleaned bottles, a bucketful of corks, fresh basil leaves and kilo upon kilo of washed tomatoes. The tomatoes were cut lengthways into quarters and pushed into the beer bottles along with the odd basil leaf until they were almost full. The bottles were then corked, using a strange gadget. The scene was like a production line, but everyone was cheerful and relaxed, laughing and chatting as they worked.

At the other side of the garden was a large oil drum placed over a tripod. On the bottom of the drum was a raffia sack, folded in two. We placed the filled beer bottles in the drum one by one. Once it was full, water was poured in and another raffia sack placed on top to act as a lid. Then a fire was lit underneath. We took it in turns to sit with the fire all night and make sure it didn't go out until the early hours of the morning, when the process was finished. Once the water had cooled, we removed the beer bottles, dried them and placed them in store cupboards, ready for use in winter.

We always made huge quantities, enough to ensure a year-round supply for us, as well as our family living in the city who could not make their own. The preservation process was perfect. Even when we found a bottle that was a couple of years old at the back of the cupboard, the tomatoes still tasted good. These tomatoes didn't taste like the tinned ones you find in the shops; they were something else. There are still families in southern Italy who preserve their tomatoes in this way each year. If I had the time now, I think I would, too.

Besides preserving whole tomatoes, we used to make tomato concentrate to use throughout the winter months in heavy-based sauces for pasta or meat dishes. The tomatoes were washed and put through a special mincer to extract the pulp. Then the pulp was placed in large, flat, terracotta dishes, covered with nets to keep the flies off and placed on the veranda under the hot August sun for the excess moisture to evaporate.

One member of the family was put in charge of this process. Their duty was to stir the pulp every couple of hours with a large wooden spoon and occasionally sprinkle a few drops of olive oil over the top to prevent a crust forming. The dishes were taken in at night and put out again first thing in the morning. After three or four days, the fresh pulp turned into a thick, delicious concentrate of pure tomato. It was transferred to terracotta jars, drizzled with oil and sealed with greaseproof paper and string.

salsa di Pomodoro leggera
light basic tomato sauce

This is the most basic Italian tomato sauce and the most widely used with pasta and other dishes. It's always handy to make a large batch and keep in the fridge – although don't leave it for more than about three days. After this time, it is better to make a fresh batch.

makes enough for 4 servings of pasta
4 tbsp olive oil
2 garlic cloves, finely chopped
2 x 400g/14oz tins of plum tomatoes, chopped
a handful of fresh basil, finely chopped
salt and freshly ground black pepper

Heat the olive oil in a large frying pan, add the garlic and sweat until softened. Then add the tomatoes and basil, season with salt and pepper and simmer gently for 25 minutes.

salsa alla crudaiola
fresh tomato sauce

This is a delicious way to flavour summer pasta dishes or to top bruschetta and crostini (see page 155). Alternatively, simply serve it as a salad to accompany fish dishes. Make sure you use ripe cherry tomatoes, good-quality extra virgin olive oil and lots of fresh basil.

makes enough for 4 servings of pasta
400g/14oz cherry tomatoes, cut into quarters
2 garlic cloves, finely chopped
a handful of fresh basil
6 tbsp extra virgin olive oil
salt and freshly ground black pepper

Mix all the ingredients together in a bowl. Leave to marinate for at least 30 minutes. If you don't like garlic, or find 2 cloves too strong, use less or omit it altogether.

If you serve the sauce with pasta you can use it as it is or gently heat it through.

pomodori in bottiglie
'fresh' tinned tomato sauce

I call this 'fresh' because although I use tinned tomatoes they are not cooked for very long and are only chopped in half, so when served they look and taste quite fresh. They taste just like the tomatoes we used to preserve in beer bottles.

makes enough for 4 servings of pasta
2 x 400g/14oz tins of plum tomatoes, chopped in half
12 fresh basil leaves
6 tbsp olive oil
3 garlic cloves, cut into thick slices
salt and freshly ground black pepper

Place the tomatoes and their juice in a bowl with half the basil, add some salt and pepper and mix well. Heat the olive oil in a large saucepan and add the garlic. When the garlic begins to change colour, remove the pan from the heat and add the tomato mixture. Place back over the heat and cook gently for 4 minutes, until the mixture is bubbling. Stir in the remaining basil leaves.

Salsa di Pomodoro corposa
heavy-based tomato sauce

This tomato sauce is used to flavour heavy, meat-based pasta dishes such as the traditional Il Ragu (see page 100). You can use it simply as it is if you prefer a heavier tomato sauce. An hour's cooking time should suffice, but if you are cooking pieces of meat in the sauce you will need about two hours. Remember, the longer you cook this sauce, the richer it will become.

makes enough for 4 servings of pasta
6 tbsp olive oil
1 onion, very finely chopped
1 celery stalk, very finely chopped
1 garlic clove, finely chopped
2 x 400g/14oz tins of chopped tomatoes
2 tbsp tomato concentrate or tomato purée, diluted in 400ml/14fl oz lukewarm water
100ml/3½fl oz red wine
a handful of fresh basil leaves, torn
salt and freshly ground black pepper

Heat the olive oil in a large saucepan, add the onion, celery and garlic and sweat until soft. Add the tomatoes, diluted tomato concentrate or purée and wine. Season with salt and pepper, add the basil and stir well. Bring to the boil, then cover the pan – but not completely, so some of the steam can escape – and reduce the heat. Simmer for about 1 hour, until the sauce is thick and silky. Stir from time to time, checking that there is enough moisture; if necessary add a little more wine or some water.

funghi
mushrooms

I love the changing seasons. It is one of the reasons I live in England. My favourite season has always been the autumn. As September arrives, the summer ends. In Minori, that means the tourists leave, the sea becomes rough and populated with different kinds of fish, the weather changes and there is no more stifling heat. That was always my signal to leave the sea and move to the mountains, where I would lose myself in the forest, picking chestnuts, walnuts and mushrooms.

The first rain brought life to the changing land. The soil developed a rich, musky smell. Out of the blue, the fruits of the earth appeared. Thousands of mushrooms. There is nothing more magical than a glorious, sunny autumnal morning spent roaming the woods in search of these elusive fungi.

I was introduced to wild herbs and mushrooms at an early age. My mother used to take me with her on her collecting trips in the hills and fields. She showed me what was good to eat, what to try and what to leave well alone. She collected herbs and mushrooms for her herbal remedies, but we usually came back with such an abundance of produce that she would also use them for cooking.

I was still fairly young when she sent me out on my own to collect mushrooms and herbs for her. Even then, mushrooms intrigued me. I loved trying to distinguish the poisonous ones from the edible ones. It was like a game. I sampled them while I was out and about. Then I thought I was immortal; now I know I was just lucky.

I would take the mushrooms back to my mother. She threw away the ones she thought were poisonous and kept the ones she knew were good. I know so much more about mushrooms now and it breaks my heart to think of the priceless specimens she threw away.

I couldn't believe the abundance of wild herbs and mushrooms in the fields and forests when I came to England. It was here that my passion grew, and I was determined to become more knowledgeable. I discovered the delights of truffles in England, not Italy – although I am certain they existed in the forests of my childhood, I just wasn't aware of them.

I still go on regular herb and mushroom collecting forays. Some days I come back with seven or eight different edible species of mushroom – pretty ones, ugly ones, colourful ones, big ones, small ones – they are all delicious. On spring days, I like to go out and search for rocket, wild garlic, dandelions, wild fennel and sorrel.

I love the fact that you can find wild food anywhere – in fields, in parks, by the sea, even on the edge of motorways and in city centres.

Remember that although many mushrooms are safe to eat, others are highly poisonous and can be fatal. If you pick your own mushrooms, ensure you can identify them with absolute certainty, or go out with an expert.

funghi misti saltati

sauté of mixed wild mushrooms

This is a simple but truly exquisite recipe, especially after a mushroom hunt when you have lots of different varieties. Nothing is more pleasurable than going into the forest on a clear, crisp, autumnal morning and looking for mushrooms. However, if you are not fortunate enough to go out and pick your own, cultivated ones will suffice if you add dried porcini to give that 'wild' flavour. Simply soak 10g/¼oz dried porcini in 120ml/4fl oz lukewarm water for an hour, then add them, together with their soaking water, instead of the stock.

This dish is delicious as a starter, with lots of bread to mop up the sauce, or as an accompaniment to game or meat dishes.

serves 4
400g/14oz mixed wild mushrooms, such
   as porcini, chanterelles, hedgehog,
   wood blewits
6 tbsp olive oil
3 garlic cloves, finely chopped
   lengthways
1 small red chilli, roughly chopped
120ml/4fl oz vegetable stock
2 tbsp roughly chopped fresh parsley
salt

Clean the mushrooms with a cloth and brush – do not wash wild mushrooms, as the flavour disappears. Roughly chop any large mushrooms.

Heat the olive oil in a frying pan, add the garlic and chilli and sweat gently until softened – do not let them brown or burn. Turn up the heat a little, add the mushrooms and stir well for about 1 minute. Then add the stock, keep stirring, and cook for 2 minutes longer, until the liquid has evaporated slightly. Stir in the parsley and salt. Remove from the heat and serve immediately.

funghi sott'olio

preserved mushrooms

Because I am only able to get local wild mushrooms in season, I love to preserve them so I can enjoy them later in the year. In Italy it is traditional to pick porcini during late summer and autumn and then preserve them to enjoy at Christmas lunch with the antipasto. If you preserve the mushrooms in small jars, they make ideal Christmas presents.

serves 10–12
2 litres/3½ pints water
500ml/17fl oz white wine vinegar
1 glass of white wine
20g/¾oz salt
2 bunches of fresh rosemary sprigs
3 cloves
2 red onions, cut into quarters
1 red chilli, left whole
1 whole garlic bulb, cut in half
2kg/4½lb mixed mushrooms (either wild or cultivated), cleaned
1 litre/1¾ pints olive oil

Place the water, vinegar, wine and salt in a large saucepan and bring to the boil. Add the rosemary, cloves, onions, chilli and garlic. Then add the mushrooms, bring back to the boil and simmer for 5 minutes.

Drain the mushrooms and the other ingredients (onions, garlic, rosemary and chilli) and spread them out on clean kitchen cloths to dry. When they are cold, pick them up carefully with tongs and place in a sterilised 2kg/4½lb preserving jar (or several smaller jars). Cover with the oil and leave without the lid on for 2 hours. Ensure that the oil has seeped through to the bottom of the jar, cover with the lid and store in a cool, dark place for 1 week before eating (it can be left for up to 3 months).

Once opened, keep refrigerated and consume within 2 weeks.

cotolette di funghi puffball

puffball cutlets

Puffballs are strange-looking creatures. They are large, white mushrooms resembling footballs and can grow to quite an extraordinary size. They grow wild in fields from the end of August until mid-October and can be found all over the English countryside. If you ever find any, the best way to cook them is to coat them in breadcrumbs and shallow-fry.

They make a hearty English breakfast with scrambled eggs and bacon, or an Italian starter or snack with some preserved vegetables.

serves 2–4
1 medium-sized puffball-weighing about 150g/5oz
2 eggs, lightly beaten with some salt and pepper
100g/4oz fresh breadcrumbs
olive oil for shallow-frying

Clean the puffball by removing any dirt with a small brush or damp cloth. Cut into slices about 1.5cm/½ in thick. Dip into the beaten egg, then coat in the breadcrumbs.

Heat some oil in a large frying pan, add the mushroom slices and fry on both sides until golden brown. Remove and drain on kitchen paper. Serve hot or cold.

tagliatelle con funghi misti
tagliatelle with mixed mushrooms

If you enjoy making the sauté of wild mushrooms on page 148 and would like to use the same method for a more substantial dish, this is ideal. Fresh or dried tagliatelle are the perfect match for mixed mushrooms. Remember that you can use cultivated mushrooms, adding soaked dried porcini to give that 'wild' taste.

serves 4
225g/8oz fresh or dried tagliatelle
400g/14oz mixed wild mushrooms, such as porcini, chanterelles, hedgehog, wood blewits
6 tbsp olive oil
3 garlic cloves, finely chopped lengthways
1 small red chilli, roughly chopped
120ml/4fl oz vegetable stock
2 tbsp roughly chopped fresh parsley
salt
freshly grated Parmesan cheese, to serve (optional)

Clean the mushrooms with a cloth and brush – do not wash wild mushrooms, as the flavour disappears. Roughly chop any large mushrooms.

Place a large saucepan of lightly salted water on the heat and bring to the boil. Add the tagliatelle and cook until *al dente* (fresh pasta will take only about 1 minute; check the instructions on the packet for dried).

Heat the olive oil in a frying pan, add the garlic and chilli and sweat gently until softened – do not let them brown or burn. Turn up the heat a little, add the mushrooms and stir well for about 1 minute. Then add the stock, keep stirring, and cook for 2 minutes longer, until the liquid has evaporated slightly. Stir in the parsley and season to taste with salt.

Drain the pasta and add to the mushroom mixture. Mix well and serve immediately, sprinkled with some Parmesan if desired.

tramezzini

snacks

Everyone snacks in Italy. Known as *merende* in my day, snacks are part of the fabric of life. Many people only drink a small black coffee before leaving the house in the morning but then stop in a bar on their way to work and buy a croissant or a sandwich. Mid-morning and mid-afternoon, they like to have a little something, quite apart from lunch. There have been *rosticcerie* – shops dedicated to snacks – in Italy for as long as I can remember, and certainly long before fast food became a way of life in Britain and the USA. *Rosticcerie* fall half-way between a restaurant and a coffee bar and sell a whole assortment of delicious nibbles: little pizzas, salami, potato and mozzarella croquettes, endless freshly made sandwiches, hot sausages and roast quail, all ready to eat.

The Italian equivalent of the kebab is a million times more delicious. We love *porchetta*, or spit-roast suckling pig, which is sold from specialist shops and stalls. The succulent slices of pork are served on hunks of rustic bread all over Italy.

All the towns and villages around Minori had a feast day for their patron saint. It was a great excuse to travel all over the region and sample local delicacies. Because there were so many villages scattered over the mountains, there was sure to be a feast day within a few kilometres every weekend during the summer. Local farmers would bring their produce to sell, housewives prepared the village speciality to serve to visitors, and local shops put on their best displays of gastronomic delights. I would meet up with a gang of friends and we would visit as many as we could reach. We called them *merende* days because we set out to try as many different delicacies as we could find.

spiedini aromatici di mozzarella e acciughe
mozzarella and anchovy skewers

This is a very tasty snack using stale bread, mozzarella and anchovies. The hot bread is nice and crisp and the anchovies add a tangy taste, making these snacks ideal to serve with pre-dinner drinks.

Use the cheaper mozzarella, such as *fior di latte*, which is ideal for cooking and melting. There is no point using the more expensive buffalo mozzarella, which should only be eaten fresh.

makes 4
12 slices of stale baguette, cut about
    1cm/½in thick
4 slices of mozzarella cheese
50g/2oz butter
5 anchovy fillets, finely chopped
a few fresh chives, finely chopped
freshly ground black pepper

Preheat the oven to 180°C/350°F/Gas Mark 4. Take 4 wooden skewers and thread 3 slices of bread through the crusts on each one, placing a piece of mozzarella on the middle slice. Put the skewers on a baking sheet and place in the oven for about 10 minutes, until the mozzarella has just melted and the bare slices of bread become crisp.

Meanwhile, make the anchovy sauce. Melt the butter in a small pan, add the anchovy fillets and mix well.

Pour a little anchovy sauce over each bare slice of bread. Sprinkle chopped chives over the mozzarella, grind over some black pepper and serve immediately.

bruschetta

bruschetta

Bruschetta is a classic Italian snack that has become increasingly popular in restaurants and pizzerias in the UK. I suppose it is Italy's answer to garlic bread. It is very simple to make and is an extremely nutritious snack at any time of day.

1–2 slices of bread per person
slices of stale, leftover bread
   (ciabatta is good)
a few garlic cloves, peeled
abundant extra virgin olive oil
chopped ripe tomatoes (optional)
fresh basil leaves, roughly torn
   (optional)
salt

Toast the bread on both sides, or grill it on a ridged chargrill pan. Remove and immediately rub the garlic cloves over one side of the bread while it is still warm – you will see the garlic melt into the toast. Sprinkle with salt, drizzle with lots of extra virgin olive oil and top with a few chopped tomatoes and fresh basil, if desired. Serve immediately.

crostini

crostini

Crostini are slices of bread (baguette is ideal) that have been grilled or slowly baked in the oven, then topped with almost anything you like. In Italy, people often serve a selection of crostini as a starter or with pre-dinner drinks. Alternatively, they are a handy way of using up stale bread to serve as a snack instead of the usual sandwich.

Good ideas for toppings include olive paste, artichoke paste (both available in good delicatessens), chicken liver pâté (a favourite in Tuscany), a little Salsa alla Crudaiola (see page 142) or a few preserved vegetables (see page 139).

carpaccio di scamorza
carpaccio of smoked scamorza cheese

I dedicate this recipe to Kate Adie, journalist and war correspondent. While at Passione for dinner one evening, she was talking about the various meals she had eaten around the world and mentioned her favourite Italian dish, which she had had about 20 years ago – a salad of very thinly sliced cheese dressed with raw vegetables and olive oil. She had had this only once, in a restaurant in Bologna, and had never found it on other menus. I quickly went downstairs to the kitchen and recreated the dish. When I took it upstairs, wow, it certainly brought back memories for her!

It's extremely simple to prepare and makes a wonderful light snack or a sophisticated starter. You can get hard-smoked scamorza cheese at most good Italian delicatessens. Just remember you will need a good sharp knife, as everything has to be sliced wafer-thin. If you have a mandoline, use that, or the finest slicer on your food processor.

serves 4
2 small smoked scamorza cheeses
½ small shallot, very finely sliced
1 small celery heart, very finely sliced
   (including the leaves)
4 button mushrooms, very finely sliced
juice of 1 lemon
4 tbsp extra virgin olive oil
freshly ground black pepper

Remove and discard the hard skin from the scamorza and cut them lengthways into extremely thin slices. Don't worry if you don't get a whole slice, as long as the pieces are wafer-thin. Arrange them evenly on serving plates and top with the shallot, celery and mushrooms. Grind over some black pepper, then drizzle over the lemon juice and olive oil. Leave to marinate for 5–10 minutes and serve with good bread.

crochette di fave
stuffed broad bean cakes

Broad beans are good not only eaten whole but also when mashed and made into a dough. This recipe takes a little time to prepare but the result is worth the work. The little cakes are delicious hot or cold, or they can be made in advance and reheated in the oven.

makes 36
300g/11oz fresh or frozen broad beans
250g/9oz plain flour
2 eggs
50g/2oz butter, softened
1 tsp dried yeast, dissolved in
    1 tbsp lukewarm water
olive oil for deep-frying
salt and freshly ground black pepper

for the filling:
250g/9oz ricotta cheese
1 egg
3 tbsp freshly grated Parmesan cheese
3 tbsp fresh chives, finely chopped
a pinch of nutmeg

Blanch the broad beans in a large saucepan of boiling water for 1 minute, then drain well and plunge in cold water. Peel off the skins. Place the beans in a food processor and whiz until mushy. Transfer to a large bowl, add the flour, eggs, butter, yeast mixture and some salt and pepper, and mix well with your hands to form a smooth dough. Cover with a clean kitchen cloth and leave in a warm place for about 30 minutes, until slightly risen.

Meanwhile, make the filling. Put all the ingredients in a bowl and mix to a smooth paste. Season with salt and pepper.

Shape the dough into balls the size of golf balls. On a lightly floured work surface, roll each ball of dough out into an oval shape about 3mm/⅛in thick. Place a tablespoon of the filling on it and roll it up, pinching the edges together to close.

Heat the olive oil in a large, deep saucepan or a deep-fat fryer. Deep-fry the croquettes, a few at a time, for 2–3 minutes, until golden brown. With a sharp knife, cut in half on the diagonal. Drain on kitchen paper and serve hot or cold.

pasta fritta
pasta snacks

This is my version of crisps! When you make a batch of fresh pasta and have some left over, roll it out, cut it into a taglierini or tagliolini shape and deep-fry. Flavoured with some salt, it makes a fun snack for children or can be served with drinks. You could also flavour it with freshly ground black pepper, a little crushed dried chilli, some dried oregano or anything else you like.

serves 4–6
leftover pasta dough (see page 30)
olive oil for deep-frying
salt

Roll out the dough with a pasta machine to make very thin sheets. Then cut out the thinnest spaghetti shape you have on your machine. As each batch comes out of the machine, roll it into neat nests.

Heat plenty of olive oil in a large saucepan or a deep-fat fryer. Add the pasta nests a few at a time and fry for about 1 minute, until golden brown. Drain on kitchen paper. Sprinkle with some salt and serve warm or cold.

The school friends I used to share my merende *with: Gennaro, Alfonso, Franco, Geraldo, and the taller boy at the back is Pepino.*

All my friends had nicknames, and they were all called after a food or snack. Alfonso was named Muscione, which means something soft, because when we raided the fig trees in the afternoons he would clamber to the top and feel the figs until he found a soft one. Then there was Sperlungone, named after a long bread, because his mother never made ordinary bread. Hers was always very long, and his roll used to reach from his mouth to his stomach. There was Muzecatella, which means little bite, named because he always took tiny bites of his snack. Biscotti earned his nickname because he liked his snacks very sweet. A very dear friend of mine is nicknamed Melanzana, which means aubergine. In all the years I knew him, he ate an aubergine sandwich every afternoon. A few years ago, someone sent me a postcard of my village. Melanzana was in the background perched on a wall, eating what I would swear was an aubergine baguette.

Lupino got his name from his love of lupins, a type of bean. To give them their flavour, lupins used to be dried and put into big cloth sacks, which were then suspended by chains from the cliffs and rocks that overhung the sea. Lupino famously jumped off the rocks armed with his penknife, with the idea of helping himself to an illicit serving of beans. He made tiny little holes in the sacks and filled his swimming trunks with the lupins. It was a very dangerous mission. The waves crashed against the rocks and he could easily have drowned.

I can remember eating all day long. We certainly weren't starving. We learned about food by talking to the local bakers, butchers and restaurateurs. We couldn't help but learn about food because the knowledge was all around us.

arancini di riso

deep-fried stuffed rice balls

These typically Sicilian snacks are a great way of using up leftover risotto. Traditionally they are filled with different stuffings, such as minced meat or mixed vegetables, and sold as take-away snacks, but to make them simpler you could omit the filling. I have chosen a simple filling of peas and mozzarella. When deep-fried, the mozzarella melts and tastes wonderful as you bit into the *arancino*. I suggest you make lots, as once you start eating them you can't stop!

makes 25
plain flour for dusting
2 eggs, beaten
breadcrumbs for coating
olive oil for deep-frying

for the risotto:
1.5 litres/2½ pints vegetable stock
3 tbsp olive oil
1 onion, finely chopped
300g/11oz Arborio or other Italian
  risotto rice
4 tbsp freshly grated Parmesan cheese
salt and freshly ground black pepper

for the filling:
1 tbsp olive oil
1 tbsp finely chopped onion
100g/4oz frozen peas
2 tbsp water
75g/3oz mozzarella cheese, diced

Make the risotto following the basic recipe on page 58, omitting the butter (or use any leftover risotto you have). Spread the risotto evenly over a baking tray and leave to cool.

Meanwhile, make the filling. Heat the olive oil in a small pan, add the onion and sweat until soft. Then add the peas, water and some seasoning. Cover with a lid and cook for a few minutes, until the peas are tender. Leave to cool.

Take a little of the risotto and form it into a ball, roughly the same size as a golf ball. You will find it easier if you wet your hands with cold water. Make an indentation in each ball and place a few peas and a couple of cubes of mozzarella in it. Reshape the ball so the filling is in the centre and completely covered by the risotto. Dust with a little flour, then coat with beaten egg and finally coat in breadcrumbs.

Heat plenty of olive oil in a large, deep saucepan or in a deep-fat fryer. Add the risotto balls a few at a time and fry for 2–3 minutes, until golden brown. Drain on kitchen paper and serve hot or cold.

la vera pizza napoletana

genuine Neapolitan pizza

You get so many varieties of pizzas these days that I don't blame the Italians for wanting to make it DOC (quality controlled) like wine. Everyone has their own taste and I respect that, but recently I saw chicken tikka pizza on an Indian take-away menu. I do think that this is going a bit far – let's leave pizza to the Italians and chicken tikka to the Indians!

I once had the opportunity of spending some time at the Pizza Academy in Naples, where they are really strict about how the dough is made and what toppings can be used. This is my recipe for the original Neapolitan pizza, which started off as a means of using up the housewife's leftovers: bread dough, tomatoes, cheese and whatever else they had in their cupboard – which I am sure was not chicken tikka!

makes 2 large pizzas
for the dough:
500g/1lb 2oz strong bread flour plus
    extra for dusting
2 tsp salt
10g/¼oz fresh yeast
325ml/11fl oz lukewarm water
a few dried breadcrumbs or some
    semolina for sprinkling

for the topping:
300g/11oz tinned plum tomatoes,
    drained
4 tbsp extra virgin olive oil, plus extra
    for drizzling
25g/1oz Parmesan cheese, freshly grated
a few fresh basil leaves, plus extra to
    garnish, or dried oregano
150g/5oz mozzarella cheese,
    roughly chopped
salt and freshly ground black pepper

Make the dough by putting the flour and salt in a large bowl. Dissolve the yeast in the lukewarm water and gradually add to the flour, mixing well until you obtain a dough. If you find the dough too sticky, just add a little more flour. Shape the dough into a ball and leave to rest, covered with a clean kitchen cloth, for 5 minutes. Knead the dough for 8–10 minutes, until smooth and elastic, then split it in half. Knead each piece for a couple of minutes and then shape into a ball. Sprinkle some flour on a clean cloth and place the dough on it, then cover with a slightly damp cloth. Leave to rise in a warm place for 30 minutes.

Meanwhile, place the tomatoes in a bowl, crush them slightly with a fork, season with salt and pepper, and mix well.

Preheat the oven to 250°C/500°F/Gas Mark 10 (if your oven doesn't go this high, just heat it to its highest setting and cook the pizzas for a few minutes longer if necessary).

Sprinkle some flour on a clean work surface and, with your fingers, spread one piece of dough into a circle about 35–40cm/14–16in in diameter. Make the dough as thin as a pancake but be careful not to tear it, making the border slightly thicker. Repeat with the other ball of dough, then sprinkle some breadcrumbs or semolina over 2 large, flat baking trays and place the pizza bases on them.

Spread a little of the tomato evenly over each base – not too much, or the pizzas will be soggy. Drizzle with the olive oil, sprinkle over the Parmesan, add a few basil leaves or some oregano and top with pieces of mozzarella. Place in the hot oven for 7 minutes (a couple of minutes longer if you prefer your pizza crisp). Remove from the oven, drizzle with a little more olive oil, scatter with extra basil leaves if using, and eat immediately.

frittata di cipolle e porri con crosta di parmigiano
leek and onion omelette rolls in a Parmesan crust

This is a fun and unusual omelette recipe. Once the omelette is cooked, you make a cheese crust by lining a good-quality non-stick frying pan with grated Parmesan and letting it cook until it melts into a whole piece but is still pliable. The omelette is placed over it and the whole thing rolled up like a swiss roll.

makes 10–12 slices
2 eggs
2 tbsp olive oil
1 small onion, finely sliced
1 leek, finely sliced (the white part only)
50g/2oz Parmesan cheese, freshly grated
salt and freshly ground black pepper

In a bowl, beat the eggs with a fork and season with salt and pepper. Heat the olive oil in a non-stick 20cm/8in frying pan, add the onion and leek, and sweat until softened. Pour in the beaten eggs and cook gently until golden brown underneath. Flip over and cook the other side. Remove from the pan and set aside.

Wipe out the frying pan so it is dry and clean. Place over a very low heat and sprinkle the Parmesan evenly over the base. Cook for 1 minute. You will notice the Parmesan sticking together and forming a crust. Gently, with a spatula, lift out the Parmesan crust and place it on a chopping board or a clean work surface. Immediately place the omelette on top, carefully roll it up with the crust and cut into slices with a sharp knife. It is important to do this quickly or the Parmesan will be too hard to work with.

Either eat straight away or serve cold as part of an antipasto – or take it on a picnic.

Not only was I the only boy in the family, I was also extremely skinny when I was young. My mother was determined to build me up, and she went out of her way to bring me *merende* throughout the day. She would embarrass me daily by tracking me down when I was out playing with my friends and calling me over to drink a concoction of freshly beaten eggs and sugar, which she prepared in front of us all. I remember my face burning as I felt my friends watching us.

Another daily ritual was the afternoon snack. But this I shared with my friends. When we met up to play after school, we all carried a paper parcel from our mothers – precious bundles ready for the inevitable moment when all of us were starving. Somehow it was always at five o'clock, and whether we were on the beach, in the mountains, in the village or the fields, all play would stop. Frantic bartering went on until everyone had the snacks they fancied, then there was a moment of silence. We were like an orchestra. Once we started to eat you could hear a symphony of appreciative 'mmms.' We even looked like musicians, holding our baguettes carefully as if they were flutes and clarinets.

I learned a great deal about food from these snack sessions, because as soon as we had eaten the first few mouthfuls, stories would begin about where the food came from. 'I killed the pig' or 'My father milled this flour' and 'My mother grew these vegetables' or 'I preserved these fruits'. We educated each other about food. Many of my childhood friends have since become chefs. I realise now that the quality of those simple afternoon snacks was outstanding. We had bread with all sorts of fillings: pork dripping and sea salt, salami, aubergine and tomato, mozzarella and fruit.

Mamma, Aunt Alfonsina, my younger sister Adriana and me, on the balcony at home in Minori.

pane

bread

In Italy bread forms the basis of every meal. In fact, Italians hold bread in such high esteem that when we want to say that someone is a good person we say they are like a piece of bread (*è come un pezzo di pane*).

At home, my father did most of the cooking but my mother baked the bread. She could easily have bought it but she insisted on making her own. I felt she was showing us how much she loved us through her baking. She put her heart and soul into it and filled the bread with her happiness as she prepared it for us to eat.

Mamma used a wood-fired oven. She always baked bread on a Thursday and there was a certain purposeful excitement in the way she lit the oven the night before. She cooked the loaves slowly so they would stay fresh all week. In the morning, she would be up at five to stoke the fire. I would hear the crackling of the burning twigs. The smell would slowly waft through the house and infiltrate my dreams. I would wake up hungry, jump out of bed and run into the smoke-filled kitchen. There I would find three or four beautiful, warm, massive round loaves on the table. The smell was irresistible and it took all my willpower not to grab the bread and tear it apart.

When I make bread now, I put a little bit of my soul into it. Baking bread is the most wonderful part of the working day for me. Early every morning at the restaurant, I spend a couple of hours making the bread for that day. I walk into the cold, empty kitchen before the rest of the world is up. The first thing I do is switch on the oven. Then I take the yeast out of the fridge. To me, it is a living thing to be cared for. It is cold and I can hear it crying out to be fed, so I give it its breakfast. I add the flour, then the water, and watch the big bubbles explode as I mix it together. It gives me such pleasure to watch. Then I leave the dough to rise.

Once it has risen, I take some of the dough and ask it what shape it would like to be today. I tease it into long rolls, round rolls, *filone*, *filoncino*, large *campagnia* loaves – so many gorgeous, voluptuous shapes. The focaccia and filled rolls are made last. I always find something delicious to top my focaccia. Sun-dried tomatoes, olives, onions and rosemary are favourites. For my rolls I choose the freshest seasonal fillings – such as grilled vegetables, wild garlic, pesto – or mixed cheese and salami.

While the bread is in the oven, I leave the kitchen and go out on to the street for some fresh air. The moment I go back downstairs is magical. The smell of bread baking never fails to overwhelm me with sweet, nostalgic memories of my childhood.

It may sound crazy but if I bake in the afternoon the bread is never as good. Maybe it is because the ingredients are living things. I think the dough knows from the way I handle it if I'm miserable. In the afternoons I am too tired to put the amount of love into the mixing that I do in the mornings. If I'm happy and energetic, the bread always tastes much better.

The Greek word for bread translates literally as everything. I couldn't agree more. I believe bread gives you everything you need.

impasto di pane
basic bread dough

I make most of my dough-based recipes from this basic dough. Bread may seem complicated and an effort to make, but I suggest you try it – there is no more appealing cooking smell than that of your own bread, and certainly no other bread can match the taste. You will find that this bread keeps for days without going mouldy. After a day or so it might go hard, but place it in a hot oven for a few minutes and it will taste freshly made again.

makes 2 loaves

1kg/2lb 3oz strong bread flour, plus extra for dusting

20g/¾oz salt

25g/1oz fresh yeast

700ml/24fl oz lukewarm water

semolina, coarse polenta or dried breadcrumbs for sprinkling

In a large bowl, mix the flour and salt together. Dissolve the yeast in the lukewarm water and pour into the flour. Mix well until you obtain a soft but not sticky dough. Turn out on to a lightly floured work surface and knead well for about 5 minutes, until smooth and elastic. Place the dough on a clean kitchen cloth, brush the top with some water to prevent it drying out, then cover with another clean cloth. Leave to rise in a warm place for about 30 minutes or until doubled in size. Knock the risen dough back down and shape it into 2 round loaves. Place on a baking sheet sprinkled with semolina or breadcrumbs, cover with a cloth and leave in a warm place again until doubled in size. Preheat the oven to 240°C/475°F/Gas Mark 9.

Place the loaves on the bottom shelf of the oven and bake for 25 minutes. The way to test if a loaf is ready is to tap it gently on the bottom: if it sounds hollow, it is ready. Remove from the oven and leave to cool. This bread is delicious eaten on the day it is baked. It will keep for about a week and is great sliced and used for bruschetta or crostini (see page 155), toast or breadcrumbs.

Breadcrumbs Place some sliced stale bread on a baking tray and bake in the oven at 120°C/250°F/Gas Mark ½ for about an hour to dry out completely. Remove from the oven and whiz in a food processor. Store in an airtight container.

As a child, I was like one of the Bisto kids when bread was being made. The smell was so enticing. There is nothing like it.

I loved having bread in the morning. My mother often made me something called a *scodella* from any leftovers. This delicious treat was simply a bowl of bread with milk, sugar and cinnamon. It was like nectar to a hungry boy.

Every day, we children were packed off with a generous wedge of bread. We would all meet up and search the orchards for ripe fruit to eat with it. My favourite was figs. When they were ready, I found fig trees, climbed to the top with my loaf and gorged on the ripe fruit. The problem with having a passion for figs was that I was nearly always caught out. The trees gave off milk, which made me sticky and scratchy. It was very difficult to remove – even though I jumped straight into the sea afterwards to try to wash it off.

When the bread was fresh and warm, my little friends and I headed for the village *pasticceria* to have scoops of chocolate ice cream to put into the middle. The result was an inspiration. The memory of the ice cream melting into the warm dough still makes my mouth water.

I was always threatened with a prison diet of bread and water when I misbehaved as a child. It was never much of a deterrent, though, because I loved bread so much that I actually looked forward to the punishment!

Me, dressed as a cowboy, aged 9.

pane rustico

bread with salami, cheese and eggs

This has to be one of my favourite types of bread. It was traditionally made by farmers' wives as a filling lunch for their husbands while working in the fields, using up all their leftovers of ham, salami, cheese and even pork fat (scratchings). I make this bread at Easter time, as the eggs, which are placed around the ring, make it look very pretty and seasonal for Easter Sunday breakfast.

Make sure the eggs are at room temperature, as if they are cold they interfere with the rising of the dough. The eggs are cooked in their shells – securing them with strips of dough prevents them exploding in the oven. The eggs come out perfectly cooked and make a delicious addition to this substantial loaf.

makes 1 large ring

100g/4oz salami, cut into small cubes
100g/4oz pancetta, cut into small cubes
100g/4oz prosciutto, cut into small cubes
100g/4oz provolone cheese, cut into
    small cubes
100g/4oz Pecorino cheese, cut into
    small cubes
100g/4oz Parmesan cheese,
    freshly grated
2 tbsp coarsely ground black pepper
600g/1lb 5oz strong bread flour, plus
    extra for dusting
1 tsp salt
25g/1oz fresh yeast
450ml/¾ pint lukewarm water
semolina or dried breadcrumbs
    for sprinkling
6 eggs, in their shells

Place all the meat and cheese in a bowl with the pepper, mix well and set aside.

Mix the flour and salt together in a large bowl. Dissolve the yeast in the lukewarm water and add to the flour. Mix with your hands, gradually incorporating all the flour to form a soft, slightly sticky dough. Turn out on to a floured work surface and knead for about 3 minutes or until smooth, adding more flour to the work surface if necessary. Break off a piece of dough about the size of a tennis ball and set aside. Spread the remaining dough out into a rough circle and add the meat and cheese mixture, kneading it into the dough until evenly combined.

Continue to knead for a couple of minutes, then roll the dough into a large sausage shape about 65cm/26in long and seal the ends to form a ring.

Sprinkle some semolina or breadcrumbs on a large, flat baking tray and place the ring on it. Make 6 deep incisions around the top of the ring with a sharp knife and with your fingers enlarge each one to make a pocket. Place an egg lying flat in each pocket.

Take the reserved piece of dough, roll it out into a rough square and cut out 12 strips approximately 7.5cm/3in long. Place 2 strips criss-cross over each egg, brushing them with a little water so they stick well. Cover the loaf with a clean cloth and leave in a warm place until doubled in size. Meanwhile, preheat the oven to 220°C/425°F/Gas Mark 7.

Bake the loaf for 30 minutes or until golden. This is delicious served hot or cold.

focaccia con aglio e rosmarino

focaccia with garlic and rosemary

I remember having focaccia as a child, although we did not know it by that name. We would flatten leftover bread dough and drizzle it with extra virgin olive oil and sea salt. This would often be my breakfast. When I became a chef, I discovered that this simple bread was commonly known as focaccia, and during my many travels over Italy I saw it being made in different ways with various toppings and even stuffed. I used to bring these ideas back to England with me and develop them further.

You can top focaccia with almost anything you like – cherry tomatoes, olives, grilled vegetables, herbs, but always with extra virgin olive oil and sea salt. In this basic recipe, I have given you just a few simple ingredients – garlic, rosemary, oil and sea salt – which together make a delicious topping. Focaccia is best served warm straight from the oven but if you make it in advance you can always reheat it in a hot oven for a few minutes just before serving. It makes an ideal accompaniment to meals instead of bread rolls, and can even be sliced in half and filled with some ham and cheese to make a substantial sandwich.

makes 1 loaf
for the dough:
500g/17½oz strong bread flour
2 tsp salt
15g/½oz fresh yeast
350ml/12fl oz lukewarm water
semolina or coarse polenta for
   sprinkling
for the topping:
2 tbsp extra virgin olive oil, plus extra
   for drizzling
2 large garlic cloves, finely chopped
needles from 3 fresh rosemary sprigs,
   finely chopped
1 tsp flaky sea salt, preferably Maldon
freshly ground black pepper

Preheat the oven to 240°C/475°F/ Gas Mark 9. Make the dough in the same way as the Basic Bread Dough (see page 172). You will need a baking tray about 37.5 x 27.5cm/15 x 11in. After the first rising, place the dough on a lightly floured work surface and roll out into a rectangular shape roughly the size of the baking tray. Warm the baking tray in the hot oven for about 10 seconds, then remove and sprinkle with semolina.

Place the rolled-out dough on the tray and pour the olive oil on to the dough. With your fingers, spread the oil all over the dough. Leave for 5 minutes, then poke the dough all over with your fingers to make indentations. Sprinkle the garlic and rosemary over the top, followed by the salt and pepper. Leave to rest in a warm place for 30 minutes (a good place is on the hob, if it is directly above the oven).

Bake for about 15 minutes, until evenly golden brown. Check the focaccia from time to time, as domestic ovens often colour one side and not the other, so turn the baking tray round accordingly. Once cooked, remove from the oven and immediately drizzle some olive oil all over. Leave to cool, then cut into squares.

This bread is delicious eaten on the day it is baked, but it will keep for a few days, and you can freshen it up in the oven for a few minutes just before serving.

panini con verdure alla griglia e parmigiano
mixed grilled vegetable and Parmesan rolls

This is an excellent way of using up leftovers. I have suggested grilled vegetables here, but you can also use ham, salami, cheese, even pesto (see page 44). The rolls look good and are very tasty – great for taking on picnics or adding to your bread basket.

makes about 18
for the dough:
500g/17½oz strong bread flour, plus
   extra for dusting
2 tsp salt
15g/½oz fresh yeast
350ml/12fl oz lukewarm water
semolina or coarse polenta for
   sprinkling
extra-virgin olive oil for drizzling
for the filling:
2 tbsp olive oil
3 tbsp freshly grated Parmesan cheese
   (or Cheddar, if you prefer)
1 large courgette, cut into strips
   and grilled
1 aubergine, cut into strips and grilled
1 yellow and 1 red pepper, roasted and
   cut into strips (see page 139)
a handful of cherry tomatoes (optional)
salt and freshly ground black pepper

Make the dough in the same way as the Basic Bread Dough (see page 172). After the first rising, place it on a lightly floured work surface and roll out into a rectangle about 3mm/⅛in thick. Drizzle with the olive oil and sprinkle the cheese all over. Cover with the grilled vegetables and season with salt and pepper. Gently roll up lengthways like a swiss roll, tucking in any filling that escapes at either end.

With a sharp knife, slice into rolls about 3cm/1¼in wide. Sprinkle some semolina or polenta on a baking tray and place the rolls on it. Place a tomato on a few of the rolls, if desired. Leave to rest for 20 minutes.

Meanwhile, preheat the oven to 240°C/475°F/Gas Mark 9. Bake the rolls on the top shelf of the oven for 12 minutes or until golden brown. Remove from the oven and immediately drizzle with extra-virgin olive oil.

schiacciata della vendammia
sweet tart with harvest grapes

At harvest time in Italy it is traditional to put aside some grapes to consume over Christmas. They become deliciously sweet and squashy and make a perfect filling for a pie. I am not suggesting you preserve grapes for this recipe, as nowadays you find them all year round. Use the sweet varieties, such as Muscatel. Don't be alarmed by the large quantity of cinnamon – the taste is not at all overpowering.

serves 4–6
20g/¾oz fresh yeast
165ml/5½fl oz lukewarm water
300g/10½oz strong bread flour, plus
    extra for dusting
1 tsp salt
dried breadcrumbs, coarse polenta
    or semolina for sprinkling
450g/1lb white or black grapes
5 tbsp extra virgin olive oil
65g/2½oz caster sugar
1 tbsp ground cinnamon
a bunch of fresh rosemary,
    plus a few sprigs to decorate
icing sugar for dusting

Dissolve the yeast in the lukewarm water and set aside. Sift the flour into a large bowl, mix in the salt and make a well in the centre. Gradually pour in the yeast mixture, mixing it with the flour to make a soft but not sticky dough. Turn out and knead on a lightly floured surface for about 10 minutes, until smooth and elastic. Divide the dough into 2 balls, cover with a clean kitchen cloth and leave to rest for 5 minutes.

Preheat the oven to 200°C/400°F/Gas Mark 6. Roll out one of the balls of dough into a round about 2mm/$^1/_{12}$in thick and 15cm/6in in diameter. Sprinkle a large baking tray with breadcrumbs or semolina then lift the dough on to it. Set aside a small bunch of 8–10 grapes and arrange the rest over the dough, leaving a border of about 2.5cm/1in all around. Drizzle with 3 tablespoons of the olive oil, sprinkle over 50g/2oz of the sugar and all the cinnamon. Then sprinkle over the rosemary needles.

Roll out the other half of dough to the same size and place this over the filling, pressing down the edges well. Trim away any excess and crimp the edges with your fingers so that the pie is well sealed. Drizzle the remaining olive oil over the top and sprinkle with the remaining sugar. Place in the oven and bake for 10 minutes, then place the reserved grapes on top with a few sprigs of rosemary. Bake for a further 10 minutes until pale gold and lightly caramelised. Dust with icing sugar and serve warm.

dolci

desserts

I have a very sweet tooth and adore puddings and cakes. When
I make them, I use traditional methods to try to recapture the tastes
of my childhood. I like to create rustic puddings flavoured with sweet
spices such as cinnamon.

It would be no exaggeration to say that I have spent my whole life
working with food. I earned my first wages at the local *pasticceria*,
which was owned by the father of a good friend of mine. He was
exactly as you would imagine the owner of a cake shop to be, with a
chubby, smiling face and a big belly from eating too many of his own
cakes. When I went round to my friend's house, I was always given a
job to do – usually skinning almonds. Not the nicest job in the world
but it paid good money – enough to fund my trips to the cinema.

The almonds were gathered from just outside Minori. Sacks full of
them were brought down from the mountains and put outside in the
sun to dry. The nuts were cracked and shelled, then given to me to
peel – one by one. I was equipped with two buckets of water, one hot
and one cold. I had to soak the almonds in the hot water, take them
out, peel them and then drop them into the cold. I ate as many as I
provided for the shop but a blind eye was turned.

It was a wonderful cake shop. When I passed it in the morning, the
smell of baking was good enough to stop you in your tracks. Italy still
has good *pasticcerie* but the local, seasonal element has disappeared.
My friend's father used fresh eggs, freshly milled flour from the
village mill and fruit from local orchards. He baked for the shop
every day: all kinds of pastries, local speciality biscuits, sponge cakes,
jam tarts, chocolate cake and ice cream. Everyone in the village loved
him, and he was often requested to make special cakes for weddings,
parties and feasts. People would come in with their own recipes or
bring in their own spices to be added to their cakes. He would nod
and smile and agree to their wishes, but I knew that he never really
stuck to the recipes he was given, and generally added a few spices
of his own. He always produced a masterpiece and the ladies of the
village adored him for it.

I was very lucky in my choice of friends. One of them, Antonio, had a father who owned a coffee shop in the village. It sold all sorts of things besides coffee, and the house speciality was a beautiful lemon sorbet. He made it from a huge block of ice, plus sugar, lemon juice and zest – nothing else. A big aluminium spoon slowly turned on the ice, mixing in the other ingredients until it was smooth and sweet like a cream. You could smell the lemons from 200 metres away.

It was Antonio's job to zest the lemons and he was always made to do this before he would come and play with me. If I was in need of a playmate, I helped him out. We would sit together grating the lemons for the zest and then squeezing out the juice. Of course, I did have an ulterior motive: his father would give us a big portion of sorbet with honey on top when we were done. I learned to make sorbet from this man. Not long ago, I returned to Italy and went to see him. He is very old now but he remembered me. 'Gennarino,' he said (which is what he called me all those years ago; it means little Gennaro), 'do you remember the lemons?'

Crostata di Limone

Amalfi Lemon Tart

This delicious lemon tart is made with puff pastry instead of the traditional shortcrust and the ready-bought variety is absolutely fine (unless you enjoy making your own puff pastry which is quite a lengthy procedure). I normally make this tart with lemons from the Amalfi Coast, which have a wonderful aroma, however, they are not easy to source so get the best unwaxed organic variety that you can find. Simple to prepare, this lemon tart makes a lovely dessert at any time.

Serves 6–8
100ml/3½fl oz water
1 tbsp caster sugar
zest of 2 Amalfi lemons, cut into julienne (thin strips)
300g/10½oz puff pastry

for the filling:
3 eggs, separated
200g/7oz caster sugar
zest and juice of 2 Amalfi lemons
25g/1oz butter, melted, plus extra for greasing
225g/8oz ricotta cheese, sieved
25g/1oz plain flour, plus extra for dusting and rolling

Preheat the oven to fan 190°C/210°F/ Gas Mark 6–7.

To remove the bitterness from the lemon strips, place the water and sugar in a small saucepan over a medium heat and stir until the sugar has dissolved. Stir in the lemon strips, increase the heat and bring to the boil. Reduce the heat and simmer for 2 minutes. Drain, discard the liquid, dry the lemon strips on kitchen paper and leave to cool.

Lightly grease a 25cm/10in loose-bottomed tart tin with a little butter and dust lightly with some flour. On a lightly floured work surface, roll out the puff pastry to a thickness of 5mm/¼in. Line the prepared tin making sure it comes slightly above the edge. Line the pastry with greaseproof paper, fill with baking beans, dried beans or rice and bake blind for 15 minutes; after 10 minutes, remove the beans and continue to bake until the pastry is golden. Remove from the oven and set aside.

Reduce the oven to fan 130°C/300°F/ Gas Mark 2.

To make the filling, beat the egg yolks and sugar together until light and fluffy and doubled in volume – an electric whisk is best for this. Add the lemon zest and juice and melted butter, and mix well. Stir in the ricotta and sift in the flour. Whisk well to remove any lumps.

In another bowl, whisk the egg whites until stiffened, then fold carefully into the ricotta mixture until well incorporated. Pour into the pastry case and bake for 45–50 minutes until set. About 15 minutes before the end of cooking time, arrange the lemon strips over the top and continue to bake.

Remove from the oven and allow to cool. Gently remove the tart from the tin and transfer to a plate to serve.

frutta cotta

dried fruit compote with rum

You can buy a wonderful array of dried fruit in supermarkets and healthfood shops and liven it up with spices and rum. This is so simple to prepare that it is worth making a large batch and storing it in sterilised airtight jars. It will keep for a couple of months. Serve with some mascarpone or whipped cream for a delicious, warming winter dessert.

serves 6–8

grated zest and juice of 1 lemon
grated zest and juice of 1 orange
2 sprigs of fresh rosemary
1 cinnamon stick
6 cloves
½ tsp fennel seeds
½ tsp black peppercorns
500g/1lb 2oz caster sugar
500ml/17fl oz water
1kg/2¼lb mixed dried fruit, such as
    prunes, apricots, figs, raisins, apples,
    pears and peaches
200ml/7fl oz dark rum

Put the citrus zest and juice, rosemary, cinnamon, cloves, fennel seeds, peppercorns, sugar and water in a large saucepan and bring to the boil, stirring occasionally to dissolve the sugar. Reduce the heat, cover the pan and simmer gently for 5 minutes. Add the hardest fruit, such as prunes, first and simmer for 3 minutes, then add the rest of the fruit and simmer for 5 minutes.

Remove from the heat and add the rum. Stir well and leave to stand, covered, for at least a day before use. Heat through gently before serving.

fragole fresche con salsa di fragole

fresh strawberries with strawberry sauce

For a simple summer dessert with minimum effort but maximum taste, this is ideal. If you like, you can serve it with good-quality vanilla ice cream.

serves 4

450g/1lb strawberries, cut into quarters
sprigs of fresh mint and icing sugar, to
   decorate (optional)

for the sauce:

20g/¾oz butter
75g/3oz caster sugar
¼ lemon
200g/7oz strawberries, cut in half

First make the sauce. Put the butter and sugar in a saucepan and place over a gentle heat. Spear the lemon quarter with a fork and use it to stir the butter and sugar until the butter has melted and the sugar has dissolved. Press the lemon with the fork to squeeze out all the juice, then discard it. Stir in the halved strawberries, then remove from the heat and push the mixture through a sieve. Leave to cool.

Pour the sauce on 4 serving plates, then top with the fresh strawberries. Decorate with sprigs of mint and sprinkle with icing sugar, if desired.

gelato passione
limoncello and strawberry ice cream

This recipe was devised by my friend Albino Barberis who makes the best ice cream this side of Milan. He came up with the idea when we opened Passione, combining limoncello liqueur, which comes from the Amalfi Coast, with wild strawberries because of my fascination for wild food. The result was outstanding and it has become a firm favourite on our dessert menu. I make it with cultivated strawberries but if you want to treat yourself to wild strawberries, then even better!

serves 6–8
250g/9oz strawberries
3 egg yolks
65g/2½oz caster sugar
300ml/½ pint double cream
150ml/¼ pint full-fat milk
250ml/8fl oz limoncello liqueur
grated zest of ½ lemon

Put a large plastic container in the freezer ready for the ice cream. Slice half the strawberries quite thinly and set aside. Blend the remaining strawberries in a blender or food processor to a purée. Set aside.

Beat together the egg yolks and sugar in a bowl. Put the cream and milk in a saucepan and bring gently to the boil. As it begins to boil, remove from the heat and beat in the egg mixture. Return to a low heat and cook for about 1 minute, stirring all the time with a wooden spoon, until slightly thickened. Remove from the heat and fold in the sliced and puréed strawberries. Then stir in the limoncello and lemon zest. Remove the container from the freezer and pour in the mixture until it is about three-quarters full (if you have extra mixture, pour it into another plastic container). Leave to cool, then place, uncovered, in the freezer.

After 30 minutes, remove and stir well, then replace in the freezer. Leave for another 30 minutes and repeat the procedure a few times until the ice cream is frozen. Alternatively, if you have an ice cream machine, churn the ice cream until it thickens, then place in a container in the freezer.

semifreddo di mandorle e cioccolato bianco

semifreddo of almonds and white chocolate

Semifreddo is a classic Italian dessert, which is served straight from the freezer but does not set as firm as ice cream. It is ideal for the warmer months and can be made in advance and kept in the freezer until you need it. I have used individual dariole moulds here but you could use one large mould, such as a loaf tin, and serve it sliced.

serves 6
3 egg yolks
75g/3oz caster sugar
75g/3oz white chocolate, finely chopped
275ml/9fl oz whipping cream
for the *croccante* (praline):
37g/1¹/₃oz caster sugar
150g/5¹/₃oz blanched almonds,
    roughly chopped
4½ tbsp water

First make the *croccante*. Place the sugar in a small, heavy-based pan over a medium heat and stir with a wooden spoon until it begins to caramelise and turn golden brown. At this stage, add the almonds and water and mix well. Remove from the heat, pour the mixture on to a lightly oiled baking tray or marble board and leave to cool.

Whisk the egg yolks and sugar together in a bowl until light and fluffy and increased in volume. Break up the cooled *croccante* quite roughly and add ²/₃ of it to the egg mixture, together with the white chocolate. Set the remaining ¹/₃ of the *croccante* aside, to decorate.

In a separate bowl, whip the cream to stiff peaks, then fold it into the mixture. Line six 9cm/3½in dariole moulds with clingfilm, fill them with the mixture and place in the freezer for at least 2 hours, until frozen. To serve, remove from the freezer and leave at room temperature for a few minutes, then turn out on to plates and peel off the clingfilm. Sprinkle with the reserved *croccante*, if wished.

panna cotta con menta fresca
fresh mint panna cotta drizzled with honey

Panna cotta literally translated means 'cooked cream' and that's basically what it is. You can try all sorts of different flavourings – this one is especially light and subtle with the cool, fresh mint. It's a very simple dessert to make, and it should be prepared in advance to give it time to set. I find it sets best if you make it the night before. It will keep for 3–4 days in the fridge.

serves 4
3 gelatine leaves
250ml/8fl oz double cream
250ml/8fl oz milk
25g/1oz caster sugar
10 fresh mint leaves, finely chopped
a couple of drops of vanilla extract
4 tbsp runny honey
a few dark chocolate shavings (optional)

Place the gelatine leaves in a bowl of cold water and leave to soften for about 5 minutes. Put the cream, milk, sugar, mint and vanilla in a small saucepan and bring gently to the boil. As soon as it begins to bubble, remove from the heat, cover with a lid and leave to rest for 5 minutes. This is done to allow the mint to infuse. Strain the cream through a fine sieve and discard the mint.

Drain the gelatine leaves and squeeze out any excess water with your hands. Add the soaked gelatine to the cream mixture and stir well, making sure that the gelatine melts. The mixture will take on an oily appearance – don't worry, this is because of the gelatine and is quite normal. Pour the mixture into 4 ramekins or dariole moulds and place immediately in the fridge. Leave for at least 4 hours, until set.

To serve, run a knife round the edge of each panna cotta and then turn the mould upside down on to an individual serving dish to tip it out. Drizzle some runny honey on top and scatter with a few chocolate shavings, if desired. If using ramekins, you don't have to tip the panna cotta out if you don't want to; just drizzle the honey on top and serve in the ramekins.

pastiera di grano
Neapolitan Easter wheat and ricotta tart

This dessert is believed to date back to pagan times, when Neapolitans would offer all the fruits of their land to the mermaid, Partenope, in spring: eggs for fertility, wheat from the land, ricotta from the shepherds, the aroma of orange flowers, vanilla to symbolise faraway countries and sugar in honour of the sweet mermaid. It is said that the mermaid would take all these ingredients, immerse herself in the sea of the Bay of Naples and give back to the Neapolitans a dessert that symbolised fertility and rebirth. The recipe as we know it today came from Neapolitan convents, and nuns would make it for rich nobles of the area.

My mother and aunts would always make it at Easter. It is still made today, at home as well as in pastry shops throughout the Campania region. In Naples, Easter wouldn't be Easter without a *Pastiera di Grano*. Wheat sounds like a strange ingredient for a tart but it really is delicious, especially with the delicate flavour of orange-flower water. Pre-cooked wheat is sold in tins in Italian delicatessens, and orange-flower water can be found in supermarkets.

serves 12

400g/14oz tin of pre-cooked wheat
120ml/4fl oz milk
½ tsp vanilla extract
250g/9oz ricotta cheese
5 egg yolks
200g/7oz icing sugar,
    plus extra for decorating
120g/4½oz mixed candied peel,
    finely chopped
1½ tbsp orange-flower water
grated zest of ½ orange
2 egg whites

for the sweet shortcrust pastry:

400g/14oz plain flour
3 eggs
100g/4oz caster sugar
150g/5oz butter, at room temperature,
    diced
grated zest of 1 lemon

First make the pastry. Sift the flour on to a work surface and make a well in the centre. Add the eggs, sugar, butter and half the lemon zest (reserve the rest for the filling) and lightly blend everything together with your fingertips until you have a smooth dough. Wrap in clingfilm, chill for 1 hour, then roll out thinly and use to line a 25cm/10in loose-bottomed tart tin, trimming the excess. Place in the fridge until ready to use. Do not discard the pastry trimmings; shape them into a ball, wrap in clingfilm and place in the fridge.

Preheat the oven to 170°C/325°F/Gas Mark 3. Place the wheat, milk, 1 tablespoon of the remaining lemon zest and the vanilla extract in a small saucepan, mix well and bring to the boil. Reduce the heat and simmer gently until the wheat has absorbed all the liquid. Remove from the heat and leave to cool.

Mash the ricotta with a fork and beat in the egg yolks until light and fluffy. Sift in the icing sugar and beat until well incorporated, then beat in the candied peel, orange-flower water, the remaining lemon zest and the orange zest. Stir in the cooled wheat mixture.

In a separate bowl, whisk the egg whites until stiff. Then fold carefully but thoroughly into the ricotta and wheat mixture.

Remove the pastry case from the fridge and pour in the mixture. Roll out the remaining pastry quite thinly and cut it into 2.5cm/1in strips roughly the length of the cake tin. Arrange the strips criss-cross over the tart roughly 2.5cm/1in apart, trimming off any excess and pressing the ends against the edge of the pastry case to seal. Place in the oven and bake for 50 minutes, until lightly browned but still moist. Leave to cool, then sift over some icing sugar to decorate.

torta al cioccolato e vino rosso

chocolate and red wine cake

Chocolate and red wine go well together, so what better way to combine them than in a cake? This cake is light, moist and simple to prepare. For a special occasion, coat with chocolate sauce (see below) and decorate with chocolate curls and a sprig of flowering rosemary.

makes a 20cm/8in cake
200g/7oz butter, softened
250g/9oz caster sugar
4 eggs, beaten
25g/1oz cocoa powder
250g/9oz plain flour
1 tsp baking powder
½ tsp ground cinnamon (optional)
100ml/3½fl oz red wine
½ tsp vanilla extract
150g/5oz dark chocolate drops

Preheat the oven to 180°C/350°F/Gas Mark 4 and lightly grease a loose-bottomed 20cm/8in cake tin.

Cream the butter and sugar together in a bowl, until light and fluffy. Gradually beat in the eggs. Then sift in the cocoa, flour, baking powder and, cinnamon if using, and fold in. Mix in the red wine and vanilla, then fold in the chocolate.

Pour the mixture into the prepared cake tin and bake for 1 hour, until a skewer inserted in the centre comes out clean. Remove from the oven and allow to cool in the tin, then carefully turn out. Coat with chocolate sauce (see below) and chocolate curls, if desired.

salsa al cioccolato

chocolate topping

This lovely, rich chocolate sauce is ideal for covering cakes, as when cooled it sets, and goes quite hard. It can also be used to pour over ice cream or panna cotta (see page 192). In both cases, use immediately after making, before it has a chance to set. If necessary, make a large batch and keep it for up to a week in the fridge; just place whatever quantity you need in a bowl set over a pan of hot water to melt before using.

makes enough to cover two cakes
120ml/4fl oz single cream
150g/5oz dark chocolate, broken up
1½ tsp cocoa powder
1½ tsp glucose syrup
25g/1oz butter
1 tbsp sugar

Place all the ingredients in a bowl set over a saucepan of hot water (make sure the bowl does not touch the water) and stir constantly until the chocolate has melted and the sauce has a smooth, silky consistency. Pour through a sieve, if necessary, to strain out any lumps of cocoa. Leave to cool slightly (only 1–2 minutes) before using to decorate the cake (above) or as you wish.

torta alle pere
pear cake

This cake is deliciously moist and can be served either as a dessert or at teatime. Use Williams pears for best results. The glaze is simple to make but you could always do without it – it doesn't really affect the taste of the cake but just gives it a nice, shiny glow!

makes a 25cm/10in cake
2 eggs
1 egg yolk
150g/5oz caster sugar
50g/2oz butter, cut into small chunks
1 tbsp runny honey
3 tbsp full-fat milk
150g/5oz plain flour
1 tsp baking powder
a pinch of salt
1 tsp vanilla extract
5 pears
4 tbsp apricot jam, to glaze (optional)

Preheat the oven to 180°C/350°F/ Gas Mark 4. Lightly grease a 25cm/ 10in round shallow cake tin with butter and line the base with a circle of greaseproof paper.

In a bowl, beat the eggs, egg yolk, sugar, butter and honey together until light and fluffy. You will find this easier and quicker with an electric beater. Gradually add the milk, beating well. Then sift the flour, baking powder and salt over the top and fold in with a metal spoon. Add the vanilla and mix. Core and dice 3 of the pears and mix them in.

Pour the mixture into the prepared cake tin. Core and thinly slice the 2 remaining pears and arrange them on top. Bake for 45 minutes, until the cake is risen and golden brown. Remove from the oven and leave to cool in the tin, then turn out. If you want to glaze the cake, make up the apricot glaze by diluting the apricot jam with a little water and then heating it gently in a saucepan, stirring until smooth. Pour the warm glaze through a sieve and brush it immediately over the top of the cake.

A tiny old lady, round as a barrel, ran the smallest, most magical shop in Minori. With a stern expression, she presided over a fabulous array of sweets, chocolates and small pastries, but there was a kindly twinkle in her small, dark eyes.

Her shop was scarcely bigger than a telephone box, yet it was packed with an amazing variety of tantalising delicacies. Everything was handmade. We children thought she was magic, and believed our parents when they told us that a fairy worked with her, sprinkling fairy dust over her sweets.

Pastries were filled with pâtisserie cream made from eggs that had been laid that morning, and flavoured with chocolate. There were tarts filled with ricotta and cherries, apples and cream, and all kinds of fruit. There was nougat, too, made with sugar, almonds and honey. The little *signora* stood with her arms folded across her chest, the trays of sweets before her covered in white muslin cloths. It was pure theatre. She waited until we were breathless with anticipation before lifting the muslin very slowly to reveal the mouth-watering displays and release the most tantalising smells.

I was lucky. I had the chance to taste her sweets now and then because my grandfather would send me on errands to her shop and always gave me a little extra money for myself. The fairy lady always chanted: 'What do you want? How much have you got? Has your grandad sent you?' When I close my eyes, I can still hear her. She would wrap my grandfather's order in beautiful crisp, coloured paper. And then she would make a smaller parcel for me. She seemed to read my mind, and always put in the very sweets I had been fantasising about. Needless to say, my parcel was opened and devoured almost as soon as I left the shop.

biscotti rococò
spicy almond biscuits

This is an old recipe from Naples. The exotic spices reflect the type of ingredients introduced to ancient Naples by the Arabic invasions. In fact, these biscuits taste more like a North African speciality than an Italian one. Stored in an airtight container, they will keep for about two weeks. They are delicious served at teatime, or after dinner as an alternative to the classic Tuscan cantuccini, for dipping into a dessert wine such as Passito di Pantelleria or Vin Santo.

makes about 40
300g/11oz plain flour
200g/7oz ground almonds
200g/7oz caster sugar
1 sachet of Easyblend yeast
25g/1oz butter, diced
2 tbsp finely grated lemon zest
2 tbsp finely grated orange zest
150ml/¼ pint sweet white wine
1 egg, beaten, plus beaten egg,
  for brushing
150g/5oz mixed candied peel,
  finely chopped
150g/5oz whole almonds,
  roughly chopped
1 tsp ground cinnamon
a pinch of ground nutmeg
1 egg, beaten, for brushing
icing sugar, for dusting

Preheat the oven to 180°C/350°F/ Gas Mark 4). Mix the flour, ground almonds, sugar and yeast together in a large bowl. Add the butter and rub it in with your fingertips until the mixture resembles breadcrumbs. Add the lemon and orange zests, the wine, egg, candied peel, almonds, cinnamon and nutmeg and mix well, preferably with your hands, to form a soft dough. Form into golf-ball shapes, then, on a lightly floured surface, roll into sausage shapes 12.5–15cm/5–6in long. Shape each one into a ring, overlapping the ends slightly and pressing them together to seal (like mini bagels).

Place on baking trays lined with greaseproof paper and brush with the beaten egg. Bake for 20–25 minutes, until golden brown. Dust with icing sugar and serve.

salsina picante con pere

pear and chilli relish

This wonderfully tangy relish makes a perfect accompaniment to very mature hard cheese such as Pecorino, or a selection of after-dinner cheeses. It also goes well with cold meats. Apart from grilling the pears, there is no cooking involved. Stored in attractive jars, the relish makes an ideal present, together with a hunk of good-quality hard cheese.

makes about 1kg/2¼lb
3 pears, weighing about 350g/12oz
icing sugar for dusting
4 large, fresh medium-hot red chillies,
    roughly chopped
500g/1lb 2oz mostarda di Cremona
    (preferably the hot variety, see
    page 203),
    any pips removed
375g/13oz marmalade,
    preferably thick-cut

Cut the pears in half and core them. Cut in half again and then again. Cut into 2mm/¹/₁₂in dice. Arrange on a large, flat baking tray and dust all over with icing sugar. Place under a hot grill for about 10 minutes, until the pears have caramelised.

Meanwhile, place the chillies, mostarda di Cremona and marmalade in a food processor and whiz until smooth (if you are using fine-cut marmalade, don't add it to the food processor). Transfer to a large bowl (fine-cut marmalade should be mixed in now). Add the caramelised pears and mix well.

Fill one large or several small storage jars with the mixture. It will keep for a couple of months.

formaggi
an Italian cheese selection

Cheese can be served before or instead of dessert, and although more popular eaten this way in northern Italy it is now also becoming the trend in the South. Traditionally in the South, cheese is consumed as part of the antipasto course.

I love the cheese course, which is often the highlight of a meal. There are so many varieties and you can combine them with different accompaniments to make it a real talking point. When buying cheese, look out for fully ripened, good-quality specimens, even if you have to travel a little to buy the best. I always bring back some cheese from Italy, as several excellent local types are not available in the UK. Nevertheless, you can get many good varieties in Italian delicatessens and specialist cheese shops nowadays.

Here are some tips on serving cheese as part of an Italian meal.

Take the cheese out of the fridge and leave it at room temperature for about 4 hours before serving. This softens it and its flavour becomes more pronounced.

If serving cheese as part of an antipasto, use a fresh one such as buffalo mozzarella, drizzled with lots of extra virgin olive oil, scamorza or caprino (Italian goat's cheese).

To make up a selection, choose a couple of hard cheeses, such as Parmesan and Pecorino, a semi-soft cheese such as Taleggio or provolone, and two soft cheeses – one blue-veined, such as gorgonzola or dolcelatte, and one plain, such as caprino. Four or five cheeses are sufficient; too many and the tastebuds get confused. Serve with some taralli (a southern Italian, crisp, twice-baked savoury biscuit), fresh bread or plain biscuits and some fresh fruit or celery. Always accompany with a good red wine or a full-bodied white.

If you serve just one cheese after dinner, it should be something quite special, such as Castelmagno or Formaggio di fossa served with my special chilli relish (see opposite). Alternatively, a good-quality gorgonzola or dolcelatte drizzled with honey and served with a few walnuts is a great way to end a meal.

Good accompaniments to cheese include pears, grapes, walnuts and fresh broad beans.

Mostarda di Cremona is also excellent with cheese. This is a preserve made of candied fruits and mustard and is available in mild and hot versions. It can be bought in jars from good Italian delicatessens.

Index

First published in the United Kingdom
in 2017 as *Passione* by
Pavilion
43 Great Ormond Street
London WC1N 3HZ

This edition published in 2018
Text © Gennaro Contaldo, 2003, 2017, 2018
Design and layout © Pavilion Books
Company Ltd, 2017, 2018
Photography © Pavilion Books Company Ltd,
2017, 2018 except where credited otherwise

All recipe photography by Kim Lightbody
Photograph on p. 2 © Patrice Hauser/Getty
Images, pp.10–11 © Atlantide Phototravel/
Getty Images, p.89 © Glenn Beanland/Getty
Images, p.183 © Larry Gatz/Getty Images;
on p.28 © The Stapleton Collection;
on pp. 4–5, 21, 42, 52, 73, 97, 105, 119, 152,
160, 167, 168, 173 © Gennaro Contaldo
Front cover photography by Kim Lightbody

ISBN: 978–1–911624-49-3

A CIP catalogue record for this book is
available from the British Library.

10 9 8 7 6 5 4 3 2 1

Reproduction by Mission, Hong Kong
Printed and bound by Times, Malaysia

This book can be ordered direct from the
publisher at www.pavilionbooks.com

acknowledgements

2003 edition: Thank you to Sarah Walmsley for patiently listening to all my stories
and putting them to paper so beautifully; to Liz Przybylski for spending many hours
in the kitchen with me, taking down the recipes and writing them up; to Heather
Holden-Brown for her enthusiasm throughout the project and for being such fun
in Italy!; to Jane Middleton, for being so thorough in checking and rechecking all
the text; and to Jo Roberts-Miller for all her hard work and efficiency in putting
the book together. To Steve and Janice Lanning for the great idea. Thank you also
to Luigi Bonomi, my agent, for making this happen!

2017 edition: Thank you to Adriana Contaldo, for helping to cook the recipes on
the shoots; to Emily Ezekiel for superb food and prop styling; to Kim Lightbody, the
photographer, for the most beautiful photographs; and finally to Polly Powell and all
the Pavilion team, especially our editor Emily Preece-Morrison, and designers Laura
Russell and Rosamund Saunders.

Gennaro
Slow Cook Italian

Gennaro
Slow Cook Italian

Gennaro Contaldo

PAVILION

Contents

Introduction

Slow cooking is one of my favourite ways to cook: it's simple, stress-free and allows you to get on with other things safe in the knowledge that slowly, slowly the stove-top or oven is doing its job. Stews and sauces bubble on the hob, a roast cooks in the oven with herbs gently infusing the meat, breads and cakes bake, all filling the house with mouth-watering smells and creating that special warmth which nothing else can.

It takes me back in time to when – only a generation or so ago – everyone cooked on coals and wood. There was no gas or electricity, and food sometimes took all day (or even all night) to cook. Soups gently simmered on wood-burning stoves, potatoes were baked in the ash from the day's fire, and whole animals were cooked in underground pits.

My mother, grandmother, aunt and sisters would leave a ragù or soup very gently bubbling on the hob so that there was always a hot meal ready, whatever time the rest of the family got home. Delicious cooking smells filled the house, giving it that warm and cosy feeling of home and all that is good and wholesome; a bad day at school or work would somehow be soothed away.

When I was in my teens, people in the village, including my family, were changing their kitchens and the latest trend was to have a new gas cooker incorporating stove-top and oven in the same unit. Huge green gas cylinders were hauled up the stairs of apartments and attached to the cooker.

There was much excitement as people talked about their new 'American' gadget that made cooking much quicker. The flame was instant and it was no longer necessary to light a fire.

Gradually, over the years, supplies of coal and wood were replaced with the cylinders. Shrewd housewives always kept a spare, especially during winter and feast times. My grandfather refused to change, and kept the same old range; this is where the family got together for Sunday lunches and special occasions until he died in the early 1980s. At the time, I could not believe he would forgo such luxury. It was not until years later, as an adult and chef, that I looked back with much fondness and nostalgia at that old kitchen range – the romance of the flickering flame, the warmth of a real fire, the smell of burning wood and ash. That's why, a few years ago, I had a rustic kitchen built in my garden with a wood-fired oven and stove; now I can recreate those slow, slow-cooked dishes of my childhood using copper pans and terracotta pots, and enjoy the oh-so-wonderful smells of freshly baked bread from the wood oven.

Pulses – soaking and simmering

Dried beans, chickpeas and lentils, soaked overnight in preparation for the next day's meal, are an essential and economical part of the slow-cooking repertoire. Pulses were especially important during the winter, when fresh vegetables were in shorter supply, and to ensure a varied diet we always kept a selection in our store cupboard – cannellini beans, borlotti beans, chickpeas, broad (fava)

beans, dried peas and lentils, as well as some local varieties. In the evening, after dinner, my elder sisters would check the beans or lentils for small stones and other impurities, rinse them well, place them in a large terracotta pot and cover them with water to soak overnight. In the morning, the water was drained and the pulses cooked in the same pot: terracotta was used for most of our slow-cooked dishes, as it not only enhanced the flavour of the food but also kept it warmer for longer. Beans and pulses are high in protein, and are so nutritious that they used to be known as 'poor man's meat'.

Nowadays, you can find all sorts of canned beans and pulses, which just need heating up, but I still love the ritual of handling the dried ones, putting them in water to soak and thinking of how to cook them. As well as retaining their texture and shape during cooking (the canned variety can get quite mushy), they taste far better. Once soaked, they are simply cooked in fresh water for an hour or so until tender (red kidney beans must be boiled hard for 10 minutes before the long simmering) and then you can use them according to your recipe. Sometimes I enjoy them as a dish in their own right, with some good extra virgin olive oil, garlic and herbs. So simple, so nutritious and so delicious.

Cheap cuts of meat

The great thing about slow cooking is that you can use economical cuts of meat from different parts of the animal – lamb neck and shanks, pork belly and shoulder, beef chuck, shin and brisket, and offal such as tongue and oxtail, for example – rather than the tender cuts that are quick to cook but expensive. Although sometimes looked down

upon, these cuts of meat make wonderful meals. When I was a child in Italy, no part of the animal was wasted, and this is still true in rural areas.

By slow cooking these tougher cuts, adding herbs and spices, you can produce a meal fit for a king, giving you maximum flavour for minimum effort while being kinder on your purse and respectful to the animal. Try the rustic mutton stew, *Montone alla contadina* (see page 80); pork in aspic jelly, *Liatina e' puorc* (see page 64); or the Sicilian-style pot-roasted beef flavoured with olives, almonds and cinnamon (see page 120). I've also come up with a simplified version of the Piedmontese dish *Bollito misto* (mixed boiled meats), using ox tongue, beef brisket and chicken rather than the traditional huge array of different meats (see page 61).

Game is fantastic for slow cooking too, and I consider myself lucky to have grown up in a family that loved to hunt. I learned not only how to hunt the animals, but also how to clean and cook them, and I still use my father's tips and recipes for rabbit, hare and pheasant. In season, I love to go out with friends on hunting trips and bring home whatever I catch. Pheasant makes a delicious ragù to serve with pasta, *Taglioni con ragù di fagiano in bianco* (see page 46), while the venison casserole, *Scottiglia di capriolo* (see page 86), can be used for almost any game, including wild boar, hare or rabbit.

Kitchen kit

Slow cooking is comfort food at its best and easiest. Ask anyone what their favourite meal is, and you will very likely be told their mum's casserole, stew, roast or bake. With

food, as with many other things in life, it's often the simple things that give the most pleasure and stay in our memories. Slow cooking goes back to basics: no major cooking skills or fancy gadgets are needed. A good, sturdy cooking pot or cast-iron casserole dish, ovenproof pans and roasting tins, plus a couple of wooden spoons, are all you really need.

A food processor or blender is undoubtedly useful, but when I was a child these items were almost unimaginable: whatever we cooked we did everything by hand, and there is always an alternative to modern gadgets – it will take longer, but the results will be just as good.

We didn't have electric slow cookers when I was a child and I still don't use one at home, preferring to use the old-fashioned stove-top. However, if you do have a slow cooker, you could use it for many of my recipes. With a slow cooker, once you've done the basic preparation you can leave the food to cook gently without worrying about things boiling dry. Cooking times are longer, so you need plenty of liquid, but you don't need to be in the kitchen to check the food as it cooks. We have included tips for recipes that work well in a slow cooker.

One-pot cooking

Dishes that are cooked all in one pot, either on the stove-top or in the oven, are great for entertaining – and they can often be made in advance so all you have to do is reheat them when you have friends round. This way, you will have more time to relax, knowing that what you have made is cooked to perfection and you don't need to keep popping into the kitchen. One-pot dishes are also ideal for busy people. Set aside a little time to make a stew, pasta sauce or soup and freeze in batches for a quick, home-cooked meal at the end of the day. Try Lamb stew with butternut squash and saffron (see page 83); Boozy baked chicken with peppers, *Pollo ubriaco* (see page 130); the wonderful Italian classic slow-cooked beef or veal with onions, *La Genovese* (see page 36), to serve with pasta; or a summer vegetable stew, *Verdure estive stufate* (see page 90).

This book is about taking it slowly but surely, enjoying the simple things, learning how to make the most of a few basic ingredients and above all relaxing and enjoying good food – *buon appetito!*

Soups

For me, soup is the ultimate comfort food. There is nothing so warming as returning home on cold winter evenings to a steaming bowl of homemade soup. Or at the weekend, after a walk in the woods, knowing you have a welcoming pot of soup waiting for you. You can make soup out of anything you like and it is an excellent way of using up leftovers. It can be made in advance and heated up when required, or made in large quantities and frozen in batches to be enjoyed when you have less time to cook. It is one of the simplest of foods, but always one of the most satisfying and pleasurable.

In Italy, soup - whether delicate or hearty - is popular and is sometimes served as a *primo* (first course) in place of pasta or risotto. Lunches in Italy are often substantial, so in the evening a lighter meal is preferred, and this is often just a broth made from homemade vegetable, chicken or beef stock with the addition of *pastina* (small pasta shapes).

I love making meat stock or broth: all the ingredients go into one large pot and cook slowly until the meat is tender; the resulting stock can be served as a soup or used as the basis for another soup or stew. The tender meat is ready to eat as a main course, or can be made into other dishes such as salads or meatballs. It's a great way to make the most of economical cuts of meat.

My favourite soups have always been hearty and substantial; beans, pulses and thickly sliced vegetables left gently bubbling on the stove, served with a slice of toasted country bread, a drizzle of good extra virgin olive oil and a sprinkling of grated Parmesan - heaven on a plate!

Zuppa di piselli secchi con lattuga
Split pea soup with lettuce

This lovely, old-fashioned soup dates from the time before frozen peas were available, and Italian housewives kept dried split peas to use when fresh peas were not in season. When cooked, their texture is quite dense, so to balance this I have kept the potatoes and pancetta in chunky pieces rather than blending the soup. However, if you prefer, you can blend it before you add the milk and egg yolk mixture at the end. The addition of lettuce gives the soup a pleasant contrasting freshness. Split peas don't normally need pre-soaking, but check the packet instructions.

Serves 4

300g/10½oz/1½ cups dried split peas
2 tbsp extra virgin olive oil
50g/1¾oz/4 tbsp butter
1 small onion, sliced
1 celery heart, sliced
85g/3oz pancetta, cubed
2 potatoes, cut into chunks
  1 litre/1¾ pints/4 cups hot vegetable broth (see page 32)
500ml/18fl oz/2cups hot water
250g/9oz lettuce
225ml/8fl oz/scant 1 cup milk
2 egg yolks, beaten
grated Parmesan, to serve

Rinse the split peas in cold water, discarding any small stones or other impurities; set aside.

Heat the olive oil and half of the butter in a large saucepan on a medium heat. Add the onion, celery and pancetta and sweat for 5 minutes, until softened.

Stir in the potatoes and split peas, add the broth and water, cover with a lid and cook on a low heat for 1½ hours, stirring from time to time to prevent the peas from sticking.

About 15 minutes before the end of cooking time, put the lettuce leaves in a pan of boiling water and simmer for 6 minutes. Drain, squeezing out excess water, and leave to cool, then slice thinly lengthways. Set aside.

Melt the remaining butter and transfer to a bowl with the milk and egg yolks, whisking well. Remove the pea soup from the heat, stir in the milk mixture and serve sprinkled with the sliced lettuce and Parmesan.

Minestra di verdure e riso

Vegetable soup with rice

This is a lighter version of the classic minestrone vegetable soup, made with spring vegetables and rice instead of the usual pasta.

Serves 4

200g/7oz Swiss chard
3 tbsp extra virgin olive oil, plus extra
    to drizzle
60g/2¼oz pancetta, finely chopped
1 garlic clove, left whole
1 onion, sliced
1 celery stalk with leaves, sliced
1 carrot, cut into chunks
1 potato, cut into chunks
1 courgette (zucchini), cut into chunks
8 cherry tomatoes
100g/3½oz/⅔ cup fresh broad
    (fava) beans
a handful of basil leaves
salt and freshly ground black pepper
2 litres/3½ pints/2 quarts hot vegetable
    broth (see page 32)
100g/3½oz/½ cup arborio rice
grated Parmesan, to serve (optional)

Separate the white stalks of the Swiss chard from the green leaves; roughly chop the stalks and leaves and set aside.

Heat the olive oil in a large saucepan, add the pancetta, garlic, onion, celery and carrot and sweat on a medium heat for 4 minutes. Add the potato, courgette, tomatoes, chard stalks, broad beans, basil, salt and pepper, stir and cook for 1 minute.

Add the broth, increase the heat and bring to the boil, then reduce the heat, partially cover with the lid and cook for 50 minutes. Add the chard leaves and rice and continue to cook on a low heat for about 20 minutes, until the rice is al dente. If you need a little more liquid during cooking or when you add the rice, add more hot stock (or hot water).

Remove from the heat, taste for seasoning and serve in individual bowls with a drizzle of extra virgin olive oil and some grated Parmesan if desired.

Minestra di ceci

Chickpea soup

If you like chickpeas, you'll love this rustic soup, flavoured with pork rind (you may need to ask for this in advance from your butcher or supermarket); you can remove the rind before serving if you prefer. Put all the ingredients in a large pot and leave it to bubble gently on the stove, just like farmers' wives used to do in rural parts of Italy; when the family came home, there was always a warm bowl of soup ready and waiting. Remember to soak the chickpeas overnight the day before you make the soup.

Serves 4

500g/1lb 2oz/2½ cups dried chickpeas, soaked in water overnight
500g/1lb 2oz pork rind, sliced into 12 x 3cm/4½ x 1-inch strips
2 onions, finely sliced
2 garlic cloves, left whole
4 large potatoes, peeled and left whole
1 tsp marjoram
10 basil leaves
5 tbsp extra virgin olive oil, plus extra to drizzle
freshly ground black pepper

Drain and rinse the chickpeas. Put them in a large saucepan together with all the remaining ingredients and 1 litre/1¾ pints/4 cups water. Bring to the boil, partially cover with a lid and cook on a low heat for 3–4 hours, or until the chickpeas are tender (the potatoes will break up and make the soup thicker). Serve with a drizzle of extra virgin olive oil.

Brodo di carne
Beef broth

When I make *brodo di carne* I always choose beef brisket, an inexpensive boneless cut from the breast of the animal. Brisket is one of the toughest cuts of beef and is perfect for slow cooking, gradually becoming tender and releasing its flavour. This is one of my favourite comfort foods, especially in cold weather. I like to cook some tortellini in the broth for a first course and then serve the boiled beef and vegetables as a main; or use the beef to make a salad (see page 58) or meatballs (see page 60). The beef broth can be made a couple of days in advance and kept in the fridge, leaving the meat and vegetables in the liquid. The beef broth can also be used as stock for soups and stews, and can be frozen.

Serves 4

1kg/2lb 4oz beef brisket
1 large onion
2 large carrots
2 celery stalks with leaves
3 turnips
3 bay leaves
6 black peppercorns
1 tsp salt

Put the meat in a large saucepan and add 3 litres/ 5¼ pints/3 quarts cold water, making sure the meat is covered – if necessary, add more water. Bring to the boil. You will notice scum appearing on the surface; remove this with a slotted spoon.

Add the rest of the ingredients, reduce the heat to low, cover with a lid and simmer very gently for 3 hours.

Remove the meat and vegetables from the pan and set aside. Strain the liquid through a fine sieve. To serve as a soup, pour the broth back into the pan and reheat, cooking some tortellini or small pasta shapes in the broth if you like. Slice the meat and cut the vegetables into chunks to serve after the broth.

Brodo di pollo
Chicken broth

For the best chicken broth, ask your butcher for a boiling chicken; in Italy this is called *gallina*, an older hen who has stopped laying eggs and is best used for making broth or stock. Otherwise, a normal roasting chicken will suffice. Chicken stock is used in many recipes, so it is worth making lots: you can freeze whatever you don't use, or even make a double quantity and freeze in batches. You can serve this as a light broth or a more substantial soup. Alternatively, this recipe makes a lovely two-course meal: you can have the broth with some *pastina* (small pasta shapes) or tortellini and then enjoy the chicken as a main course with the carrots and onion and some extra vegetables. The chicken can be eaten hot or cold; try it in a salad (see page 62).

Serves 4-6

1.5kg/3lb 5oz chicken
2 carrots
1 large onion
2 celery stalks with leaves
a handful of parsley
1 tsp sea salt
4 black peppercorns

Put all the ingredients in a large saucepan and add 3 litres/5¼ pints/3 quarts cold water, making sure the chicken is covered – if necessary add more water. Bring to the boil, then reduce the heat to low, cover with a lid and simmer gently for 2 hours.

Remove the chicken and vegetables from the pan and set aside. Strain the liquid through a fine sieve for a clear broth. Taste for seasoning and add a little more salt if necessary. To serve as a soup, pour the broth back into the pan and reheat, cooking some tortellini or small pasta shapes in the broth if you like. For a more substantial soup, add chopped cooked vegetables, shredded chicken and some pasta.

Brodo di pollo con polpettine di pollo
Chicken broth with chicken dumplings

This hearty soup is a delicious one-course meal – comfort food at its best. It's based on chicken broth (opposite); the cooked chicken is made into dumplings, which are then simmered in the broth.

Serves 4-6

chicken and broth from chicken broth
  recipe (opposite)
100g/3½oz country bread with crusts
  removed, very finely chopped
100g/3½oz Parmesan, grated, plus
  extra to serve
1 tbsp chives, finely snipped
salt and freshly ground black pepper
2 eggs

Remove the chicken skin and take all the flesh off the bones, breaking the flesh into pieces. Put the chicken in a food processor and whizz until minced (ground). Alternatively, chop it very finely with a sharp knife.

In a bowl, combine the chicken, bread, Parmesan, chives, salt and pepper to taste, and the eggs. Shape into balls about the size of walnuts and set aside.

Strain the broth into a large saucepan, bring to the boil, add the chicken dumplings and simmer on a medium heat for a couple of minutes. Remove from the heat and serve the broth in bowls with about four or five dumplings per person; sprinkle with a little grated Parmesan and black pepper if desired.

Brodo 'e purpo
Octopus broth

This dish was once typical of street food in Naples, and I have given its name in Neapolitan dialect. It is still eaten as street food but is not as common as it used to be. It is considered to be a winter dish, served with lots of black pepper and a squeeze of lemon juice, and often used as a cold remedy. You can enjoy the broth as a starter and serve the octopus as a main course salad (see page 66). You will need to order the octopus from your fishmonger.

Serves 4

1 whole octopus, weighing about
    1.2kg/2lb 10oz
1 tsp salt
4 bay leaves
15 black peppercorns
freshly ground black pepper, to serve
freshly squeezed lemon juice, to serve
    (optional)

Rinse the octopus under cold running water and set aside.

Put 1.5 litres/2½ pints/1½ quarts water, the salt, bay leaves and peppercorns into a large saucepan and bring to the boil. Hold the octopus by its head and dip it into the hot water several times – this is done to curl the tentacles. Put the octopus in the boiling water, cover with a lid and simmer on a medium–low heat for about 1¼ hours, until tender.

Carefully remove the octopus and set aside on a plate, together with a little of the broth; use to make Octopus salad (see page 66). Serve the broth in cups or bowls with lots of freshly ground black pepper and a drizzle of lemon juice, if desired.

Zuppa di cipolle con fontina
Onion soup with fontina cheese

A Tuscan version of onion soup, called *carabaccia*, which dates back to ancient times, includes cinnamon, almonds and basil. I have kept my onion soup simple, and to give it that extra Italian flavour I have used fontina cheese for the topping. The inclusion of white wine, and the slow cooking on a gentle heat, really brings out the taste of the onions. Easy to make, this nutritious and flavoursome soup is a welcome winter warmer.

Serves 4

1 bay leaf
3 sprigs of thyme
50g/1¾oz/4 tbsp butter
1.3kg/3lb onions, finely sliced
2 garlic cloves, left whole
30g/1oz/3 tbsp plain (all-purpose) flour
1 litre/1¾ pints/4 cups beef broth (see page 21)
400ml/14fl oz/1²⁄₃ cups dry white wine
salt and freshly ground black pepper

for the topping
4 slices of ciabatta bread
150g/5½oz fontina cheese, finely chopped

Tie the herbs together and set aside.

Heat the butter in a large saucepan on a medium heat, add the onions, garlic and tied herbs and sweat for 5 minutes. Stir in the flour, whisking well to prevent lumps, then pour in the broth and wine. Add a pinch of salt and cook on a low heat, partially covered, for about 1¼ hours.

Preheat your grill (broiler) to hot. Remove the soup pan from the heat and discard the herbs and garlic. Divide the soup among four heatproof bowls, place a slice of ciabatta on top of each and sprinkle with the fontina.

Put the bowls of soup under the grill for 2 minutes, until the cheese melts and turns golden. Sprinkle with black pepper and serve at once.

Zuppa di borlotti sul pane
Borlotti bean and vegetable soup served on bread

Poor families traditionally served bean soup on bread to add bulk to the family meal. Sometimes the soup was poured into the empty cavity of bread rolls – the scooped-out bread being used for breadcrumbs or in other dishes. This is a nutritious recipe packed with vegetables, and the red onion added at the end gives the soup crunch. If you don't have borlotti beans, you can use cannellini.

Serves 4

250g/9oz/1¼ cups dried borlotti beans, soaked in water overnight
6 sage leaves
2 garlic cloves, left whole
4 tbsp extra virgin olive oil, plus extra to drizzle
2 carrots, sliced
2 celery stalks, sliced
400g/14oz ripe tomatoes, roughly chopped
140g/5oz chicory, roughly chopped
2 small leeks, sliced
100g/3½oz savoy cabbage, shredded
salt and freshly ground black pepper
1.2 litres/2 pints/5 cups hot water
1 tbsp chopped fresh parsley
4 slices of country bread, toasted
1 small red onion, thinly sliced

Drain the beans, rinse and put them in a large saucepan. Add the sage, garlic and enough water to cover the beans. Bring to the boil, then reduce the heat, cover with a lid and simmer for 1 hour, or until the beans are tender and cooked (check the packet instructions). Drain the beans and discard the garlic. Mash a quarter of the beans and set aside.

Heat the olive oil in a large saucepan on a medium heat, add the carrots, celery and tomatoes and sweat for a couple of minutes. Add the chicory, leeks and cabbage, season, cover with a lid and cook on a low heat for 15 minutes. Add the hot water and continue to cook for a further 15 minutes. Add the whole beans, mashed beans and parsley and continue to cook gently for 30 minutes.

Remove from the heat and taste for seasoning. Put a slice of toasted bread in each of four bowls and pour over the bean soup. Top with a few slices of red onion, drizzle with olive oil and serve.

Zuppa di orzo e cavolo nero
Pearl barley and cavolo nero soup

I love pearl barley and often use it in soups or as a substitute for rice. *Cavolo nero* is a loose-leafed Tuscan cabbage with very dark green, almost black, leaves – hence its Italian name, which translates as 'black cabbage'. As well as being tasty, both pearl barley and cavolo nero are very nutritious, and this easy-to-prepare soup is a complete meal in itself. Both ingredients can be found in good supermarkets.

Serves 4

150g/5½oz pearl barley
3 tbsp extra virgin olive oil, plus extra
    to drizzle
1 onion, finely chopped
400g/14oz cavolo nero, roughly
    chopped
1 large potato, peeled and cubed
115g/4oz tomatoes, chopped
1 litre/1¾ pints/4 cups vegetable broth
    (see page 32)
salt and freshly ground black pepper
4 slices of country bread, toasted, to
    serve (optional)
grated Parmesan, to serve (optional)

Rinse the barley and put it in a saucepan; add cold water to cover. Bring to the boil, then reduce the heat, cover with a lid and simmer for 1 hour, until the barley is cooked. Drain well and set aside.

Heat the olive oil in a large saucepan, add the onion and sweat for 5 minutes. Stir in the cavolo nero, potato and tomatoes. Add the cooked barley and the broth and season with salt and pepper. Bring to the boil, then reduce the heat to low, cover with a lid and cook for 40 minutes.

Remove from the heat, add a drizzle of olive oil and serve with toasted country bread and grated Parmesan if desired.

Zuppa di barbabietole e sedano rapa
Beetroot and celeriac soup

These are two of my wife Liz's favourite vegetables, so she decided to combine them while testing recipes for this book. Wow, what a taste! And so simple to make; just put all the vegetables in a pot and leave to slow cook until tender, whizz and serve. Can be enjoyed at any time, but it's an elegant soup for a dinner party.

Serves 4

500g/1lb 2oz celeriac (celery root), peeled and cut into large chunks
150g/5½oz beetroot (beets), peeled and cut into large chunks
1 large potato, peeled and cut into large chunks
1 celery stalk with leaves, roughly chopped
1 onion, roughly chopped
1.3 litres/2¼ pints/5½ cups vegetable broth (see page 32)
salt and freshly ground black pepper
a handful of parsley, finely chopped
natural yogurt, to serve (optional)

Put all the vegetables in a large saucepan together with the broth, bring to the boil, then reduce the heat, partially cover with a lid and simmer gently for 1 hour, until tender.

Remove from the heat and blend until smooth. Add salt and pepper to taste. Serve in individual bowls, sprinkled with parsley and a swirl of yogurt if desired.

Brodo di verdure
Vegetable broth

Vegetable broth or stock is at the base of many traditional Italian dishes – risotto, soups and stews – or it can simply be served as a soup. Ready-made stock can be very good, but nothing beats the fresh flavour of your own homemade broth, made with the freshest of vegetables. It is worth making a double quantity and freezing in batches. Being the lightest of all broths, it is popular for weaning babies or if you are feeling fragile, possibly with the addition of some tortellini or pastina (small pasta shapes). Or you can simply drink it as it is!

Serves 4

1 onion, peeled
1 courgette (zucchini)
1 carrot
1 celery stalk with leaves
1 leek
1 potato, peeled
2 cherry tomatoes
a handful of parsley, including stalks
2 tbsp extra virgin olive oil
1 tsp sea salt

Put all the ingredients in a large saucepan, add 1.5 litres/2½ pints/1½ quarts water and bring to the boil. Reduce the heat, cover with a lid and simmer gently for 1¼ hours. Taste for seasoning and add more salt if necessary.

Remove from the heat and strain the broth through a fine sieve, pressing down well on the vegetables with the back of a spoon. Serve hot, or reheat, adding some small pasta shapes to cook in the broth if you like.

Pasta

Pasta is the best-loved dish of all Italians and its popularity has spread worldwide – no wonder, as it makes a satisfying meal and many pasta dishes are quick to cook. However, there are lots of sauces and baked pasta dishes that require long, slow cooking. One of the best examples has to be ragù: there are many variations of ragù, but all are based on the principle of meat or other ingredients cooked very slowly so that they become superbly tender and their flavour creates a wonderful sauce. During hunting season, I will use whatever I have caught – perhaps pheasant, pigeon, hare or rabbit – cooked slowly to make a deliciously rich sauce to serve with pappardelle or tagliatelle.

My family's slow-cooked ragù, which we enjoyed for Sunday lunches, would take at least 12 hours to cook. My *zia* (aunt) Maria was the expert and she would start her ragù on Saturday and leave it to cook very, very gently on the smallest of flames on the stove all through the night for a ragù that was cooked to absolute perfection – the meat so tender and crumbly and the dense sauce with its unforgettable consistency and taste.

I love pasta dishes that can be served as two courses, such as the southern Italian ragù (see page 38) and *La Genovese* (see page 36), where a large piece of meat is cooked slowly and the resulting sauce is served with pasta as a first course followed by the meat as a main. These are some of my favourite dishes to cook, especially when I have a crowd for dinner. Not only are they simple to prepare, they go a long way and you know they will please everyone!

When I was growing up in southern Italy, *pasta al forno*, or baked pasta, was a must for special occasions like Christmas, weddings and christenings. At these times, the wood fire would be lit well in advance and large terracotta dishes would be baked for hours. A lasagne made with tomato sauce, meatballs, boiled eggs and lots of local salami and cheese was a sure favourite at these grand occasions. Baked pasta dishes can be made in advance and slowly cooked in the oven, and they don't mind waiting around before you serve them. They are ever-popular for Sunday lunches, at parties, or when you have lots of people round.

La Genovese con pennette

Slow-cooked onion sauce with pasta, followed by veal

Although the title suggests otherwise, this is a Neapolitan classic and, like ragù, is a Sunday lunch favourite in the Campania region. The recipe has age-old roots and there are various stories about its origins. One says it was prepared in *osterie* (inns) at the port of Naples by cooks from Genova for Genovese sailors. Large pieces of meat were slow-cooked with onions in order to create a flavoursome pasta sauce and a main course to feed the hungry sailors. Nowadays everyone has their own version. Beef is commonly used, but I prefer the milder taste of veal, which marries well with the onions; after long, gentle cooking these become sweet, with a meltingly soft texture that is perfect for a pasta sauce.

Serves 4

800g/1lb 12oz veal joint
salt and freshly ground black pepper
2 garlic cloves, sliced
100ml/3½fl oz/scant ½ cup extra virgin
  olive oil
2.5kg/5lb 8oz large onions, sliced
1 celery stalk, finely chopped
1 large carrot, finely chopped
85g/3oz salami, finely chopped
3 sage leaves
1 sprig of rosemary
2 bay leaves
200ml/7fl oz/scant 1 cup dry white
  wine
350g/12oz pennette pasta
30g/1oz pecorino (romano) cheese,
  grated

Rub the veal all over with salt and pepper, make some incisions in the meat and poke in the garlic slices.

Heat the olive oil in a large saucepan on a medium heat. Add the veal and brown well all over. Remove from the pan and set aside.

Add the onions, celery, carrot, salami and herbs, season with salt and pepper and sweat for about 30 minutes on a low heat.

Put the meat back in the pan, add the wine and allow to evaporate. Reduce the heat to very low, cover with a lid and cook for 3 hours, until the meat is very tender. Check from time to time to make sure it isn't sticking to the pan, turning the meat and stirring the onions.

Remove the meat from the pan and set aside. Using a potato masher, mash the onions slightly and taste for seasoning.

Cook the pennette in lightly salted boiling water until al dente, drain and toss with the onions. Serve with grated pecorino cheese and freshly ground black pepper. Slice the veal and serve as a main course with a green salad.

Il ragù antico
Slow-cooked ragù

Simbolo della domenica in famiglia ('the symbol of Sunday with the family')

This dish is a very popular and traditional Sunday lunch in most southern Italian families. When I was growing up, Sunday just wasn't Sunday without *il ragù*. The weekend would traditionally begin with the housewife's early trip to the butcher to obtain the perfect cuts of meat; with the package firmly clutched under her arm, she would begin to imagine how it would be cooked. Once at home, surrounded by children, grandparents and the odd neighbour or two, she would begin preparations for this weekly ritual – discussions would erupt among the women as to what should go in, how the meat should be sealed and so on. Just like in the film *Saturday, Sunday and Monday* (1990), when Sophia Loren goes to the butcher and ends up in a fiery discussion with other housewives as to what makes the perfect ragù! Ultimately, the ragù would be left slowly, slowly bubbling away on the stove, in a large terracotta pot, for most of Saturday and sometimes even throughout the night – a cooking time of 12 hours or more was quite normal. As the ragù gently simmered, the women went about making fresh pasta and gossiping, or in some families the rosary was recited. The smell of the bubbling ragù, the warmth from the wood-fired stove, the squeals of playing children and the animated voices of the women gave the serene feeling of home, family and the sign that the weekend was truly under way.

Traditionally the ragù was made with various cuts of beef – shin, knuckle, chuck – with the precious addition of *nervetti* (tendons) to give more flavour, as well as cuts of pork such as ribs and shanks. Home-preserved bottled tomatoes, made at the end of summer, gave the ragù its unique taste.

The secret to simmering a perfect ragù is to put it on an extremely low heat, partially cover the pot and listen for that gentle 'plop, plop, plop' sound during cooking. When the sauce and olive oil separate and the oil comes to the top, you know the ragù is ready.

The ragù is enjoyed as two courses, the first course being the rich tomato sauce served with pasta, followed by the meat. Pasta shapes such as *ziti* or *candele* were popular, but this varied from village to village; in my home village, Minori, we preferred *fusilli*. Not the mass-produced twist shapes found in the shops today, but long, thin curls made by rolling the pasta around umbrella spokes. I know ladies who still make *fusilli* like this today and when I go back to visit, I make sure I bring back a bagful to enjoy with my version of *il ragù*.

Serves 4-6

3 tbsp extra virgin olive oil
1 onion, finely chopped
600g/1lb 5oz beef shin, cut into about
  six chunks
4 pork ribs
500g/1lb 2oz stewing pork, cut into
  chunks
75ml/2½fl oz/5 tbsp red wine
1 tbsp tomato purée (paste), mixed with
1 tbsp lukewarm water
400g/14oz can chopped tomatoes
500ml/18fl oz/2 cups tomato passata
  (strained tomatoes)
a handful of basil leaves
salt and freshly ground black pepper

Heat the olive oil in a very large saucepan, add the onion and sweat for a couple of minutes on a medium heat. Add all the meat and brown well all over.

Add the wine and allow to evaporate. Then add the tomato purée and stir to coat the meat. Add the canned tomatoes and cook for a minute, then add the passata, basil, salt and pepper. Bring to the boil, then reduce the heat to very, very low, partially cover with a lid and cook for 6 hours. Check the liquid level (top up with a little stock or water if necessary) and stir very carefully from time to time.

After 3 hours, remove the ribs and pork and set aside.

About 20 minutes before the end of cooking time, return the ribs and pork to the sauce to heat through.

Remove the pan from the heat and leave to rest for 10 minutes. Using a slotted spoon, remove the meat and set aside. Use the tomato sauce to dress freshly cooked pasta and serve the meat as a main course.

For a slow cooker

Traditionally this is always cooked in a large pot, and all the meat is browned together so the flavours begin to mingle. When using a slow cooker you may find it easier to brown the meat in batches.
Sweat the onion and brown the meat as above. Continue as above and bring to the boil, then transfer everything to a large slow cooker pot, press the meat beneath the liquid, cover and cook on Low for 8-9 hours (there's no need to remove the ribs and pork from the slow cooker). Serve as above.

Ragù Bolognese
Classic Bolognese ragù

Although one of the most popular pasta sauces worldwide, the Bolognese is so often made badly outside of Italy: too much tomato, not cooked for long enough and usually served with spaghetti, hence the term 'spag bol' - unheard of in Italy! Because of all these differences and others, the Bolognese association of the *Accademia Italiana della Cucina* decided in 1982 to declare an official recipe. Although the original recipe used a whole cut of meat which was cut into tiny pieces, the *Accademia* allows for minced meat for ease of preparation. Only double- or triple-concentrated tomato purée is used (the kind sold in tubes in the supermarket is usually double-concentrated) and the addition of milk towards the end of cooking takes away any acidity from the tomato. The thick meat sauce would fall off the thin strands of spaghetti and so the Bolognese always serve it with tagliatelle; this ragù is also used for lasagne. For a rich, dense sauce, slow-cook for at least 2 hours. It is always worth making more than you need so you can freeze some in batches.

Serves 4

3 tbsp extra virgin olive oil
30g/1oz butter
1 onion, finely chopped
1 celery stalk, finely chopped
1 carrot, finely chopped
150g/5½oz pancetta, cubed
200g/7oz minced (ground) beef
200g/7oz minced (ground) pork
200ml/7fl oz/scant 1 cup red wine
1½ tbsp tomato purée (paste)
200ml/7fl oz/scant 1 cup beef stock
   (see page 21) - or use a stock cube
100ml/3½fl oz/scant ½ cup full-fat milk

Heat the olive oil and butter in a large saucepan, add the onion, celery, carrot and pancetta and sweat on a gentle heat for about 10 minutes, until the onion has softened.

Add the meat and brown all over. Increase the heat, add the wine and allow to evaporate. Dilute the tomato purée in a little of the stock and stir into the meat. Reduce the heat to low, cover with a lid and cook on a gentle heat for 2 hours, checking and adding a little extra stock from time to time to prevent the sauce from drying out.

About 10 minutes before the end of cooking time, stir in the milk.

Serve with freshly cooked tagliatelle.

For a slow cooker
Sweat the vegetables and pancetta and brown the meat as above. Add the wine and allow to evaporate, then dilute the tomato purée in 350ml/12fl oz/1½ cups stock, bring to the boil and transfer to a medium slow cooker pot. Cover and cook on Low for 8-9 hours. Stir in the milk and cook for 10 minutes. Serve as above.
For a large slow cooker pot, make double the quantity: cooking times remain the same.

Tagliatelle con ragù d'agnello in bianco con finocchietto

Tagliatelle with lamb and wild fennel

When we talk about ragù, we tend to think of the traditional sauce made with beef and tomatoes. This is a much lighter version, made *in bianco* ('in the white' – as Italians refer to dishes not cooked in tomato sauce). Italians tend to eat this dish in the spring, when lamb is at its best and wild fennel is found in abundance. Rather than using minced (ground) lamb, I use a piece of lamb cut into small bite-size pieces, keeping its texture, and slow-cook it on a gentle heat. The simple combination of lamb, wild fennel and a sprinkling of pecorino is delicious.

Serves 4

4 tbsp extra virgin olive oil
1 onion, finely sliced
1 celery stalk, finely sliced
400g/14oz lamb, cut into small pieces
100ml/3½fl oz/scant ½ cup dry white
  wine
salt and freshly ground black pepper
a handful of wild fennel, roughly
  chopped
300ml/10fl oz/1¼ cups vegetable stock
  (see page 32) – or use a stock cube
325g/11½oz dried tagliatelle pasta
40g/1½oz pecorino (romano) cheese,
  grated

Heat the olive oil in a large saucepan, add the onion and celery and sweat on a low heat for 20 minutes, stirring from time to time, until softened.

Increase the heat, add the lamb and brown well all over. Add the wine and allow to evaporate. Season and add a couple of fennel sprigs and 100ml/3½fl oz/scant ½ cup of the stock. Reduce the heat to very low, cover with a lid and cook for 1 hour, checking from time to time and gradually adding a little more of the stock. After about 55 minutes, stir in the remaining fennel.

When almost ready to serve, bring a large saucepan of lightly salted water to the boil and cook the tagliatelle until al dente. Drain, reserving a little of the cooking water. Add the pasta and a couple of tablespoons of the cooking water to the sauce and mix well. Remove from the heat, sprinkle with the pecorino and serve.

Maltagliati con cannellini e olive
Fresh pasta strips with cannellini beans and olives

I love cannellini beans, especially the dried beans that need to be soaked overnight. Once the beans are soaked, this dish is really easy to make, and the beans and prosciutto give a wonderful aroma as they cook together. The addition of fresh crunchy celery, olives and tomatoes makes this fresher and lighter than a typical *pasta e fagioli* (pasta and beans) dish. Delicious served next day and can also be enjoyed cold.

Serves 4

300g/10½oz/1½ cups dried cannellini
  beans, soaked in water overnight
200g/7oz piece of prosciutto, cubed
1 celery stalk, finely chopped
20 green olives, finely chopped
2 tomatoes, deseeded and finely
  chopped
leaves from 2 sprigs of rosemary, finely
  chopped
1 garlic clove, finely chopped
4 tbsp extra virgin olive oil, plus extra
  to drizzle
300g/10½oz fresh pappardelle, roughly
  chopped into 10cm/4-inch long strips
30g/1oz Parmesan, grated, plus extra,
  shaved, to serve
a small handful of basil leaves, torn
  if large
salt and freshly ground black pepper

Rinse the beans and put them in a large saucepan with the prosciutto; add 2 litres/3½ pints/2 quarts cold water and bring to the boil. Reduce the heat, partially cover with a lid and cook on a very low heat for 1 hour, or until the beans are tender but not falling apart.

Combine the celery, olives, tomatoes, rosemary, garlic and olive oil and add to the beans. Increase the heat, bring to the boil and add the pasta, then reduce the heat to medium and cook for 2–3 minutes, until the pasta is al dente. Remove from the heat, stir in the Parmesan and basil, taste for seasoning and leave to rest for 5 minutes. Serve with black pepper, a drizzle of extra virgin olive oil and a few Parmesan shavings.

Pappardelle con sugo di lepre
Pappardelle with hare sauce

Hare meat is rich and dark like beef or venison. If you are a hunter yourself, you know how rare it is to catch a hare, but if you do get the chance or can buy hare from a good butcher, then I urge you to try this dish. The recipe was created by one of my chefs, Davide Bargione, who, like me, loves hare. The sauce can be made in advance and reheated.

Serves 6

1 hare, cut into 12 pieces
salt and freshly ground black pepper
500g/1lb 2oz fresh or dried pappardelle
grated Parmesan, to serve (optional)

for the marinade
1 litre/1¾ pints/4 cups red wine
150ml/5fl oz/⅔ cup white wine vinegar
1 garlic head, cloves separated and
   crushed
2 cinnamon sticks
1 tsp fennel seeds, lightly crushed
20 black peppercorns, lightly crushed
3 sprigs of rosemary
6 bay leaves
juice of 1 lemon
2 large celery stalks, roughly chopped
2 onions, roughly chopped

for the sauce
3 tbsp extra virgin olive oil
1 onion, finely chopped
2 celery stalks, finely chopped
1 carrot, finely chopped
bouquet garni of thyme, bay leaf,
   rosemary and parsley
2 tbsp tomato purée (paste)
200ml/7fl oz/scant 1 cup red wine
1.2kg/2lb 10oz (3 x 400g/14oz cans)
canned chopped tomatoes
500ml/18fl oz/2 cups hot vegetable stock
   (see page 32) - or use a stock cube

Wash the hare thoroughly under cold running water and pat dry with kitchen paper. Put the hare in a large bowl together with the rest of the marinade ingredients, cover with clingfilm (plastic wrap) and leave in the fridge for at least 12 hours.

Remove the hare from the marinade, pat dry and season with salt and pepper. To make the sauce, heat the olive oil in a large saucepan and brown the hare all over. Remove the meat and set aside. In the same pan, sweat the onion, celery, carrot and bouquet garni together with the vegetables, garlic and herbs from the marinade for about 3 minutes. Stir in the tomato purée, add the wine and allow to evaporate. Return the hare to the pan, add the tomatoes, stock, some salt and pepper, and bring to the boil. Reduce the heat, cover with a lid and cook gently for 1½ hours.

At the end of the cooking time, remove the chunks of meat and set aside until cool enough to handle. Remove the meat from the bones, discard the bones, chop the meat finely and return to the sauce and heat through.

Meanwhile, bring a large saucepan of lightly salted water to the boil and cook the pappardelle until al dente. Drain, mix with the hare sauce and serve immediately, with a little grated Parmesan if desired.

Tagliolini con ragù di fagiano in bianco

Tagliolini with pheasant

This is one of my favourite dishes after a morning's shooting; I love getting together with all the other hunters and tucking into this tasty pasta dish. I often don't bother to marinate the pheasant, as I like the gamey flavour. As the sauce is *in bianco* ('white', or without tomato) the dish is quite light and shows off the full flavour of the meat. The sauce can be made in advance and reheated thoroughly before adding the pasta.

Serves 4

1 pheasant, cleaned, boned and cut into chunks (ask your butcher to do this)
salt and freshly ground black pepper
plain (all-purpose) flour, to dust
5 tbsp extra virgin olive oil
100ml/3½fl oz/scant ½ cup dry white wine
1 onion, finely chopped
1 celery stalk, finely chopped
1 carrot, finely chopped
1 sprig of rosemary
350ml/12fl oz/1½ cups hot vegetable stock (see page 32) – or use a stock cube
350g/12oz fresh or dried tagliolini pasta

for the marinade
400ml/14fl oz/1⅔ cups dry white wine
½ onion, roughly chopped
1 celery stalk, roughly chopped
1 carrot, roughly chopped
1 sprig of rosemary

Put the chunks of pheasant in a bowl together with all the marinade ingredients, cover with clingfilm (plastic wrap) and leave in the fridge overnight.

Remove the meat from the marinade, carefully remove the skin and discard. Dry the meat with kitchen paper, season with salt and pepper and dust with flour. Discard the marinade.

Heat half of the olive oil in a frying pan on a medium–high heat, add the pheasant and brown well all over, then add the wine and allow to evaporate.

In another frying pan, heat the remaining olive oil and sweat the onion, celery, carrot and rosemary until the vegetables have softened. Add the browned meat to the vegetables and mix together. Add the stock, some salt and pepper and bring to the boil, then reduce the heat, cover with a lid and cook gently for 50 minutes. Check from time to time and if necessary add more hot stock.

When almost ready to serve, cook the tagliolini in lightly salted boiling water until al dente. Drain, reserving a little of the cooking water, and add the pasta to the pheasant sauce, then toss well with a few tablespoons of the cooking water. Serve immediately.

Paccheri con sugo di coniglio
Paccheri with rabbit sauce

Paccheri are a traditional Neapolitan pasta in the shape of large, round tubes, which marry very well with a thick sauce like this. The sauce can be made in advance and reheated thoroughly before adding the pasta. Rabbit is quite a bland meat so it needs to be livened up with spices or herbs: here I've inserted cloves into an onion, which gives the sauce a spicy taste. This is a simple one-pot meal that will give you two courses: the pasta is served with the sauce as a starter and the rabbit follows as a main course, perhaps served with a green salad.

Serves 4

3 cloves
1 onion, peeled, left whole
4 tbsp extra virgin olive oil
1 carrot, finely chopped
1 garlic clove, left whole
½ red chilli, finely chopped
2 sage leaves
1kg/2lb 4oz rabbit, cut into chunks on the bone
750ml/1¼ pints/3 cups tomato passata (strained tomatoes)
salt
350g/12oz paccheri or lumaconi (large shells) pasta
grated pecorino (romano) cheese, to serve

Insert the cloves into the onion. Heat the olive oil in a large saucepan on a medium–high heat, add the onion, carrot, garlic, chilli and sage leaves and stir-fry until golden. Remove and discard the garlic. Add the rabbit and brown on all sides. Stir in the passata and some salt, reduce the heat, cover with a lid and simmer gently for 2 hours.

Remove the rabbit pieces and set aside. Strain the sauce and put it back in the saucepan to keep it warm, together with the rabbit.

Meanwhile, cook the paccheri in plenty of lightly salted boiling water until al dente. Drain, add to the sauce, mix well and serve with freshly grated pecorino cheese.

Lasagne con ragù di verdure
Lasagne with slow-cooked vegetable ragù

This is a lighter version of the classic lasagne, with vegetables replacing the meat Bolognese ragù. The vegetables are cooked on a very low heat so they do not go mushy and the flavours infuse well.

Serves 4

3 tbsp extra virgin olive oil
1 shallot, finely sliced
1 leek, finely sliced
1 celery stalk, finely sliced
1 carrot, finely sliced
1 turnip, finely sliced
150g/5½oz pumpkin, cubed
85g/3oz mushrooms, sliced
100g/3½oz curly endive, roughly
   chopped
1 garlic clove, crushed
1 sprig of marjoram
1 sprig of thyme
salt and freshly ground black pepper
3 tbsp canned chopped tomatoes
250ml/9fl oz/1 cup vegetable stock
   (see page 32) - or use a stock cube
butter, to grease and finish
8-10 fresh lasagne sheets
100g/3½oz Parmesan, grated

for the white sauce
40g/1½oz/3 tbsp butter
40g/1½oz/5 tbsp plain (all-purpose)
   flour
500ml/18fl oz/2 cups full-fat milk
a pinch of freshly grated nutmeg

Heat the olive oil in a large saucepan, add the shallot and leek and sweat on a medium heat for 3 minutes. Add the celery, carrot, turnip, pumpkin, mushrooms, endive, garlic, herbs and black pepper. Stir in the tomatoes and stock, reduce the heat to minimum, then cover with a lid and cook for 1 ½ hours, stirring from time to time.

Preheat the oven to 200°C/400°F/gas mark 6.

To make the sauce, melt the butter in a saucepan, remove from the heat and whisk in the flour very quickly to avoid lumps, then gradually add the milk, whisking well. Return to the heat and cook on a medium heat for 3–4 minutes, whisking all the time until the sauce begins to thicken. Remove from the heat and stir in some salt, pepper and nutmeg.

Grease an ovenproof dish, about 20 x 25cm/8 x 10 inches, with butter and spread a little of the white sauce on the bottom. Arrange a layer of lasagne sheets on top, followed by some vegetable ragù, a little white sauce, and a sprinkling of grated Parmesan. Continue making layers like this until you have used all the ingredients, ending with white sauce and grated Parmesan. Top with small knobs of butter. Cover with foil and bake in the oven for 20 minutes.

Remove the foil and cook for another 10 minutes to brown the top. Remove from the oven and leave to rest for 5 minutes before serving.

Pasta e patate arraganate al forno
Baked pasta and potatoes

My sister, Adriana, makes this dish; it is a cross between *pasta e patate* (pasta and potatoes), which was a much-loved dish in our family, and *patate arraganate* (sliced potatoes baked in the oven with oregano and tomatoes). It's a thrifty way to use up small amounts of dried pasta from your store cupboard, making a tasty, nutritious meal for a family midweek supper.

Serves 4

500g/1lb 2oz potatoes, cut into chunks
60g/2¼oz Parmesan: 30g/1oz roughly
 cut into cubes; 30g/1oz grated
250g/9oz dried pasta, broken up

for the sauce
1 tbsp extra virgin olive oil
1 onion, roughly chopped
1 celery stalk with leaves, roughly
 chopped
600g/1lb 5oz canned chopped
tomatoes
a handful of fresh basil leaves, plus
 extra to serve
a pinch of dried oregano
 salt and freshly ground black pepper

First, make the sauce: heat the olive oil in a saucepan and sweat the onion and celery for a couple of minutes. Add the tomatoes, then rinse out the can with 200ml/7fl oz/scant 1 cup water and add to the pan. Stir in the basil, oregano, salt and pepper and cook on a medium heat for 25 minutes.

Meanwhile, preheat the oven to 180°C/350°F/gas mark 4.

Put the tomato sauce and potatoes in an ovenproof dish about 20 x 25cm/8 x 10 inches, dot with pieces of Parmesan, cover with foil and bake for 45 minutes.

Cook the pasta in plenty of salted boiling water for 2 minutes, then drain, reserving about 200ml/7fl oz/scant 1 cup of the cooking water. Add the pasta to the sauce and potatoes, together with the reserved pasta cooking water. Sprinkle with grated Parmesan and scatter over a few basil leaves, then return to the oven for 15 minutes, without the foil. Remove from the oven and leave to rest for 5 minutes before serving.

Pasta e fagioli
Pasta and beans

This dish is popular throughout Italy and each region, town, village and family have their own versions. The dish was a staple in most rural homes, slowly bubbling away in large terracotta pots over the ash of the fireplace to provide a warm, nutritious meal when the family returned home from a hard day working in the fields. This particular recipe is typical of the Abruzzo region, where it is normally made with fresh eggless tagliatelle-type pasta. *Pasta e fagioli* dishes are not traditionally served with grated cheese, but if you prefer you can grate some Parmesan or pecorino to sprinkle on when serving.

Serves 4

250g/9oz/1¼ cups dried borlotti beans, soaked in water overnight
3 tbsp extra virgin olive oil, plus extra to drizzle
½ onion, finely chopped
1 celery stalk, finely chopped
1 small carrot, finely chopped
½ red chilli, finely chopped (optional)
400g/14oz can chopped tomatoes
150g/5½oz tomato passata (strained tomatoes)
salt and freshly ground black pepper
250g/9oz dried tagliatelle, broken up

Drain and rinse the beans, put them in a saucepan with enough cold water to cover and bring to the boil. Reduce the heat to low, partially cover with a lid and cook for about 1 hour, or until the beans are tender. Drain, reserving a couple of tablespoons of the cooking water. Take about a quarter of the beans and mash them with the cooking water. Set aside.

Heat the olive oil in a saucepan, sweat the onion, celery, carrot and chilli, if using, for a couple of minutes, then add all the tomatoes, salt and pepper and cook on a medium heat, partially covered with a lid, for 20 minutes. Add all the beans and the reserved cooking water and continue to cook for 10 minutes, stirring from time to time.

Meanwhile, bring a large saucepan of lightly salted water to the boil and cook the tagliatelle until al dente. Drain, reserving a little of the cooking water, and add to the sauce, mixing well together; if necessary add a little of the cooking water. Remove from the heat and leave to rest for 5 minutes, then serve in individual bowls with a drizzle of extra virgin olive oil.

Light dishes
& leftovers

———

'Slow cooking' conjures up images of heavy meals for colder months,
but the idea of taking things slowly can also create light, fresh-tasting dishes
for snacks and summer eating.

Marinating is a form of 'slow cooking' that doesn't need the stove or oven,
but it does need several hours for the flavours to mingle and marry.
It's a simple technique with stunning results: as the food absorbs the flavourings,
the taste improves. The dishes are enjoyed cold as an *antipasto*, snack or light
but satisfying meal and can include all sorts of ingredients, from pumpkin in the
antipasto di zucca to mackerel marinated with mint, and rabbit in a Tuscan salad.

While writing and testing recipes for this book, I encountered lots of slow-cooked
dishes that could effortlessly be made into other meals. Once you've made a beef
or chicken broth, for example, you can transform the main ingredient into another
course or a meal for another day. Boiled beef can be transformed into a salad,
meatballs or even burgers. Boiled chicken also makes a delicious salad.
When I was brought up, food was never wasted and I still maintain those values.
My sister Adriana is a genius at this and comes up with some amazing dishes
using leftovers that most people would bin! Not only is it part of our culture
never to waste food, but it also makes cooking a fun and imaginative process.

———

Antipasto di zucca arrostita marinata
Pumpkin antipasto

This lovely roasted pumpkin makes an ideal antipasto served alongside some Parma ham and lots of good bread or crostini. The vinegar marinade gives the pumpkin a 'kick' and gets your taste buds going. This can be rustic or more elegant: marinate the pumpkin in four small ramekins and turn out onto serving plates. It can be made the day before and left in the fridge overnight – but serve at room temperature.

Serves 4

extra virgin olive oil, to grease and drizzle
850g/1lb 14oz peeled and deseeded pumpkin, finely sliced
salt
150ml/5fl oz/²⁄₃ cup white wine vinegar
3 small shallots, finely sliced
2 small bay leaves
6 black peppercorns
a handful of basil leaves, plus extra to garnish

Preheat the oven to 180°C/350°F/gas mark 4. Lightly grease a baking sheet with olive oil, put the pumpkin slices on top, sprinkle with salt and drizzle with more olive oil. Roast in the oven for 30 minutes, until golden and cooked through but not mushy. Remove and leave to cool.

Put the vinegar, shallots, bay leaves and peppercorns in a small pan and bring to the boil. Remove from the heat and leave to cool.

In a non-metallic container, make layers of pumpkin, basil leaves and the vinegar marinade. Leave to marinate for at least 4 hours – or overnight in the fridge. Bring to room temperature before serving, drizzle over some extra virgin olive oil and scatter over a few fresh basil leaves.

Sardine marinate all'arancia
Sardines marinated in orange

Sardines are so good for you, and I am pleased to see they are now readily available on most supermarket fish counters ready cleaned and filleted and excellent value! Fish is often made in this way in Italy, known as *al carpione*; once cooked it is left to marinate and it was a popular way to preserve fish before the arrival of fridges. It makes an excellent antipasto served with a crunchy raw fennel salad.

Serves 4

1 egg
salt and freshly ground black pepper
70g/2½oz dried breadcrumbs
1 tbsp finely chopped parsley
4 sardines, 50-60g/about 2oz each,
  cleaned and filleted
plain (all-purpose) flour, to dust
vegetable oil for shallow frying

for the marinade
3 tbsp extra virgin olive oil
125g/4½oz shallots, finely chopped
2 tbsp white wine vinegar
grated zest and juice of 1 large orange

for the fennel salad
1 large fennel bulb, finely sliced
4 tbsp extra virgin olive oil

Put the egg in a bowl, season and beat well. Put the breadcrumbs on a plate and combine with the parsley. Dust the sardines in flour, shake off excess flour, dip into the egg mixture, then coat well with the breadcrumbs, gently pressing and flattening with the palms of your hands.

Heat some oil in a large frying pan. When hot, cook the sardines for a couple of minutes on each side until golden. Drain on kitchen paper and set aside.

For the marinade, put the olive oil in a small saucepan on a medium heat, add the shallots and cook until they have softened and are slightly golden. Stir in the vinegar and leave to infuse for a minute. Remove from the heat and leave to cool. Stir in the orange juice and zest. Pour over the sardines, cover with clingfilm (plastic wrap) and leave to marinate for at least 2 hours – or up to 3 days in the fridge; serve at room temperature.

For the fennel salad, put the sliced fennel in a bowl and mix well with olive oil, salt and pepper. Serve with the sardines.

Insalata di coniglio alla Toscana
Tuscan rabbit salad

I love the tangy taste that comes from cooking the rabbit in vinegar and wine; it is then marinated, resulting in tender, flavoursome pieces of meat. Served in a salad with bulgur wheat and beans, it makes a perfectly balanced, simple meal. If you prefer, you can substitute chicken for the rabbit. To use dried borlotti beans, soak them in water overnight, then drain and simmer in fresh water for about 1 hour, or until the beans are tender (check the packet instructions). Drain and leave to cool.

Serves 4-6

700ml/1¼ pints/3 cups white wine
    vinegar
700ml/1¼ pints/3 cups dry white wine
½ tsp salt
1kg/2lb 4oz rabbit pieces on the bone
250g/9oz bulgur wheat
200g/7oz fresh or frozen broad (fava)
    beans
200g/7oz cooked or canned borlotti
    beans
1 small red onion, finely sliced
juice of 1 lemon

for the marinade
500ml/18fl oz/2 cups olive oil
3 garlic cloves, squashed and left whole
6 sage leaves
2 rosemary sprigs
1 red chilli, finely sliced

In a large saucepan, heat 700ml/1¼ pints/3 cups of water with the vinegar and wine. Add the salt and rabbit, bring to the boil, then reduce the heat and simmer for about 35 minutes, until the rabbit is tender and cooked through.

Combine the ingredients for the marinade and set aside.

Remove the rabbit from the pan and leave until cool enough to handle, then remove the flesh from the bones. Put the meat in the marinade, cover with clingfilm (plastic wrap) and leave to marinate for 2 hours.

Meanwhile, cook the bulgur wheat for about 15 minutes, until al dente – check the packet instructions. Drain and leave to cool. Cook the broad beans for about 10 minutes (less if using frozen beans), until tender but not mushy, drain and leave to cool.

Combine the cooked bulgur wheat, broad beans, borlotti beans and red onion, adding as much or as little of the olive oil from the marinade as you like, together with lemon juice to taste, and toss well. Place on a serving dish and top with the pieces of marinated rabbit.

Insalata di manzo bollito
Cold beef salad

This is a lovely light dish made from the boiled beef used to make beef broth (see page 21). The resulting meat is very tender and perfect served cold as a salad, with good bread.

Serves 4-6

1 quantity of beef from beef broth (see page 21)
1 bunch of spring onions (scallions), trimmed and roughly chopped
200g/7oz cherry tomatoes, halved or quartered, depending on size
20g/¾oz/2 tbsp black olives
salt and freshly ground black pepper
5 tbsp extra virgin olive oil
juice of 1 lemon
200g/7oz rocket (arugula)
40g/1½oz Parmesan shavings

Drain the beef from the broth, leave to cool, then chop into bite-size pieces and set aside.

Place the beef in a bowl together with the spring onions, tomatoes and olives and toss well with salt, pepper, olive oil and lemon juice. Add the rocket and stir in carefully. Divide among four or six plates and just before serving top with Parmesan shavings.

Polpette di carne
Meatballs

This is a fantastically simple recipe you can make with the beef cooked for the beef broth (see page 21); in the past, Italian housewives would always make *polpette* this way or with leftover roast beef. When we have leftover boiled or roast beef, my wife Liz often makes meatballs or burgers for the children. These meatballs can also be frozen. *Polpette* are delicious eaten as they are or with a tomato sauce, served with pasta or added to a lasagne. If you turn the beef into burgers, serve with some good bread buns, salad and cheese and enjoy, as my girls do, a homemade treat!

Makes about 40 meatballs or 20 burgers

1 quantity of beef from beef broth
  (see page 21)
3 tbsp extra virgin olive oil
2 onions, finely chopped
a handful of parsley, finely chopped
115g/4oz bread, grated into fine crumbs
100g/3½oz Parmesan, grated
salt and freshly ground black pepper
3 eggs
plain (all-purpose) flour, to dust
olive oil for frying

Drain the beef from the broth and chop into large chunks; put the chunks in a food processor and whizz until well minced (ground). Alternatively, chop the beef very finely with a sharp knife.

Heat the olive oil in a frying pan, add the onions and sweat on a low heat for about 10 minutes, until softened. Leave to cool.

Combine the minced beef with the cooled onion, parsley, breadcrumbs, Parmesan, salt and pepper to taste, and the eggs. Shape into balls about the size of walnuts; alternatively shape into burgers. Place on a lightly greased baking tin or dish, cover with clingfilm (plastic wrap) and place in the fridge for about an hour. Alternatively, place in a container, seal and freeze for later use.

Dust the meatballs with a little flour, heat some oil in a frying pan and fry the meatballs in the hot oil until lightly browned on all sides. Do this in batches, depending on the size of your pan. Drain on kitchen paper and keep warm until all are cooked. If you are making burgers, fry them for a couple of minutes on each side. Serve with pasta or buns and salad.

Bollito misto con salsa verde

Mixed boiled meats served with salsa verde

This typical Piemontese dish is usually made for special occasions involving large numbers of people. Traditionalists insist on seven prime cuts of beef and veal, seven lesser meats such as chicken, ox tongue and sausage, served with seven sauces, boiled vegetables and a bowl of the broth in which the meats were cooked. However, the recipe is adapted by different families to suit their needs. *Zampone* or *cotechino* sausage is usually included in *bollito misto* - you will find it in Italian delis. Here is my simplified version of this dish, with a tangy salsa verde (green sauce). You can also serve it with *mostarda di Cremona* (a traditional condiment of candied fruits in mustard, sold in Italian delis), horseradish sauce, mustard and pickled vegetables. The meats are simmered together in a large pan; the resulting broth is served as a starter with tortellini pasta (or kept as a stock for other dishes), and the meats are served as a main course.

Serves 10

500g/1lb 2oz ox tongue
500g/1lb 2oz piece of beef brisket
1 small chicken, weighing about
   1.2kg/2lb 10oz
1 large onion
2 celery stalks with leaves
2 carrots
4 cherry tomatoes
a handful of parsley, including stalks
salt
10 black peppercorns
6 potatoes, peeled and left whole
1 vacuum-packed zampone or
   cotechino sausage

for the salsa verde
2 large handfuls of parsley
50g/1¾oz baby gherkins (cornichons)
50g/1¾oz capers
1 garlic clove
4 anchovy fillets
40g/1½oz bread, soaked in a little
   lukewarm water
yolk from 1 hard-boiled egg
5 tbsp extra virgin olive oil

Wash the ox tongue under cold running water and pat dry with kitchen paper. Place in a large saucepan with cold water to cover, bring to the boil, skim off the scum, then reduce the heat, cover with a lid and cook gently for 1 hour, removing the scum from time to time.

Add the beef brisket and continue to simmer for 1 hour.

Add the chicken, onion, celery, carrots, tomatoes, parsley, salt and peppercorns and cook for 30 minutes. Add the potatoes and cook for another 30 minutes. At the same time, bring another saucepan of water to the boil, add the zampone or cotechino and cook according to the packet instructions.

To make the salsa verde: very finely chop the parsley, gherkins, capers, garlic, anchovies, bread and egg yolk – you can do this in a food processor, but I prefer the slight crunchiness you get by chopping with a knife. Put the chopped ingredients into a bowl and combine with the olive oil. This can be made 2–3 days ahead and stored in the fridge, but serve at room temperature.

When the meats are cooked, remove from the liquid and set aside. Leave the tongue to cool a little before peeling off the skin, then slice. Slice all the other meats and arrange on a large serving dish. Serve with the salsa verde (you can also serve the potatoes and vegetables).

Insalata di pollo con giardiniera
Chicken salad with preserved vegetables

This is a lovely dish made from the chicken cooked in the Chicken broth recipe (see page 22). Serve as an antipasto or a main course with lots of good bread to dip into the dressing. You will need to marinate it overnight in the fridge and you can leave the finished dish to infuse for another day. If you want a short cut, instead of preparing the vegetables, use a jar of ready-made preserved *giardiniera*, which is an Italian mixed vegetable pickle sold in good delis.

Serves 4

1 cooked chicken from chicken broth
  (see page 22)
a sprig of thyme, a couple of sage
  leaves and slices of red chilli, to
  garnish (optional)

for the marinade
300ml/10fl oz/1¼ cups olive oil
3 garlic cloves, left whole
1 red chilli, sliced
4 sprigs of thyme
2 sprigs of rosemary
4 sage leaves

for the vegetables
200ml/7fl oz/scant 1 cup red wine
  vinegar
salt
100g/3½oz green beans, topped
  and tailed
2 celery stalks, sliced
2 small carrots, finely sliced
10 baby onions, peeled and left whole
100g/3½oz celeriac (celery root),
  peeled and cut into bite-size chunks
¼ red pepper, cut into chunks
  (optional)
a few cauliflower florets (optional)

Remove the chicken from the broth and leave to cool. Remove the skin and bones and break the flesh into pieces. Place in a dish and set aside.

Put all the marinade ingredients into a saucepan and heat gently, but do not bring to the boil. Remove from the heat and pour over the chicken, cover with clingfilm (plastic wrap) and leave in the fridge overnight.

Remove the chicken from the fridge and leave at room temperature for about 20 minutes.

Meanwhile, to cook the vegetables, put 400ml/14fl oz/ 1⅔ cups water in a saucepan with the vinegar and a couple of good pinches of salt, bring to the boil, add the vegetables and blanch for 5 minutes. Drain and leave to cool.

Add the vegetables to the chicken mixture and toss well. Garnish with herbs and chilli if desired. Serve immediately or leave in the fridge to infuse for up to 24 hours, but serve at room temperature.

Liatina e' puorc
Pork in aspic jelly

Gelatine or aspic jelly was used in ancient Rome as a stiffening agent in the kitchen; in medieval times meat and fish gelatines were served at grand banquets. Gelatine, these days, is mostly used by producers of marshmallows and gummy sweets and is sold in thin leaves for home use when making jellies or panna cotta. But it is derived from the feet (and other parts) of pigs and calves. Until relatively recently in rural areas of Italy, nothing was wasted when a pig was killed, and parts like the trotter, ear, tail and even snout were used in dishes like this. We used to eat this dish when I was a boy in Italy; that's why I have kept the title in Neapolitan dialect. Jellied pork is still popular in the Campania region and Sicily. It is very simple to prepare and most butchers will be happy to sell you the pig's parts for a minimal cost.

Serves 10-12

1 pig's trotter
1 pig's ear
1 pig's tail
1kg/2lb 4oz mixed pork meat, such as chops, stewing chunks, neck
10 bay leaves, plus a few extra to garnish
1 tbsp salt
3 tbsp white wine vinegar
juice of ½ lemon
freshly ground black pepper
30g/1oz pine kernels
30g/1oz sultanas (golden raisins)

First clean the pig's trotter, ear and tail under cold running water, scrubbing well and ensuring all hairs and impurities are removed. Put the pieces in a large saucepan with the pork meat, 10 bay leaves and the salt and cover with cold water. Bring to the boil, skim off the scum, then reduce the heat, partially cover with a lid and gently simmer for 2¾ hours, removing any scum from time to time.

Add the vinegar and simmer for a further 15 minutes. Remove the pork meat and leave to cool. Discard the trotter, ear and tail. Strain the liquid through a fine sieve, add the lemon juice and set aside.

Using your fingers, tear the cooled meat into pieces, discarding any fat. Put the pieces of meat in a large terrine, sprinkle with some black pepper, half the pine kernels and sultanas and three or four bay leaves. Pour over the liquid and leave in a cool place to set for about an hour, then scatter over the remaining pine kernels, sultanas and a couple more bay leaves. Cover with clingfilm (plastic wrap) and leave in a cool place overnight to set completely. If you are making this on a warm day, place in the fridge once set, otherwise leave at room temperature.

Sgombro marinato alla menta
Marinated mackerel with mint

A really easy dish using one of my favourite fish, mackerel. It makes a delicious antipasto or light lunch, served with lots of good bread to mop up the oil. It's not a dish you can hurry: the fish is first steam-cooked in parchment paper and then marinated, first in vinegar and then in olive oil. The longer you leave it in the oil, the more the flavour improves: it can be kept, covered, in the fridge for up to a week.

Serves 4

800g/1lb 12oz mackerel fillets
salt
400ml/14fl oz/1⅔ cups white wine
  vinegar
1 garlic clove, finely sliced
a handful of mint leaves
abundant olive oil, to marinate

Take a large sheet of baking parchment and wrap each fillet separately, tying them with kitchen string into a parcel – this is to prevent them from breaking during cooking. Place in a pan of salted water, bring to the boil, reduce the heat and simmer for 3 minutes. Alternatively, cook the fillets in a steamer.

Remove, drain the parcels and open carefully. Put the fillets in a non-metallic container or dish, pour over the vinegar, cover with clingfilm (plastic wrap) and leave in the fridge to marinate for at least 4 hours.

Carefully remove the mackerel and place in a clean container together with the garlic and mint leaves, and cover with olive oil. Cover with clingfilm (plastic wrap) and leave in the fridge overnight.

Remove from the fridge and bring to room temperature before eating. Serve with lots of good bread.

Insalata di polipo
Octopus salad

This is one of my favourite meals. It's made from the octopus cooked in the octopus broth recipe (see page 25). The flesh is cut into pieces and simply tossed in extra virgin olive oil and lemon juice. It can be made the day before and kept, covered, in the fridge – but get it out 30 minutes before you want to eat, as it is best served at room temperature.

Serves 4-6

1 cooked octopus from octopus broth
  (see page 25)
8 tbsp extra virgin olive oil
juice of 1 large lemon
a good pinch of salt
2 garlic cloves, finely sliced
bunch of parsley, roughly chopped
1 small red chilli
12 large green olives, sliced in half

Take the drained octopus and set aside about 100ml/3½fl oz/scant ½ cup of the broth and leave to cool.

Put the octopus on a chopping board and chop into bite-size pieces – you can use scissors to cut the tentacles. Place the pieces in a large bowl. Add the rest of the ingredients, including the reserved broth, mix well, and leave to rest for at least 30 minutes. Serve with lots of good bread.

Carciofi ripieni
Filled artichokes

Artichokes are very popular in Italy, especially in the south, where they grow in abundance. The season begins in spring and they are often eaten at Easter time. I love artichokes; they are light and digestible and can be cooked in so many different ways. In this slow-cooked stove-top dish they are filled with a tasty mixture of pancetta and vegetables.

Serves 4

4 globe artichokes
juice of 1 lemon
1-2 small carrots, scrubbed and halved
1 celery stalk with leaves
1 small onion, halved
1 potato, scrubbed
2 cherry tomatoes
a pinch of salt

for the filling
4 tbsp extra virgin olive oil, plus extra
 to drizzle
40g/1½oz pancetta, cubed
2 shallots, finely sliced
1 garlic clove, chopped
1 small courgette (zucchini), finely
 diced
½ aubergine (eggplant), finely diced
a handful of parsley, roughly chopped
15g/½oz/2 tbsp pine nuts
40g/1½oz Parmesan, grated
freshly ground black pepper
a small bunch of basil leaves (optional)

First clean and prepare the artichokes: using a sharp knife, remove the bottom outer leaves and cut off the stalks. Trim the base so the bottom is flat and the artichoke can stand upright. With your fingers, gently open out the artichoke leaves until you can see the hairy choke. With a small teaspoon, remove and discard the choke, which is inedible. Place the artichokes in a bowl of water with the lemon juice in order to prevent discoloration while you prepare the filling.

To make the filling, heat the olive oil in a saucepan, add the pancetta and fry until crisp, remove and set aside. Add the shallots and garlic to the pan and sweat until softened, ensuring you don't burn the garlic; remove and set aside. In the same pan, stir-fry the courgette and aubergine for 8–10 minutes, until soft but not mushy. Remove from the heat and combine with the pancetta, shallots, parsley, pine nuts, Parmesan and pepper.

Remove the artichokes from the water and turn them upside down to drain. Open them up and fill the cavity with the pancetta mixture; tie with string to ensure the filling does not fall out and, if you like, tuck a few basil leaves into the top of each artichoke. Place in a pan large enough to hold all four artichokes snugly.

Add the carrots, celery, onion, potato and tomatoes. Sprinkle the artichokes with a little salt, drizzle with olive oil and fill the pan with water to come halfway up the artichokes. Put the pan on a medium–high heat and bring to the boil, then immediately reduce the heat to low, cover with a lid and simmer gently for 1¼ hours. Lift the artichokes out of the pan using a slotted spoon and serve one per person, with a little of the broth. And don't forget to eat the potato and carrot!

Stews

——

Stews are popular all over the world; they are warming, welcoming, and a wonderful way to use economical cuts of meat. Pieces of meat that are slowly cooked in a sauce with herbs, spices and seasonings are often far more tender and tasty than a quickly grilled steak, and with the inclusion of vegetables can be a meal in themselves – or serve with polenta (cornmeal), rice, mashed potatoes or lots of good bread to mop up the juices.

The classic Italian way of preparing a stew begins with a *soffritto*, a gently fried mix of onion, celery and carrot – this important step forms the base of the stew, ensuring maximum flavour. The sealing or browning of the pieces of meat is equally important, giving a rich flavour and adding colour to the stew. It is important to cook the stew on a very gentle heat because boiling will toughen the meat. To enhance the flavour, stews are best made the day before and gently reheated when required.

You can usually find ready-cut chunks of meat clearly marked 'for stewing' in supermarkets, or your butcher will cut the meat for you. If you are beginning with a larger piece of meat, it should be cut into cubes of roughly 4–5cm/1½– 2 inches; pieces that are too small will fall apart and may dry out during cooking.

The following are ideal cuts for stewing:
Lamb: scrag end and middle neck, shoulder, knuckle/shank
Beef: neck , chuck, blade, brisket, thick flank , thin flank, skirt,
shin/shank ,topside, silverside, knuckle
Pork: shoulder – although you can use any cut, shoulder is the most economical

Italian stews are as varied as the country: from a rich Tyrolean goulash originating in the Austrian-influenced Alpine region of Trentino-Alto Adige, to my slow-cooked vegetable stew using the typical sun-drenched ingredients of the southern regions – you will find a dish to satisfy every taste and mood.

——

Goulash Tirolese

Tyrolean beef stew

This classic stew from the Trentino-Alto Adige or South Tyrol region of northern Italy is slow cooked with onions, cumin and paprika - its distinct central European flavour is influenced by neighbouring Austria. The gradual addition of stock gives this stew a gentle flavour; pancetta is added, so be careful not to make your stock too salty. This dish is traditionally served with runny polenta (cornmeal). It is also delicious with a piece of good country bread whose soft part is removed, cubed and toasted; the goulash is served in the bread crust and the toasted bits sprinkled on top - a dish fit for an Austrian king!

Serves 4

3 tbsp extra virgin olive oil
2 large onions, sliced
100g/3½oz pancetta, cubed
about 1 litre/1¾ pints/4 cups hot
  vegetable stock (see page 32) -
  or use a stock cube
1kg/2lb 4oz stewing beef, cut into
  chunks
2 garlic cloves, sliced
1 tsp cumin seeds, crushed
1 tsp paprika
2 sprigs of thyme
polenta (cornmeal) or toasted country
  bread, to serve

For a slow cooker
Cook the onions, pancetta and beef as above. Once the beef is browned add 750ml/1¼ pints/3 cups stock, the garlic, cumin, paprika, thyme and pancetta. Bring to the boil, stirring, then transfer to a large slow cooker pot, press the meat beneath the liquid, cover and cook on Low for 8-9 hours.

Heat the olive oil in a large saucepan and sweat the onions on a medium heat for about 5 minutes, stirring all the time to prevent sticking, until softened. Remove and set aside.

Add the pancetta to the pan and cook on a medium heat until coloured but not burnt. Remove from the pan and set aside. Return the onions to the pan, add about 3 tablespoons of stock and cook for a minute or so until the liquid has evaporated.

Add the beef, increase the heat and brown the meat all over. Add 100ml/3½fl oz/scant ½ cup of stock, reduce the heat to low, cover with a lid and cook very gently for 30 minutes, then add another 100ml/3½fl oz/scant ½ cup of stock and continue to cook for 30 minutes.

Stir in the garlic, cumin, paprika, thyme and pancetta. Add 400ml/14fl oz/1⅔ cups of stock, cover with a lid and cook over a low heat for a further 1 hour, gradually adding more stock and stirring from time to time to ensure the meat doesn't stick.

Remove from the heat and serve with toasted country bread or runny polenta.

Stufato di manzo al cioccolato
Slow-cooked marinated beef with chocolate

Although adding chocolate to savoury dishes is a South American tradition, it has become increasingly popular in Italian dishes – cocoa powder is even added to pasta dough! I must say I am not too keen on these gimmicky recipes; however, the addition of a little good-quality dark chocolate to slow-cooked beef does enrich the sauce.

Serves 4

1kg/2lb 4oz stewing beef, cut into
  chunks
2 onions, sliced
2 carrots, sliced
3 bay leaves
1 garlic clove, left whole, crushed
250ml/9fl oz/1 cup red wine
2 tsp red wine vinegar
3 tbsp extra virgin olive oil
a handful of parsley, finely chopped
2 sprigs of thyme, finely chopped
400ml/14fl oz/1²/₃ cups beef stock
  (see page 21) – or use a stock cube
30g/1oz dark chocolate, grated
salt and freshly ground black pepper
3 potatoes, cut into chunks

Rinse the beef under cold running water and pat dry. Place in a bowl with the onions, carrots, bay leaves and garlic. Pour in the wine and vinegar, cover with clingfilm (plastic wrap) and put in the fridge to marinate for 8 hours or overnight.

Discard the garlic clove, drain the liquid and set aside. Heat the olive oil in a large saucepan and brown the beef well all over. Add the onions, carrots and bay leaves and sweat for about 4 minutes, until the onion has softened. Stir in the parsley and thyme, pour in the marinade liquid and stock and stir in the chocolate, some salt and pepper. Reduce the heat, partially cover with a lid and cook on a low heat for 1½ hours.

Remove the lid, add the potatoes and cook on a medium heat for a further 30 minutes, until the potatoes are cooked and the liquid has reduced slightly. Serve immediately.

For a slow cooker
Marinate the beef as above. Brown the beef, then add the vegetables, herbs, marinade liquid and 300ml10fl oz/1¼ cups beef stock, then the chocolate and salt and pepper. Bring to the boil, stirring, then transfer to a large slow cooker pot, press the meat beneath the liquid, cover and cook on Low for 8-9 hours. Cook the potatoes in a saucepan of boiling water for 15 minutes until just tender. Drain and stir into the slow cooker pot. Cover and cook on Low for 30 minutes. Stir before serving.

Spezzatino casalingo
Everyday beef and vegetable stew

This is the family stew my wife Liz normally makes at home – nothing fancy or complicated, just good old-fashioned comfort food. It is delicious, nutritious and good value for money, using economical pieces of stewing beef and root vegetables. If you don't have red wine to hand or don't want to open a new bottle, simply replace with more stock. Serve with mashed potatoes for a satisfying meal.

Serves 4

800g/1lb 12oz stewing beef, cut into
  chunks
salt and freshly ground black pepper
plain (all-purpose) flour, to dust
5 tbsp extra virgin olive oil
2 onions, finely sliced
2 large carrots, cut into chunks
2 parsnips, cut into chunks
2 sprigs of thyme
50ml/2fl oz/3 tbsp red wine
400ml/14fl oz/1²/₃ cups beef stock
  (see page 21) – or use a stock cube
2 tsp tomato purée (paste)

Rub salt and pepper all over the chunks of beef and dust lightly with flour. Heat 2 tablespoons of the olive oil in a large saucepan, add the beef and brown well all over on a high heat. Remove the meat and set aside.

In the same pan, heat the remaining olive oil and sweat the onions on a medium heat for a couple of minutes. Add the carrots, parsnips and thyme and sweat for another 2 minutes.

Return the meat to the pan, increase the heat to high, add the wine and allow to evaporate. Add the stock and tomato purée, reduce the heat to low, cover with a lid and cook gently for 1 hour 45 minutes, stirring from time to time.

Remove from the heat and serve immediately with mashed potatoes or with some good crusty bread.

For a slow cooker
Dust the beef with flour and brown as above. Using a slotted spoon, transfer to a large slow cooker pot. Sweat the vegetables as above, add the wine and evaporate. Add the stock and tomato purée, bring to the boil, stirring, then pour over the meat and press the meat and vegetables beneath the liquid. Cover and cook on Low for 8-9 hours. Stir before serving.

Ossobuco alla Milanese in bianco
Braised veal shins

There are two ways of making this classic Milanese dish – with or without tomatoes. The latter, known in Italian as *in bianco*, is actually the original version: the veal is slowly braised with vegetables, white wine and stock and garnished with gremolada for extra flavour and colour. Veal shin or knuckle is a cheap, tough cut but extremely flavoursome and ideal for slow cooking. The name *ossobuco* in Italian means 'bone with a hole', a reference to the hollow marrow bone at the centre of the cross-cut veal shin. Ask your butcher for veal shin for ossobuco and he will cut the pieces for you for this excellent dish. In Milan, this is traditionally served with risotto alla Milanese – saffron risotto.

Serves 4

4 cross-cut slices of veal shin, about
    300g/10½oz each
plain (all-purpose) flour, to dust
50g/1¾oz/4 tbsp butter
3 tbsp extra virgin olive oil
1 onion, finely chopped
1 carrot, finely chopped
150ml/5fl oz/⅔ cup dry white wine
salt and freshly ground black pepper
500ml/18fl oz/2 cups veal or chicken
    stock (see page 22) – or use a stock
    cube

for the gremolada
1 garlic clove, finely chopped
a handful of parsley, finely chopped
grated zest of ½ lemon

Using kitchen scissors, slightly snip the skin around the veal shins (this is done to prevent the meat from curling up during cooking). Dust the meat with flour, shake off any excess and set aside.

Heat the butter and oil in a large saucepan, add the onion and carrot and gently sweat until softened. Increase the heat to medium, add the veal shins and brown on both sides. Add the wine and allow to evaporate. Season with salt and pepper, add the stock, reduce the heat, partially cover with a lid and cook on a low heat for 1½ hours, or until the meat is tender.

Meanwhile, prepare the gremolada by combining all the ingredients together.

When the veal is cooked, remove from the heat and leave to rest for 5 minutes. Sprinkle with the gremolada and serve.

For a slow cooker
Sweat the vegetables and brown the meat as above, add the wine and evaporate. Add the salt, pepper and stock, bring to the boil, then transfer to a large slow cooker pot, make sure the veal is beneath the stock, then cover and cook on Low for 6-7 hours. Serve as above.

Spezzatino di maiale

Pork stew

A homey stew that is a complete meal in itself. The addition of pancetta or bacon enhances the flavour of the pork. It can be made the day before and reheated when required, adding the peas after you have reheated the stew. Serve with good bread to mop up the sauce.

Serves 4

650g/1lb 7oz stewing pork,
  cut into chunks
salt and freshly ground black pepper
plain (all-purpose) flour, to dust
3 tbsp extra virgin olive oil
1 onion, finely chopped
1 celery stalk, finely sliced
2 carrots, halved lengthways and cut
  into chunks
3 fresh sage leaves
50g/1¾oz pancetta slices or streaky
  bacon, roughly chopped
75ml/2½fl oz/5 tbsp dry white wine
250ml/9fl oz/1 cup vegetable stock
  (see page 32) – or use a stock cube
400g/14oz potatoes, cut into chunks
150g/5½oz/generous 1 cup frozen peas

Season the pork with salt and pepper and dust with flour, shake off any excess flour and set aside.

Heat the olive oil in a large saucepan. Add the onion, celery, carrots, sage and pancetta and sweat on a medium heat. Add the pork and brown well all over.

Add the wine and allow to evaporate. Add 100ml/ 3½fl oz/scant ½ cup stock, reduce the heat to low, cover with a lid and cook for 30 minutes.

Add the remaining stock. After 15 minutes, add the potatoes and cook for another hour.

Five minutes before the end of cooking time, add the peas. Remove from the heat and serve.

For a slow cooker
Heat the oil in a large deep frying pan and sweat the vegetables and pancetta as above. Add the floured pork and brown, then add the wine and evaporate. Pour in 250ml/9fl oz/1 cup stock and bring to the boil, stirring. Cut the potatoes into 2.5cm/1 inch chunks (these can take longer to cook than meat so don't make any bigger) and place in a large slow cooker pot, pour over the hot pork mixture and press the meat and potatoes beneath the liquid. Cover and cook on Low for 8–9 hours. Stir in the frozen peas, with a little extra hot stock, if needed. Cover and cook on Low for 20 minutes.

Cassoeula
Braised pork and cabbage

This dish from the Lombardy region of northern Italy was traditionally made on the feast of Saint Anthony on 17 January to mark the end of the pig slaughtering season. No part of the pig was ever wasted and the cheaper cuts, such as trotters, skin, ears, nose, ribs and tail, were used to make this stew – the better parts were for curing into hams and salami. This dish is still popular today and I have adapted it with more readily available cuts of pork. Serve with runny polenta (cornmeal), as they do in Lombardy, or mashed potatoes for a perfect winter warmer. The addition of Parmesan rind gives the stew an extra bit of flavour. When you finish a piece of Parmesan, don't discard the rind; wrap it in clingfilm (plastic wrap) and store in the fridge to add to soups and stews.

Serves 4

1 onion, finely chopped
4 carrots, roughly chopped
2 celery stalks, roughly chopped
4 pork ribs, about 100g/3½oz each
225g/8oz pork loin steaks, cut into strips
200g/7oz pork sausages
50g/1¾oz salami, cubed
800ml/28fl oz/3½ cups vegetable stock (see page 32) – or use a stock cube
200g/7oz tomato passata (strained tomatoes)
1kg/2lb 4oz savoy cabbage, roughly chopped
a few pieces of Parmesan rind (optional)
salt and freshly ground black pepper

Heat 100ml/3½fl oz/scant ½ cup water in a large saucepan, add the onion, carrots and celery, cover with a lid and steam-fry on a medium heat for 4 minutes.

Add the ribs, loin, sausages and salami. Combine the stock and passata and add to the saucepan. Add the cabbage and the Parmesan rind, if using, some salt and pepper, cover with a lid and cook on a gentle heat for 2 hours. Remove from the heat, season with salt and pepper to taste and serve.

For a slow cooker
Steam-fry the onion, carrots and celery as above. Add the ribs, loin, sausages and salami. Mix the stock with the passata and add to the meat with the Parmesan rind, salt and pepper. Bring to the boil then transfer to a large slow cooker pot. Cover and cook on Low for 7 hours. Add the cabbage, ladle over some of the hot liquid, then cover and cook on Low for 1–1¼ hours until the cabbage is very tender. Stir before serving.

Montone alla contadina
Rustic mutton stew

I love mutton. As a boy, I remember, during the winter months, farmers would bring mutton to the village to sell and my father would always buy some to be slow-cooked with lots of herbs in a casserole. Mutton cut into chunks for stewing is now available from supermarkets; not only is it more economical than lamb, I find it more flavoursome, especially when making stews. It is ideal for slow-cooking and with the addition of potatoes is a complete one-pot meal.

Serves 4

4 tbsp extra virgin olive oil
1 large onion, finely sliced
2 garlic cloves, finely sliced
1kg/2lb 4oz mutton pieces
200ml/7fl oz/scant 1 cup red wine
2 bay leaves
4 sage leaves
2 sprigs of rosemary
salt and freshly ground black pepper
1 litre/1¾ pints/4 cups vegetable stock
   (see page 32) – or use a stock cube
1 tbsp tomato purée (paste)
600g/1lb 5oz potatoes, peeled and cut
   into chunks

Heat the olive oil in a large saucepan, add the onion and garlic and sweat for a couple of minutes. Add the mutton and brown well all over. Reduce the heat, add the wine, and allow to evaporate gradually on a low heat for about 15 minutes.

Stir in the herbs, some salt and pepper and 600ml/ 20fl oz/2½ cups of stock and cook on a low heat, partially covered with a lid, for 2 hours.

Add the remaining stock with the tomato purée and potatoes and cook for a further 25 minutes, until the potatoes are cooked. Remove from the heat, season with salt and pepper to taste and serve.

For a slow cooker
Sweat the onion and garlic, brown the meat and evaporate the wine as above. Add the herbs, salt and pepper and tomato purée, then add 750ml/1¼ pints/3 cups stock and bring to the boil. Cut the potatoes into 2.5cm/1 inch chunks and place in a large slow cooker pot, add the meat and onion, then pour in the liquid. Press the meat and potatoes beneath the liquid, cover and cook on Low for 8-10 hours. Serve as above.

Agnello con i fagioli
Lamb stew with beans

This rustic lamb stew is a perfect winter warmer and a complete meal in one pot. I really like to use dried beans, which need to be soaked overnight and cooked before being added to the stew. However, to save time, you could use canned beans and add them towards the end of the cooking time.

Serves 4

150g/5½oz/¾ cup dried white kidney beans or cannellini beans, soaked in water overnight
3 tbsp extra virgin olive oil
1 onion, finely chopped
375g/13oz shoulder of lamb, cut into chunks
40g/1½oz pancetta, diced
1 carrot, diced
1 clove
1 bay leaf
100ml/3½fl oz/scant ½ cup dry white wine
3 tbsp canned chopped tomato
300ml/10fl oz/1¼ cups vegetable stock (see page 32) - or use a stock cube

to serve
country bread, toasted and drizzled with extra virgin olive oil

Drain the beans and put them in a large saucepan with plenty of cold water, bring to the boil, then reduce the heat, partially cover with a lid and simmer for 1½ hours, or until tender but not mushy. Drain the beans and set aside.

Meanwhile, heat the olive oil in a large saucepan, add the onion and sweat for about 3 minutes until softened. Add the lamb and brown all over. Add the pancetta, carrot, clove and bay leaf and stir-fry on a medium heat for 5 minutes. Pour in the wine and allow to evaporate. Add the tomato and cook for 3 minutes, then add the stock. Reduce the heat, cover with a lid and cook on a low heat for 2 hours.

Add the beans and cook for a further 15 minutes. Serve with slices of toasted country bread.

For a slow cooker
Heat the oil in a large deep frying pan, sweat the onion and brown the lamb as above. Add the pancetta, carrot, clove and bay leaf, then the wine, and evaporate as above. Add the tomato, 300ml/ 10fl oz/1¼ cups stock, salt and pepper. Bring to the boil, stirring, then transfer to a large or medium slow cooker pot, press the meat beneath the liquid, cover and cook on Low for 7-8 hours. Drain 2 x 380g/13oz cartons cannellini beans (or use about 500g/ 1lb 2oz cooked dried beans), stir into the slow cooker pot with a little extra hot stock, if needed. Cover and cook on Low for 30 minutes. Stir before serving.

Spezzatino d'agnello con zucca e zafferano

Lamb stew with butternut squash and saffron

This hearty lamb stew with butternut squash and potato is full of colour – orange from the squash, yellow from saffron and a hint of red from tomato and chilli. Simple to prepare, this one-pot meal makes a delicious family meal or an informal dinner with friends.

Serves 4

700g/1lb 9oz stewing lamb, cut into
  chunks
salt and freshly ground black pepper
3 tbsp extra virgin olive oil
1 onion, finely chopped
2 garlic cloves, finely chopped
1 red chilli, halved lengthways
2 sprigs of rosemary
4 small sage leaves
a pinch of saffron, diluted in 1 tbsp
  water
2 tbsp canned chopped tomatoes
4 tbsp dry white wine
200ml/7fl oz/scant 1 cup vegetable
stock (see page 32) – or use a stock
  cube
200g/7oz potato, cut into large chunks
400g/14oz butternut squash, peeled
  and cut into large chunks

Rub the lamb all over with salt and pepper. Heat the olive oil in a large saucepan, add the meat and brown on all sides, then remove and set aside.

Add the onion, garlic and chilli to the pan and sweat for a couple of minutes. Return the lamb to the pan, then add the herbs, saffron and tomato. Add the wine and allow to evaporate. Add the stock, cover with a lid and cook on a very slow heat for 1 hour.

Add the potato and butternut squash and continue to cook for 30 minutes. Remove from the heat and leave to rest for a couple of minutes before serving.

For a slow cooker

Brown the meat, sweat the vegetables and add the herbs, saffron and tomato as above; add the wine and allow to evaporate. Add 350ml/12fl oz/1½ cups stock and bring to the boil, stirring. Cut the potato and squash into 2.5cm/1 inch chunks. Put the potatoes into a large slow cooker pot, pour over the lamb mixture, press the lamb beneath the liquid and scatter the pumpkin on top. Cover and cook on Low for 8–9 hours. Stir before serving.

Coniglio marinato all'agrodolce
Sweet and sour marinated rabbit

I love rabbit and can't understand why it is not more widely available. The meat is tender, light and very digestible; in Italy, rabbit is given to weaning babies, convalescents and the elderly. You can order rabbit from good butchers, or if, like me, you shoot, the countryside is full of them. I often marinate rabbit because it rids the meat of that slightly gamey taste it can have; it can be marinated the day before and left in the fridge overnight. Once cooked, the rabbit is finished with a tangy sweet and sour sauce, giving the meat a real kick. Delicious served with slices of toasted country bread. If you prefer, chicken can be substituted for the rabbit.

Serves 4

1kg/2lb 4oz rabbit pieces on the bone,
   cleaned with a damp cloth
plain (all-purpose) flour, to dust
5 tbsp extra virgin olive oil
1 small onion, finely chopped
salt and freshly ground black pepper
5 tbsp vegetable stock

for the marinade
1 small onion, finely sliced
175ml/6fl oz/¾ cup red wine
a handful of parsley, finely chopped
2 bay leaves
8 black peppercorns
1 garlic clove, left whole
1 tsp thyme leaves
salt

for the agrodolce
20g/¾oz/1½ tbsp caster (superfine)
   sugar
a knob of butter
4 tbsp red wine vinegar
30g/1oz/3 tbsp sultanas (golden
   raisins), soaked in lukewarm water for
   about 20 minutes, then drained
15g/½oz/2 tbsp pine nuts

Put all the marinade ingredients in a small saucepan and bring to the boil, then remove from the heat and leave to cool. Put the rabbit in a dish, pour over the marinade, cover with clingfilm (plastic wrap) and leave in the fridge for at least 2 hours.

Remove the rabbit from the marinade, pat dry and dust with flour.

Heat the olive oil in a large frying pan, add the onion and sweat for a minute, then add the rabbit and brown all over. Pour over the marinade and cook on a low heat, uncovered, for about 15 minutes until the liquid has evaporated. Add salt, pepper and stock, cover with a lid and cook for 25 minutes on a medium–low heat until the rabbit is cooked through and the sauce has reduced.

Meanwhile, for the agrodolce, put the sugar and 2 tablespoons water in a small saucepan on a medium heat and stir until the sugar has dissolved. Stir in the butter until melted, then the vinegar and sultanas and bring to the boil for a minute. Pour this over the cooked rabbit, mixing it with the sauce, sprinkle with the pine nuts and serve.

Scottiglia di capriolo
Venison casserole

Scottiglia is a slow-cooked Tuscan stew or casserole that is usually made with whatever the hunter has managed to catch, so you could substitute wild boar, rabbit or hare for the venison in this recipe. Many supermarkets now sell farmed venison; 'casserole venison' is cut up ready for stewing. The meat is first marinated overnight for maximum tenderness and flavour and then slow-cooked for a rich-tasting casserole. Delicious served with runny polenta (cornmeal).

Serves 4

1kg/2lb 4oz venison haunch or
  casserole venison, cut into 4-5 cm/
  1½-2-inch chunks
plain (all-purpose) flour, to dust
6 tbsp extra virgin olive oil
2 sprigs of rosemary
3 sage leaves
2 bay leaves
1 onion, sliced
2 garlic cloves, crushed
1 celery stalk, chopped
2 carrots, roughly chopped
salt and freshly ground black pepper
300ml/10fl oz/1¼ cups beef stock (see
  page 21) – or use a stock cube

for the marinade
75ml/2½fl oz/5 tbsp red wine vinegar
250ml/9fl oz/1 cup red wine
15 juniper berries
15 black peppercorns
3 bay leaves

Put the venison in a bowl. Combine all the marinade ingredients and pour over the meat, cover with clingfilm (plastic wrap) and leave in the fridge overnight.

Remove the venison from the marinade, reserving the liquid, and pat the meat dry. Dust the meat with flour and shake off any excess.

Heat the olive oil in a large saucepan on a high heat, add the meat and brown well all over. Reduce the heat, add the herbs, onion, garlic, celery, carrots and sweat for a couple of minutes. Season with salt and pepper. Add the marinade and cook on a high heat for a couple of minutes. Add the stock, reduce the heat to low, cover with a lid and cook for 2½ hours, until the meat is tender. Serve with runny polenta.

For a slow cooker
Marinate the venison as above. Drain, dust with flour and brown the meat, then transfer to a large slow cooker pot. Sweat the herbs, vegetables and garlic, season, then add the marinade and stock. Bring to the boil, pour over the venison, cover and cook on Low for 8-9 hours. Stir before serving.

Pollo alla cacciatora

Hunter's chicken

This classic Italian dish is renowned all over the world and often seen on the menus of Italian restaurants. The title *alla cacciatora* ('in the style of the hunter') suggests it was probably first made with game birds or rabbit. However, as with many Italian dishes, it also has roots in the *cucina povera*, when people used whatever meagre ingredients they had to hand; in this case, a chicken or, more likely, an old hen, was slaughtered for a special occasion and, to make it go further, enriched with whatever vegetables and herbs were available in the garden as well as a splash of homemade wine. It is made all over Italy and here I have recreated it in the way it is normally made in my region of Campania, using lots of herbs and fresh tomatoes. I like to serve this rustic dish with slices of toasted country bread drizzled with extra virgin olive oil.

Serves 4

750g/1lb 10oz chicken thighs and drumsticks
salt and freshly ground black pepper
3 tbsp extra virgin olive oil
1 large onion, finely sliced
1 garlic clove, crushed and left whole
1 small red chilli, sliced
2 sprigs of rosemary
2 sprigs of thyme
a handful of parsley, roughly chopped
2 bay leaves
4 sage leaves
125ml/4fl oz/½ cup dry white wine
1½ tbsp tomato purée (paste), dissolved in 3 tbsp lukewarm water
175g/6oz cherry tomatoes, halved

Rub the chicken pieces all over with salt and pepper. Heat the olive oil in a large saucepan, add the chicken and seal well all over.

Add the onion, garlic, chilli and herbs and cook for a couple of minutes on a medium heat. Add the wine, increase the heat and allow the wine to evaporate slightly. Add the diluted tomato purée, then stir in the cherry tomatoes. Reduce the heat to low, cover with a lid and cook gently for 1¼ hours, until the chicken is cooked through; the flesh should come away from the bone and there should be no sign of pink when you pierce the thickest part. Serve hot.

For a slow cooker

Heat the oil in a large deep frying pan and cook the chicken as above. Continue as above, add the tomatoes, plus 300ml/10fl oz/ 1¼ cups chicken stock. Bring to the boil, then transfer to a large slow cooker pot. Cover and cook on Low for 7-8 hours or until there are no pink juices when the chicken is pierced with a small knife.

Verdure estive stufate
Summer vegetable stew

This simple but very tasty vegetable stew puts the flavours and colours of the Mediterranean on a plate. The slow, gentle cooking brings all the flavours of the vegetables and other ingredients together. I like to make this with lots of chilli and serve with couscous for a light but nutritious meal. It can be made in advance and in summer can be eaten cold if desired. Although it uses what I consider to be summer vegetables, it can be made at any time of the year.

Serves 4

4 tbsp extra virgin olive oil
2 red onions, finely sliced
2 celery stalks with leaves, sliced
3 garlic cloves, sliced
1 red chilli, finely chopped
5 anchovy fillets
1 tbsp capers
140g/5oz/¾ cup green olives
1 red (bell) pepper, cut into thick slices
1 yellow (bell) pepper, thickly sliced
1 aubergine (eggplant), cut into chunks
2 courgettes (zucchini), cut into chunks
200g/7oz green beans, sliced in half
3 tbsp dry white wine
300g/10½oz cherry tomatoes, halved
a handful of basil leaves
salt

Heat the olive oil in a large saucepan, add the onions, celery, garlic and chilli and sweat on a medium heat for a couple of minutes. Add the anchovy fillets and stir with a wooden spoon until dissolved. Add the capers and olives. Stir in the peppers, aubergine, courgettes and beans. Add the wine and allow to evaporate. Add the tomatoes, basil leaves and a pinch of salt. Reduce the heat, cover with a lid and cook gently for 1 hour. Serve with couscous.

For a slow cooker
Follow the recipe above and once all the ingredients are in the pan, heat through, stirring gently, then transfer to a large slow cooker pot. Cover and cook on High for 2-3 hours, stirring once halfway through cooking and again just before serving.

Savoury
bakes

When I was growing up, slow-baked dishes were very popular in Italy; they were often cooked in the wood-fired oven as it cooled down after the bread had been baked. Dishes such as *gattó di patate* and *timballo di riso* could be left in the low oven to cook for a long time, sometimes all day, ready for the evening meal.

People who didn't have an oven at home would bring their savoury dishes to the local bakery to put in the hot ovens once the day's bread was all made; the dishes would be left for most of the day and collected later, nicely cooked and warm – and all for free!

This method of cooking was traditionally used on the eve of the feast of All Saints – these days known as Hallowe'en. Food was cooked during the day and night, but tradition dictated that it was forbidden to cook on 1 November; that day was dedicated to visiting the cemetery to honour deceased relatives and families needed a warm cooked meal ready upon their return from the cemetery.

Most of the bakes in this chapter can be made in advance and reheated when required; some can also be enjoyed cold. Many are meals in themselves and are ideal to serve at parties.

Patate alla birra
Potato bake with beer

A light, simple potato dish, ideal to accompany roast meats – or it can be eaten as a meal by itself. The subtle taste of malt in the beer marries really well with the potatoes, onions and smoked bacon. This can be made a day in advance and reheated.

Serves 4-6

1kg/2lb 4oz potatoes, peeled and thinly
   sliced
200ml/7fl oz/scant 1 cup lager beer
2 tbsp extra virgin olive oil
salt and freshly ground black pepper
2 large onions, thinly sliced
200g/7oz smoked bacon cubes
85g/3oz pecorino (romano) cheese,
   grated

Preheat the oven to 200°C/400°F/gas mark 6.

Put the potatoes in a large bowl and toss together with the beer, olive oil, salt and pepper.

Lift the potatoes out of the beer mixture and line the bottom of an ovenproof dish with a layer of potatoes, followed by a layer of sliced onions; sprinkle over a few cubes of bacon and some of the grated pecorino. Continue layering in the same way until all the ingredients are used, finishing with grated pecorino. Pour over the beer mixture, cover with foil and bake in the oven for 1 hour. Remove the foil and bake for another 30 minutes.

Remove from the oven and leave to rest for a couple of minutes before serving.

Cipolle ripiene
Baked filled onions

Onions are perfect for slow cooking – their flavour becomes delicate and subtle. They can be filled with all sorts of different ingredients; I love this combination of mortadella, walnuts and thyme, which I sometimes use as a stuffing for chicken. This dish can be eaten by itself, served with a green salad, or as an accompaniment to roast meat. It can be made in advance and reheated when needed.

Serves 2-4

4 large onions
115g/4oz mortadella, finely chopped
85g/3oz/¾ cup walnuts, finely chopped
85g/3oz Parmesan, grated
1 tsp finely chopped thyme leaves
salt and freshly ground black pepper
2 eggs, beaten
extra virgin olive oil, to drizzle
2 tbsp dried breadcrumbs
100ml/3½fl oz/scant ½ cup vegetable
   stock (see page 32) - or use a stock
   cube

Preheat the oven to 180°C/350°F/gas mark 4.

Peel the onions and slice off the tops at about a third of the way down, then scoop out the cavities. Finely chop the scooped-out onion and combine with the mortadella, walnuts, Parmesan, thyme, some salt and pepper and the eggs; set aside.

Put the onions in an ovenproof dish and sprinkle a little salt and pepper inside them. Fill each onion with the mortadella mixture, drizzle with a little olive oil and sprinkle with the breadcrumbs. Pour the stock into the bottom of the dish, cover with foil and bake in the oven for 1 hour. Remove the foil and bake for another 15 minutes.

Remove from the oven and leave to rest for 5 minutes before serving.

Gattó di patate con porcini e speck
Mashed potato cake with porcini and speck

The *gattó di patate* is a typically Neapolitan dish whose name derives from the French *gâteau*, meaning 'cake'. Apparently it was first made in Naples in 1768 for the wedding of Marie Caroline (sister of Marie Antoinette) to Ferdinand, King of Naples; French cuisine was highly influential in Europe at that time. In southern Italy, *gattó* is traditionally made with mozzarella and pieces of leftover salami and prosciutto. This is a south-meets-north version, a southern speciality using northern ingredients – dried porcini mushrooms, speck (smoked cured ham) and Taleggio cheese. Of course, if you prefer, you can use mozzarella and a mix of prosciutto and salami. Once baked, it is left to rest in the warm oven for at least 30 minutes – this way all the flavours come together for maximum taste – and enjoyed at room temperature. It tastes even better the next day, eaten cold. This is a meal in itself, served with a mixed side salad.

Serves 4-6

1kg/2lb 4oz floury (starchy) potatoes, such as red Desirée, scrubbed
100g/3½oz/7 tbsp butter, plus extra to grease
150g/5½oz piece of speck or Parma ham, cubed
100g/3½oz Parmesan, grated
2 eggs
2 egg yolks
salt and freshly ground black pepper
3 tbsp dried breadcrumbs, plus extra to dust
3 tbsp extra virgin olive oil
2 garlic cloves, crushed
40g/1½oz dried porcini mushrooms, soaked in warm water for 20 minutes
85g/3oz button mushrooms, halved
1 tbsp chopped fresh parsley
200g/7oz Taleggio cheese, roughly chopped

Boil the potatoes in their skins until cooked through, drain, leave until cool enough to handle, then peel off the skins. Mash the potatoes together with 75g/2¾oz/ 5 tbsp of the butter. Add the speck, Parmesan, eggs and yolks and combine well. Season with salt and pepper to taste. Set aside.

Preheat the oven to 180°C/350°F/gas mark 4. Grease an ovenproof dish with butter and dust with breadcrumbs.

Heat the olive oil in a frying pan, add the garlic and cook on a medium heat for a couple of minutes, then discard the garlic. Drain the porcini, add to the pan and stir-fry for 4 minutes. Add the button mushrooms, parsley, salt and pepper to taste and cook for a further 2 minutes. Remove from the heat and set aside.

Put half of the mashed potato mixture in the prepared dish, cover with the mushroom mixture and the Taleggio cheese, and then the remaining potato mixture. Dot with the remaining butter and sprinkle with breadcrumbs. Bake in the oven for 1 hour, until the top is golden brown.

Switch the oven off and leave to rest for at least 30 minutes before serving.

Tiella Pugliese con cozze
Baked rice with mussels

This typical peasant dish from Puglia, the heel of Italy, is said to have Spanish influences. It was often made with 'poor', but nourishing, local ingredients, to easily and cheaply feed a large family at the end of a long working day in the fields. It is unclear whether the word *tiella* derives from the dish it was cooked in or the cooking method. No matter; it has over time become the name of this dish, of which there are many variations, made with vegetables, meat or fish, depending on availability. However, the two main ingredients, rice and potatoes, are always present. This version using mussels comes from Bari, the capital city of the Puglia region. The uncooked rice is scattered over the layers of ingredients and the end result is an interesting type of baked risotto with a lovely subtle seafood flavour.

Serves 4

250g/9oz fresh mussels, scrubbed, any open or broken shells discarded
2 handfuls of parsley, finely chopped, plus extra to serve
1 garlic clove, finely chopped
1 onion, finely sliced
salt and freshly ground black pepper
100ml/3½fl oz/scant ½ cup extra virgin olive oil
250g/9oz potatoes, peeled and thinly sliced
250g/9oz cherry tomatoes, halved
10g/¼oz pecorino (romano) cheese, grated
150g/5½oz/¾ cup arborio rice

Preheat the oven to 170°C/325°F/gas mark 3.

Put the mussels in a pan, cover with a lid and cook on a high heat for a couple of minutes until the shells open. Remove from the heat and leave to cool slightly, discarding any mussels whose shells remain closed. Combine the parsley and garlic and set aside.

Line an ovenproof dish with the sliced onion, followed by half of the parsley mixture, sprinkle with salt and pepper and drizzle with 2 tablespoons olive oil. Cover with half of the potatoes, the mussels, tomatoes, 2 tablespoons olive oil and the remaining parsley mixture. Sprinkle with the pecorino, then scatter in the raw rice, the remaining potatoes and the remaining olive oil. Pour in 400ml/14fl oz/1⅔ cups water, ensuring you cover all the ingredients – you may need less or more water.

Cover with foil and bake for 1¼ hours, until the potatoes are very tender when pierced with a skewer. Serve hot, sprinkled with parsley.

Calamari ripieni
Filled baked squid

I love squid and whenever I'm on the coast in Italy, whether at a restaurant or at my sister's house, I make sure to have them - in a salad, stewed with tomatoes, in pasta, or filled and slow-baked like this. Made this way, they are ideal as a light lunch served with a side salad.

Serves 4

4 large squid (calamari), including tentacles
3 tbsp extra virgin olive oil, plus extra to drizzle
2 garlic cloves, finely chopped
4 anchovy fillets
1 tbsp capers
200ml/7fl oz/scant 1 cup white wine
salt and freshly ground black pepper
100g/3½oz bread, finely chopped
40g/1½oz/5 tbsp pine nuts
grated zest of ½ lemon
1 tbsp chopped fresh parsley

Thoroughly clean the calamari – you can ask your fishmonger to do this – ending up with four perfect sack-like calamari ready to fill. Roughly chop about half of the tentacles and set aside.

Preheat the oven to 180°C/350°F/gas mark 4. Lightly oil a baking dish.

Heat the olive oil in a saucepan, add the garlic, anchovies and capers and sweat for a few minutes, stirring with a wooden spoon until the anchovies have dissolved. Add the chopped tentacles and stir-fry for about 5 minutes, then add the wine and allow to evaporate; season with salt and pepper to taste. Remove from the heat and leave to cool.

Stir in the bread, pine nuts, lemon zest and parsley. Fill each squid with this mixture and tuck the reserved tentacles into the ends, place in the baking dish, drizzle with extra virgin olive oil, cover with foil and bake in the oven for 45 minutes. Remove the foil and bake for another 15 minutes, until lightly golden. Serve hot.

Peperoni al forno ripieni al risotto
Baked peppers filled with risotto

I love roasted peppers, and this nutritious filling makes them a healthy complete meal. Filling peppers with rice is quite common in Mediterranean countries, but I find they can be a little bland; I have made a quick risotto with some summer vegetables to use as the stuffing and the addition of mint gives a pleasant refreshing flavour. You can make this dish very colourful by using red, yellow, green and orange peppers. I have suggested one pepper per person, but if, like me, you are greedy, double the quantities – you can always enjoy them cold or heated up the next day.

Serves 4

2 tbsp extra virgin olive oil, plus extra to drizzle
½ onion, finely chopped
150g/5½oz/¾ cup arborio rice
½ courgette (zucchini), cubed
½ aubergine (eggplant), cubed
2 tsp tomato purée (paste)
700ml/1¼ pints/3 cups hot vegetable stock (see page 32) – or use a stock cube
30g/1oz Parmesan, grated
salt and freshly ground black pepper
4 large (bell) peppers
1 ball of mozzarella (about 125g/4½oz), cubed
a handful of fresh mint leaves, torn

Preheat the oven to 180°C/350°F/gas mark 4. Heat the olive oil in a saucepan, add the onion and sweat on a medium heat until softened. Stir in the rice until each grain is coated with oil. Stir in the courgette, aubergine and tomato purée, then add a little stock and cook until absorbed.

Gradually add the remaining stock, stirring all the time, for 12–15 minutes. The rice should still be quite firm. Remove from the heat, stir in the Parmesan, taste for seasoning and leave to cool slightly.

Slice the tops off the peppers, keeping the stems so they look like little hats, and set aside. Put the peppers in a lightly oiled baking dish. Half-fill them with the risotto, add a few cubes of mozzarella, gently pressing it into the filling, and some mint. Add the remaining risotto and more mozzarella, pressing it in. Put the 'hats' on the filled peppers, drizzle with a little olive oil, cover with foil and bake for 45 minutes. Remove the foil and bake for another 15 minutes.

Remove from the oven and leave to rest for 5 minutes before serving. Can also be enjoyed cold.

Timballo di riso estivo
Baked rice with peppers, aubergines and tomato

A light rice dish slowly baked in the oven together with summer vegetables. You can roast the peppers in advance: place in a hot oven until the skins blacken, remove from the oven and leave until cool; the skins will easily come off. You can also grill the aubergines in advance, either under a hot grill (broiler) or on a hot griddle pan. Once the vegetables are cool, put them in the fridge until required. The *timballo* can be eaten warm or enjoyed cold the next day.

Serves 4

250g/9oz/1¼ cups arborio rice
salt and freshly ground black pepper
400g/14oz aubergine (eggplant), thinly
   sliced, grilled (see above)
4 tbsp extra virgin olive oil
1 small yellow (bell) pepper, roasted
   and peeled (see above)
1 small red (bell) pepper, roasted and
   peeled (see above)
400g/14oz tomatoes: half roughly
   chopped, half thinly sliced
1 garlic clove, finely chopped
small handful of parsley, roughly
   chopped
8 basil leaves, roughly torn
150g/5½oz mozzarella, roughly sliced

Preheat the oven to 170°C/325°F/gas mark 3. Bring a saucepan of lightly salted water to the boil and cook the rice for 8 minutes. Drain and leave to cool.

Lightly brush the grilled aubergine slices with olive oil and set aside.

Roughly chop the roasted peppers, place on a plate, sprinkle with salt and drizzle with olive oil.

Place the chopped tomatoes in a bowl and combine with the garlic, parsley, basil, a generous tablespoon of olive oil, some salt and pepper and leave to marinate for 10 minutes. Stir in the cold cooked rice.

Lightly grease an ovenproof dish with olive oil and line with the aubergines. Add half of the rice mixture, followed by the peppers, mozzarella and a few tomato slices, then the remaining rice mixture. Put the remaining tomato slices on top, drizzle with olive oil, cover with foil and bake for 50 minutes. Remove the foil and bake for another 5 minutes.

Remove from the oven and leave to rest for 5 minutes before serving. Can also be enjoyed cold.

Patate al forno tartufate
'Posh' baked potatoes

When I was a child, I remember that once all the baking was done in the wood-fired oven, my grandfather would often throw in a few potatoes – so as not to 'waste' the heat and ash. The result was a delicious hot potato, which we would eat as a treat with just a little salt. It was not until I arrived in England that I realized baked potatoes were very popular with all sorts of fillings. Potatoes and truffle marry really well together, so why not combine the humble spud with decadent truffle for a real treat?

Serves 4

4 baking potatoes
salt and freshly ground black pepper
5 tsp truffle oil
40g/1½oz Parmesan, grated
100g/3½oz fontina cheese, grated
1 tsp thyme, very finely chopped

Preheat the oven to 200°C/400°F/gas mark 6.

Wash and dry the potatoes, prick them all over with a fork or skewer, then rub all over with salt and a little of the truffle oil – about 1 teaspoon should be enough for all the potatoes. Wrap each potato in foil and bake in the oven for about 1¼ hours, until cooked through.

Remove from the oven, slice or cut the tops off the potatoes and carefully spoon out most of the soft potato into a bowl. Mix the spooned-out potato with truffle oil, Parmesan, fontina, thyme and some salt and pepper. Put the filling back in the skins and return to the oven for a few minutes to allow the cheese to melt. Serve hot.

Carote al forno con erbe
Baked herby carrots

Simple to prepare, baked carrots infused with herbs are a wonderful way to serve this popular root vegetable. This is an ideal accompaniment to main courses, especially roast meats. If you prefer to keep the carrots whole you will need to increase the cooking time.

Serves 4

2 shallots, finely sliced
1 celery stalk, roughly chopped
500g/1lb 2oz carrots, cut into large
 chunks
2 tbsp extra virgin olive oil, plus extra
 to drizzle
salt and freshly ground black pepper
2 bay leaves
3 sprigs of thyme
8 sage leaves
2 tbsp finely chopped fresh parsley
150ml/5fl oz/⅔ cup vegetable stock
 (see page 32) - or use a stock cube

Preheat the oven to 180°C/350°F/gas mark 4. Put the shallots and celery in an ovenproof dish and put the carrots on top.

In a bowl, combine the olive oil, salt and pepper and pour over the carrots. Scatter with the herbs and pour over the stock. Leave to infuse for about 15 minutes.

Cover with foil and bake in the oven for 1 hour. Remove the foil, drizzle with extra virgin olive oil and bake for another 15 minutes. Remove from the oven and leave to rest for 5 minutes before serving.

Roasts &
pot roasts

———

I love the smell of roasted meat slowly cooking in the oven – just by the smell I know it's a Sunday morning. Since living in England, I have become accustomed to enjoying a 'roast dinner' and look forward to the weekly ritual, whether it's traditional roast beef and Yorkshire pudding, pork with apple sauce or a stuffed roast chicken, all served with lovely roast potatoes and vegetables.

Italians enjoy roasts too, but as they tend to be served after a *primo* (first course) of perhaps pasta or risotto, there is less need for so many accompaniments and the meat is often simply served with a salad. Classic Italian roasts of beef, veal, pork and lamb tend to be laden with herbs, which really enhance the flavour of the meat; my *Arrosto di manzo alle erbe* (see page 110) is a good example.

Oven roasting is a very similar process to spit roasting – cooking meat over an open fire – which has been done since ancient times. Spit roasting ensured that no part of the meat dried out as it turned on the spit and fat and juices ran over the surface of the meat. Spit roasting whole lambs, goats and pigs remains popular in Sardinia. *Porceddu* (suckling pig) infused with local myrtle leaves is cooked in this way in rural areas of the island and for celebrations like weddings. Another ancient method still used in inland parts of Sardinia is *incarralzadu*, in which the animal is cooked underground in a large hole and a fire made above. Sardinians have always been very traditional in their ways, probably because of their island location, and this way of cooking is still very much alive and celebrated today.

Oven roasting, where the heat takes a long time to reach the centre of the food, is mostly used to cook tender joints of meat. Pot-roasting allows you to use tougher, more economical, cuts of meat and is very popular in Italy; in this method, a large piece of meat is first browned, then cooked slowly with liquid. Both methods are very simple: once in the pot or roasting tin, you can more or less leave the meat to its own devices – just remember to baste the oven joint and ensure there is enough liquid for the pot roast.

———

Arrosto di manzo alle erbe
Roast beef with herbs

Delicious, easy to prepare, full of the fresh flavour of herbs, roast beef Italian-style is the perfect Sunday lunch. Italians usually enjoy a first course of pasta or risotto followed by the roast beef served with a simple salad.

Serves 4-6

2 carrots, sliced lengthways
1.4kg/3lb 2oz topside of beef
100ml/3½fl oz/scant ½ cup extra virgin
   olive oil
3 garlic cloves, finely chopped
needles from 3 sprigs of rosemary,
   finely chopped
small bunch of thyme, finely chopped
2 tbsp finely chopped marjoram
a handful of parsley, finely chopped
salt and freshly ground black pepper

Preheat the oven to 200°C/400°F/gas mark 6.

Put the carrots in a roasting tin and place the beef on top (this prevents the meat from sticking to the tin). Combine the olive oil, garlic, herbs, salt and pepper and pour over the meat, rubbing well. Roast in the oven for 20 minutes, then cover with foil and continue to roast for 1¼ hours, turning the meat over after 30 minutes.

Remove from the oven and leave to rest for 10 minutes. Slice and serve.

Brasato al Barolo
Braised beef in Barolo wine

This classic Piemontese dish, made with the region's famous Barolo wine, is fit for a king. It can, of course, be made with other, less expensive, full-bodied red wines, but for a special occasion I like to use Barolo. The meat is first marinated overnight with vegetables, herbs and wine before being slow-cooked with the same ingredients, giving the meat its richness. Delicious served with polenta (cornmeal), as is traditional in Piedmont, and also good with mashed potatoes.

Serves 4

1kg/2lb 4oz shoulder/blade or topside
  of beef
4 tbsp extra virgin olive oil
30g/1oz/2 tbsp butter
salt and freshly ground black pepper

for the marinade
1 garlic clove, left whole
2 bay leaves
2 sprigs of rosemary
8 black peppercorns
1 large onion, finely sliced
2 celery stalks, finely chopped
1 bottle of Barolo wine

Gently dry the beef with kitchen paper, then put it in a bowl together with all the marinade ingredients. Cover with clingfilm (plastic wrap) and leave in the fridge for 12 hours or overnight.

Remove the meat from the marinade and pat dry with kitchen paper. Strain the marinade, reserving the liquid, vegetables and herbs.

Heat the oil and butter in a large flameproof pot, add the beef and brown well all over. Remove and set aside. In the same pot, add the vegetables and herbs from the marinade and sweat on a medium heat for about 3 minutes. Return the meat to the pan, add some salt and pepper and cook on a medium heat for 5 minutes. Increase the heat, add the wine from the marinade and bring to the boil, then reduce the heat to low, partially cover with a lid and cook gently for 2½ hours, until the meat is tender, turning the meat over from time to time.

Remove the meat and set aside. Increase the heat and cook the sauce for about 5 minutes, until it has reduced slightly. Slice the meat and serve with the vegetables and sauce, with polenta or mashed potatoes.

For a slow cooker
Marinate the beef. Drain and brown as above. Lift the beef out of the pan and put into a medium slow cooker pot. Sweat the vegetables and herbs from the marinade, then add the marinade, salt and pepper, bring to the boil then pour over the beef. Cover with a lid and cook on High for 4 hours, turning the beef once, then reduce the heat to Low and cook for 1 hour. Pour the sauce into a saucepan and boil for 15-20 minutes to reduce and thicken. Serve as above.

Manzo di Rovato all'olio

Pot-roasted beef with extra virgin olive oil

This ancient dish, originating from the town of Rovato in Lombardy, northern Italy, is about 500 years old. At the time it was a dish cooked for the wealthy: they could afford not only meat but also 'exotic' ingredients such as anchovies and capers brought to Rovato by merchants travelling from Venice to Milan. The meat used for this dish is known in Italy as *cappello del prete* (priest's hat), which is a triangular cut of beef from the outer part of the shoulder, ideally suited to slow cooking; chuck eye is the nearest equivalent and a good butcher should be able to provide it. The olive oil is an important part of the dish, so please do use good-quality extra virgin. The extra sauce can be served the next day with some runny polenta.

Serves 4

200ml/7fl oz/scant 1 cup extra virgin olive oil
1.2kg/2lb 10oz chuck eye or chuck beef joint or feather steak
2 tbsp capers, rinsed
4 anchovy fillets
2 onions, finely chopped
1 celery stalk, finely chopped
3 carrots, finely chopped
500ml/18fl oz/2 cups dry white wine
3 courgettes (zucchini), sliced
30g/1oz Parmesan, grated
20g/¾oz/scant ¼ cup dried breadcrumbs
salt and freshly ground black pepper

Heat the olive oil in a large flameproof pot, add the beef and brown well on all sides on a high heat. Add the capers and anchovies and cook on a medium heat, stirring with a wooden spoon until the anchovies have dissolved. Stir in the onions, celery and carrots, pour in the wine, cover with a lid and cook on a low heat for 1 hour.

Add the courgettes and continue to cook for a further 1 hour.

Remove the meat from the pot and set aside. Using a food processor or blender, blend the vegetables and liquid until smooth. Stir in the Parmesan and breadcrumbs and season with salt and pepper to taste. Slice the meat and serve with the sauce.

For a slow cooker

Brown the meat, add the capers, anchovies and vegetables as above, then add 400ml/14fl oz/1²/₃ cups of wine. Bring to the boil, then transfer everything to a large slow cooker pot. Cover and cook on High for 4 hours. Turn the beef over, then add the sliced courgettes and cook on Low for 1–1½ hours. Blend the sauce and serve as above.

Braciolone Palermitano
Filled rolled beef cooked in tomato sauce

This traditional southern Italian Sunday lunch dish is one of my favourites and very reminiscent of my childhood. Each region makes its own version and my family would make it with local cheese and salami. This is a Sicilian version, hence the Italian title, using caciocavallo cheese; if you can't find it in your Italian deli, you can substitute provolone, pecorino (romano) or Parmesan. Beef brisket is ideal for slow cooking and the tasty filling turns this economical cut of meat into a meal fit for a king. Italians usually serve the tomato sauce with pasta for a starter and the meat as a main course with a green salad. If you have leftover tomato sauce, you can freeze it for another time.

Serves 4-6

700g/1lb 9oz beef brisket
2 slices of mortadella
3 tbsp extra virgin olive oil
1 small onion, finely chopped
100g/3½oz fresh breadcrumbs
50g/1¾oz caciocavallo cheese, grated
70g/2½oz salami, finely chopped
20g/¾oz sultanas (golden raisins),
   soaked in lukewarm water to soften,
   drained
20g/¾oz/generous 2 tbsp pine nuts
a handful of parsley, roughly chopped
salt and freshly ground black pepper

for the sauce
3 tbsp extra virgin olive oil
1 small onion
a handful of basil leaves
175ml/6fl oz/¾ cup red wine
1 tbsp tomato purée (paste), diluted
   with a little lukewarm water
1kg/2lb 4oz tomato passata (strained
   tomatoes)

Put the beef flat on a board. Make a cut halfway through the centre of the meat, then carefully slice horizontally through both sides of the meat so that it opens out like a book. Flatten slightly with a meat tenderizer, line with the mortadella slices and set aside.

Heat the olive oil in a saucepan, add the onion and sweat until softened. Stir in the breadcrumbs until all the oil has been absorbed, remove from the heat and leave to cool. Add the cheese, salami, sultanas, pine nuts and parsley and combine well together. Season with salt and pepper to taste. Spread the mixture over the mortadella. Carefully roll the meat and tie securely with kitchen string to ensure the filling does not escape. Set aside.

To make the sauce, heat the olive oil in a large flameproof pot, add the meat and brown well on all sides. Add the onion and sweat until softened. Stir in the basil leaves, add the wine and allow to evaporate, then add the diluted tomato purée, passata, and salt and pepper to taste. Bring to the boil, reduce the heat, cover with a lid and cook on a low heat for 3 hours. Halfway through cooking, very carefully turn the meat over, and from time to time baste the meat with the tomato sauce.

Carefully remove the meat from the sauce, place on a serving dish, discard the string and carve into slices, serving with a little of the sauce. Use the remaining sauce to dress freshly cooked pasta.

Pastizada alla Veneta

Venetian pot roast

This classic Venetian pot-roast, traditionally made with horsemeat, is slow-cooking at its best; the meat is left to marinate overnight in vinegar and spices before being slow-cooked with a little white wine, Marsala and the spices from the marinade. The end result is very tender beef with the aromatic flavour of the spices. Carve fairly thick slices, otherwise the beef will fall apart. Serve with runny polenta (cornmeal) for a hearty Venetian meal.

Serves 4

1.5kg/3lb 5oz topside of beef
100ml/3½fl oz/scant ½ cup extra virgin
  olive oil
1 onion, finely chopped
salt and freshly ground black pepper
4 tbsp dry white wine
4 tbsp Marsala wine
200ml/7fl oz/scant 1 cup beef stock
  (see page 21) or vegetable stock (see
  page 32)

for the marinade
500ml/18fl oz/2 cups red wine vinegar
2 garlic cloves, left whole
2 celery stalks, sliced
2 sprigs of rosemary
2 cloves
a pinch of ground cinnamon
a pinch of salt
6 black peppercorns

Combine the marinade ingredients, pour over the beef, cover with clingfilm (plastic wrap) and leave in the fridge to marinate overnight.

Remove the meat from the marinade, pat dry with kitchen paper and set aside. Strain the marinade, reserving the vegetables and herbs. Cut a piece of greaseproof (waxed) paper slightly larger than the diameter of your cooking pot and lightly grease.

Heat the olive oil in a flameproof pot, add the onion and the vegetables from the marinade and sweat on a medium heat for 5 minutes. Remove the vegetables and set aside. Add the beef and brown well all over; season with salt and pepper. Add the wine, Marsala and stock, reduce the heat, then cover with the greaseproof paper and the lid and cook on a gentle heat for 2½ hours.

Remove the meat and set aside on a board. Pass the sauce through a fine sieve into a small pan and, using a small whisk, beat the sauce so it is well amalgamated. Carve the meat into thick slices, pour over the sauce and serve with runny polenta.

Stufato di manzo alla Siciliana
Sicilian pot roast

This recipe evolved from memories of a pasta dish I once enjoyed in Sicily. To the pesto of almonds and olives, I added a hint of cinnamon, giving it that subtle North African flavour which is so often present in Sicilian dishes. Once the pesto is inserted into the beef, the meat is left to slow cook in stock. Delicious served with couscous or steamed rice.

Serves 4

70g/2½oz green olives, finely chopped
70g/2½oz flaked almonds, finely
  chopped
½ tsp ground cinnamon
salt and freshly ground black pepper
800g/1lb 12oz beef brisket
3 tbsp extra virgin olive oil
1 onion, finely chopped
1 garlic clove, finely chopped
a handful of parsley, finely chopped
2 tbsp tomato purée (paste)
100ml/3½fl oz/scant ½ cup red wine
700ml/1¼ pints/3 cups hot beef stock
  (see page 21) - or use a stock cube

Combine the olives, almonds, cinnamon, salt and pepper. Make incisions all over the beef with a skewer or sharp knife and insert the mixture well inside, also placing some between the meat and the outer fat; if the filling looks as though it might fall out, tie the meat securely with kitchen string.

Heat the olive oil in a flameproof pot and brown the beef on all sides. Add the onion, garlic and parsley and sweat for a couple of minutes. Mix the tomato purée with the wine and add to the meat, together with the stock. Bring to the boil, reduce the heat, cover with a lid and cook gently for 3 hours, until the meat is tender and cooked through.

Remove the meat and set aside. Increase the heat and cook the sauce for a few minutes, without a lid, until it has reduced and thickened slightly. Slice the meat and serve with the sauce, and a dish of couscous or rice.

For a slow cooker
Make up the recipe as above, adding 600ml/20fl oz/2½ cups beef stock. Bring to the boil, then transfer everything to a medium slow cooker pot. Cover and cook on High for 5 hours, turning the meat over once during cooking. If you are not ready to serve the beef, then reduce the heat to Low and cook for up to 1 hour. Serve as above.

Porchetta natalizia
Festive stuffed pork belly

I love making porchetta and often make a large one for special occasions or when I have lots of guests. It can be made in advance and sliced when required, and is delicious eaten cold. The traditional porchetta, popular street food in the region of Rome, is a whole piglet, cooked on a spit, sliced thickly and served as a substantial sandwich. To enrich the porchetta further, I have added a filling of minced pork and chicken livers. It's an unusual cut of pork and you will need to order the meat from your butcher in advance, but it is surprisingly simple to prepare.

Serves 4-6

3kg/6lb 8oz jacket of pork (loin and belly, boned)
salt and freshly ground black pepper
5 tbsp vin santo
grated zest of 2 lemons
2 tbsp extra virgin olive oil, plus extra to rub
1 onion, finely chopped
175g/6oz minced (ground) pork
175g/6oz chicken livers, finely chopped
350g/12oz bread, soaked in lukewarm water
10 sage leaves, roughly chopped
needles from 2 sprigs of rosemary, roughly chopped
leaves from 2 sprigs of thyme
15g/½oz/2 tbsp pine nuts
30g/1oz/3 tbsp sultanas
6 slices of mortadella

Unroll the jacket of pork and lay it on a board, skin side down. Season and rub well into the meat. Drizzle the vin santo and sprinkle the lemon zest over and massage in well. Roll, wrap in clingfilm (plastic wrap) and rest in the fridge for 30 minutes.

Meanwhile, heat the olive oil in a pan and sweat the onion for a couple of minutes. Add the minced pork and brown, stirring well, then add the chicken livers and brown all over. Remove from the heat and leave to cool.

Preheat the oven to 220°C/425°F/gas mark 7. Lightly grease a roasting dish with olive oil.

Squeeze the excess water from the bread and chop finely. Add the bread to the cooled meat, together with the herbs, pine nuts and sultanas and mix well.

Discarding the clingfilm, open out the pork on a board. Line with 3 slices of mortadella, add the stuffing and top with the remaining mortadella. Carefully roll up the meat and tie securely with string. Massage all over with olive oil, salt and pepper and place in the roasting dish. Roast in the oven for 30 minutes.

Cover the meat with foil, turn the oven down to 150°C/300°F/gas mark 2 and continue to roast for 3 hours. Remove the foil, turn off the oven and leave to rest in the oven until it cools down.

You can serve immediately, carved into slices, or serve cold later. It will keep for up to a week wrapped in foil in the fridge.

Stinco di maiale all'arancia
Roasted pork shins with oranges

Stinco (shin or shank) is popular throughout Italy, both for slow roasting and, in the case of pork shins, also for curing into salami and sausages. When buying pork shanks, bear in mind that although they look quite large, the majority of the weight consists of bone, so one shank has only enough meat for two people. The meat is well suited to long, slow cooking and the fact that it is on the bone makes this pork cut extremely tasty. The addition of oranges really brings out the flavour of the meat in this simple-to-prepare and unusual Sunday roast.

Serves 4

2 pork shins, about 1.5kg/3lb 5oz each
salt and freshly ground black pepper
4 tbsp extra virgin olive oil
2 red onions, finely sliced
2 carrots, sliced lengthways
2 sprigs of rosemary
400ml/14fl oz/1⅔ cups dry white wine
300ml/10fl oz/1¼ cups vegetable stock
  (see page 32) – or use a stock cube
4 oranges, plus grated zest and juice of
  2 oranges
125g/4½oz/generous ½ cup granulated
  sugar

Preheat the oven to 200°C/400°F/gas mark 6. Put the shins in a roasting tin, rub all over with salt and pepper and drizzle with the olive oil. Roast in the oven for 1 hour.

Add the vegetables, rosemary, wine and stock to the roasting tin and continue to cook for another 1½ hours.

Meanwhile, prepare the oranges and sauce. Peel 4 oranges and cut into 1cm/½-inch slices. Bring some water to the boil in a small pan, add the orange slices, boil for 1 minute, then remove, drain and set aside. Put the juice of 2 oranges in a small pan with the sugar and 125ml/4fl oz/½ cup water and cook on a medium heat, stirring all the time, until the sugar has dissolved. Remove from the heat and set aside.

About 15 minutes before the end of the pork's cooking time, add the orange slices to the roasting tin and pour over the orange sauce.

When the pork shins are cooked, put them on a large serving dish together with the vegetables, orange slices and juices. Sprinkle all over with orange zest and leave to rest for 5 minutes. Carve and serve.

Lonza di maiale con miele e noci
Roast pork loin with honey and walnuts

Pork loin is a popular cut for roasting. You can buy it on the bone, with the loin ribs attached, or boneless and tied with string to keep it together. In this recipe I have wrapped pancetta over a boneless joint to keep the pork moist during cooking; the addition of onion, walnuts and honey gives this dish its delicious flavour.

Serves 4

850g/1lb 14oz boneless pork loin joint
extra virgin olive oil, to grease
salt and freshly ground black pepper
6 slices of pancetta or streaky bacon
1 onion, finely sliced
50g/1¾oz walnuts
3 tbsp runny honey
100ml/3½fl oz/scant ½ cup dry white wine
100ml/3½fl oz/scant ½ cup hot vegetable stock (see page 32) - or use a stock cube

Preheat the oven to 150°C/300°F/gas mark 2.

Grease a roasting tin with a little olive oil and add the pork. Rub the pork all over with salt and pepper and arrange slices of pancetta over the meat side of the joint. Roast in the oven for 30 minutes.

Add the onion and walnuts to the roasting tin and brush the honey over the meat. Continue to cook for another 1½ hours, basting with the juices from time to time.

Remove from the oven, put the meat on a board and set aside. Put the roasting tin on a medium heat, add the wine and stir with a wooden spoon until the wine has evaporated. Stir in the hot stock and reduce by half, until the sauce has thickened slightly. Slice the meat and arrange on a serving dish, pour over the sauce and serve.

Cappone natalizio
Christmas capon

Capons are castrated roosters; larger than chickens but smaller than turkeys, they are eaten for Christmas in northern Italy, where they are bred specially for this time of year. Traditionally castrated on the day of Saint Rocco (16 August), the capons are then fattened up for four months. During this time they loose their rooster-like qualities, become calmer and more manageable, and develop more tender and succulent flesh. I really like capon and usually have one, stuffed with a mixture of seasonal fruits and nuts, for Christmas lunch.

Serves 6

2kg/4lb 8oz capon
salt and freshly ground black pepper
extra virgin olive oil, to drizzle
8 slices of pancetta

for the stuffing
140g/5oz dried apricots, finely chopped
140g/5oz prunes, finely chopped
12 walnuts, finely chopped
300g/10½oz chestnuts, cooked and
 finely chopped
250g/9oz salami, finely chopped
a handful of thyme leaves
140g/5oz bread, soaked in a little
 lukewarm water, drained and roughly
 chopped
50g/1¾oz Parmesan, grated
200ml/7fl oz/scant 1 cup Marsala wine

Preheat the oven to 200°C/400°F/gas mark 6.

Rub salt and pepper all over the capon and inside the cavity and set aside.

Combine all the stuffing ingredients, season with salt and pepper to taste and use to fill the cavity of the capon. Drizzle a little olive oil in a roasting tin, add the capon, cover with pancetta slices and drizzle with a little more olive oil. Cover with foil and roast for 1½ hours, basting with the juices from time to time. Remove the foil and pancetta slices and roast for another 30 minutes or until thoroughly cooked. To test whether the capon is cooked, insert a skewer in the thigh – if the juices run clear, it is done.

Remove from the oven and leave to rest for 10 minutes. Carve and serve with the stuffing.

Cosciotto d'agnello con piselli e cipolline

Roast leg of lamb with peas and baby onions

For a special occasion or Sunday lunch, this dish is a must. The combination of baby onions, black olives, anchovies, garlic and peas marry well with the succulent lamb. If you can't find Taggiasca olives, substitute Greek Kalamata olives, which give a distinct tangy taste. For 4 people, half a leg of lamb is sufficient.

Serves 4

1.2kg/2lb 10oz half leg of lamb
salt and freshly ground black pepper
a little extra virgin olive oil
150ml/5fl oz/⅔ cup dry white wine
300g/10½oz baby onions or shallots, peeled
24 Taggiasca olives, pitted
2 garlic cloves, left whole, crushed
4 anchovy fillets, roughly chopped
150g/5½oz/generous 1 cup frozen peas

Preheat the oven to 200°C/400°F/gas mark 6. Rub the lamb all over with salt, pepper and a little olive oil. Place in a roasting dish and roast for 20 minutes.

Add half the wine and cook for a further 20 minutes. Add the remaining wine, onions, olives, garlic and anchovies, cover with foil and continue roasting for 1 hour 10 minutes.

Stir in the peas and roast for 10 minutes. Remove the foil and roast for a further 10 minutes.

Remove from the oven and leave to rest for 5 minutes. Put the lamb on a board, carve and serve with the vegetables and juices.

Anatra arrosto con ripieno di mela e salvia

Roasted duck with apple and sage

Duck and apple is a perfect marriage, and this dish makes a great alternative for Christmas or for a Sunday lunch. For this recipe, I have used the excellent English Gressingham duck. Keep the drained-off fat and use for roast potatoes to accompany the duck.

Serves 4

1 oven-ready duck, weighing about
    1.8kg/4lb
salt and freshly ground black pepper
30g/1oz/2 tbsp butter
1 onion
8 sage leaves, finely chopped, plus a
    few extra
3 tbsp fresh breadcrumbs
2 egg yolks
2 Granny Smith apples, peeled, cored
    and roughly chopped
100ml/3½fl oz/scant ½ cup dry white
    wine

Preheat the oven to 180°C/350°F/gas mark 4.

Wipe the duck clean inside and out, season the cavity with salt and pepper and set aside.

Melt the butter in a saucepan, add the onion and sweat on a medium heat for 3 minutes. Add 2 tbsp water and continue to cook for 2 minutes until the onion has softened. Remove from the heat, stir in the chopped sage, breadcrumbs, egg yolks, apples, and some salt and pepper and combine well. Fill the cavity of the duck with this stuffing.

Prick the duck skin all over and sprinkle with salt – this will release the fat and make the duck skin nice and crisp. Put the duck on a rack in a roasting tin and roast for 45 minutes.

Pour off the fat and reserve to make roast potatoes. Drizzle the duck with the wine, scatter with a few sage leaves and continue to roast for about 1¼ hours, until the duck is cooked; test by inserting a skewer in the thigh – if the juices run clear, it is done.

Remove from the oven, pour off the fat and leave to rest for 5–10 minutes. Carve and serve with the stuffing.

Pollo ubriaco con peperoni
Boozy baked chicken with peppers

This is a really simple dish to prepare: put all your ingredients in a roasting dish and pop in the oven to do the rest. All the flavours infuse together and the alcohol and mustard give the chicken a real kick! Excellent for an easy Sunday lunch or midweek meal served with steamed rice.

Serves 4

150ml/5fl oz/⅔ cup dry white wine
1 tbsp English mustard
850g/1lb 14oz chicken thighs and
  drumsticks
100g/3½oz prosciutto, roughly chopped
10 baby onions or shallots, peeled
225g/8oz baby vine tomatoes, halved
1 yellow (bell) pepper, thinly sliced
1 red (bell) pepper, thinly sliced
2 garlic cloves, left whole
salt and freshly ground black pepper
2 tbsp port
2 tbsp brandy
2 tbsp extra virgin olive oil
1 tbsp chopped fresh parsley

Combine the wine and mustard and set aside.

Put the chicken pieces in an ovenproof dish with the prosciutto, onions, tomatoes, peppers and garlic, sprinkle with salt and pepper and toss together. Pour over the white wine mixture, port, brandy and olive oil and toss again. Cover with foil and set aside for the flavours to infuse for 20 minutes. Preheat the oven to 170°C/325°F/gas mark 3.

Place in the oven and bake for 1 hour, basting from time to time. Remove the foil and continue to cook for another 30 minutes.

Remove from the oven, garnish with parsley and serve.

Verdure miste arrostite
Mixed roasted root vegetables

When I cook roasted meat or poultry, I like to make a tray of roasted vegetables as an accompaniment. I usually put in whatever vegetables are lying around, toss them with some extra virgin olive oil, seasoning and herbs and slow-roast them in the wood-fired oven. I tend not to peel vegetables like potatoes and carrots because a lot of essential nutrients are in the skin, but I leave it to you. You can use whatever root vegetables you like: if you don't have celeriac, for example, use extra carrots or parsnips. In warmer months, I use vegetables such as peppers, courgettes (zucchini), aubergines (eggplants) and baby new potatoes.

Serves 4

4 large potatoes, scrubbed and cut
   into quarters
2 large carrots, scrubbed and cut in
   half lengthways
2 parsnips, peeled and cut in half
   lengthways
300g/10½oz celeriac (celery root),
   peeled and cut into large chunks
2 fennel bulbs, halved or quartered
   depending on size
2 red onions, peeled, halved or
   quartered depending on size
8 tbsp extra virgin olive oil
salt and freshly ground black pepper
2 sprigs of rosemary
2 sprigs of thyme
2 bay leaves

Preheat the oven to 200°C/400°F/gas mark 6.

Put all the vegetables in a large roasting tin, toss with extra virgin olive oil, salt, pepper and the herbs. Cover with foil and place in the hot oven for 1 hour. Remove the foil and put back in the oven for about 20 minutes, until all the vegetables are cooked through.

Remove from the oven and serve with roasted meat.

Breads

For centuries, bread has been the staple of virtually every country and culture worldwide. The basic ingredients of flour, yeast and water and the ritual of kneading and proving the dough remains the same whether you make your dough by hand or use a machine.

My mother used to bake bread once a week in the big wood-fired oven; she would make enough to last the week. On bread-baking day, I would wake up to the wonderful aroma and rush downstairs to tear open a loaf of warm, freshly baked bread. Often she would make savoury breads, adding bits of leftover salami and cheese, similar to *pane contadino* (see page 136), or sometimes she would sweeten dough with some sugar and dried fruit as a treat for *merenda* (tea time).

In Italy every town and village has at least one *panetteria* (bakery) that bakes an array of breads and dough-based products each day – by lunchtime they have usually sold out. Years ago, if you did not have your own oven, boys would carry their family's precious cargo of bread dough to the *panetteria* on planks of wood covered in tea towels, to be placed in the hot oven and returned home as hot loaves.

Like most Italians, I enjoy bread with all my meals, from breakfast to supper, and could not imagine life without this most basic of foods. Italians consider bread to be almost sacred and never allow it to be thrown away; stale bread is always used up as bruschetta, fillings or made into breadcrumbs.

For me, making dough and baking bread is deeply satisfying. I love to wake up early and light the wood-fired oven in my garden. I then prepare the ingredients – I usually use fresh yeast, which I crumble into the flour, add water and watch the big bubbles explode as I mix it together. While the dough is rising I check the fire, add a few more logs if necessary, have my breakfast and get on with other things. This is the slowness when making bread. When the moment comes to shape the dough I like to be creative and use up leftovers such as grilled vegetables in *girelle* (see page 144) or use herbs from the garden in *panini al rosmarino* (see page 142). I love the smell of bread baking and it never fails to overwhelm me with sweet, nostalgic memories.

Pane contadino
Rustic farmers' bread

This is a country bread traditionally made by rural housewives for their husbands working in the fields. It was made using up leftovers of ham, salami, cheese and pork lard. In my region, we usually make this type of bread, with the addition of boiled eggs, at Easter; it is known as *casatiello* and is often made in large quantities to give away to friends and family. You can use any type of cured meats and hard cheese you have available – when I tested this recipe I didn't have any other Italian cheese, so I used up some Gruyère that I had in the fridge and the result was just as tasty.

Serves 6

500g/1lb 2oz/4 cups strong (bread) flour
1 x 7g sachet of dried yeast
3g salt
3g black pepper
2 tbsp extra virgin olive oil, plus extra to brush
300ml/10fl oz/1¼ cups lukewarm water
70g/2½oz pancetta, cut into small cubes
70g/2½oz coppa (or prosciutto), cut into small cubes
40g/1½oz salami, cut into small cubes
70g/2½oz Gruyère cheese, cut into small cubes
30g/1oz pecorino (romano) cheese, grated
30g/1oz Parmesan, grated

In a large bowl, combine the flour, yeast, salt, pepper and olive oil. Gradually add the water and mix well to form a dough. Knead on a lightly floured surface for 10 minutes, then leave to rest for about 5 minutes.

Meanwhile, mix together the cured meats and cheeses.

Open up the dough slightly, incorporate the cured meats and cheeses and knead for about 5 minutes, making sure all the ingredients are well combined. Form into a long sausage shape about 65cm/26 inches long and seal the ends together to form a ring. Place on a baking sheet, cover with a clean tea towel and leave to rise in a warm place for about 1 hour, until it has doubled in size.

Meanwhile, preheat the oven to 200°C/400°F/gas mark 6.

Brush the top of the bread with olive oil, reduce the oven temperature to 180°C/350°F/gas mark 4 and bake the bread for 35 minutes.

Remove from the oven and leave to rest for 10 minutes before serving.

Focaccia di patate alla Pugliese
Pugliese potato focaccia

Each Italian region has its own varieties of bread and focaccia. Puglia, the heel of Italy, is renowned for its amazing bread from the town of Altamura, but equally delicious is the potato-based focaccia. The addition of mashed potatoes makes the dough incredibly soft, and with its topping of cherry tomatoes this is a wonderful snack.

Makes 1 x 30cm/12-inch round focaccia

12g/¼oz fresh yeast
  185ml/6½fl oz/generous ¾ cup lukewarm water
400g/14 oz/3¼ cups '00' flour
100g/3½oz potato, cooked and mashed
1 tsp salt

for the topping
100g/3½oz cherry tomatoes, halved
3 tbsp extra virgin olive oil
salt and freshly ground black pepper
1 tsp dried oregano
small handful of fresh basil leaves

Dissolve the yeast in a little of the water. Put the flour, mashed potato and salt in a large bowl, add the yeast-and-water mixture and gradually add the remaining water to form a smooth dough. Knead on a lightly floured surface for 5 minutes. Form into a ball, cover with clingfilm (plastic wrap) or a clean tea towel and leave to rise in a warm place for about 1½ hours, until it has doubled in size.

Meanwhile, preheat the oven to 200°C/400°F/gas mark 6.

Line a large baking sheet with greaseproof (waxed) paper or baking parchment, place the dough on top and, using your fingers, gently spread the dough to form a rough 30cm/12-inch circle; it will not be as thin as a pizza base. Top with the tomatoes, drizzle with olive oil, sprinkle with salt and pepper, oregano and the basil leaves. Bake for 30 minutes.

Remove from the oven and leave to rest for 5 minutes before serving. Enjoy hot or cold.

Focaccia allo stracchino
Cheese focaccia

This has to be one of the best focaccia around! It originates from Liguria and dates back to the Saracen raids in the ninth and tenth centuries, when locals fled the coastal areas to the safety of the mountains, where only basic ingredients such as flour, oil and cheese were available. Nowadays in Liguria this delicious cheese-filled focaccia is served warm as street food. Stracchino or crescenza, a soft cow's milk cheese, is used for this recipe. If you can't find it in your Italian deli, you can use Taleggio or, for a stronger flavour, dolcelatte. Make sure you stretch the dough as much as you can to get a really thin focaccia. Delicious served hot from the oven with a slice of mortadella.

Serves 4

500g/1lb 2oz/4 cups strong (bread) flour
1 x 7g sachet of dried yeast
6g sea salt
3 tbsp extra virgin olive oil, plus extra to grease and brush
250ml/9fl oz/1 cup lukewarm water
250g/9oz stracchino cheese, roughly chopped
salt and freshly ground black pepper

Mix the flour, yeast and salt in a large bowl. Make a well in the centre, add the olive oil and gradually add the water, mixing well with your hands to form a dough. Knead on a lightly floured surface for 15 minutes, until smooth and elastic. Cover with a clean tea towel and leave to rise in a warm place for 1 hour, until it has doubled in size.

Preheat the oven to 220°C/425°F/gas mark 7. Grease a 33 x 30cm/13 x 12-inch baking sheet with olive oil.

Divide the dough in two, making one piece a little bigger than the other. Take the larger piece and roll out into a roughly rectangular shape, then stretch by hand until it is about 3mm/⅛ inch thick. Line the greased baking sheet with the dough and pinch the edge to raise it to about 2cm/¾ inch high. Dot with pieces of cheese and sprinkle with a little salt and pepper.

Roll out the other piece of dough to the same thickness. Place over the cheese, pressing down with your fingertips and sealing the edges well. Brush olive oil all over the top and bake for 20 minutes, until golden.

Remove from the oven and leave to rest for a couple of minutes, then slice and serve.

Focaccine con cipolle rosse
Savoury buns with red onion

Although the Italian title suggests otherwise, these are not the thin bread we know as 'focaccia'- quite a few savoury breads in Italy are called focaccia. Very simple to make, the dough includes softened red onion, and is shaped into round buns and decorated with more red onion and a black olive. Delicious to eat by themselves or sliced and filled with mortadella or prosciutto to enjoy for lunch or a snack.

Makes 10 buns

4 tbsp extra virgin olive oil, plus extra
   to brush
1 large red onion, finely chopped, plus
   2 red onions, finely sliced, to garnish
700g/1lb 9oz/5½ cups strong (bread)
   flour
1 x 7g sachet of dried yeast
10g/¼oz/2 tsp salt
350ml/12fl oz/1½ cups lukewarm water
10 black olives, to garnish

Heat the olive oil in a pan, add the chopped onion and sweat for a few minutes until the onion has softened.

In a large bowl, combine the flour, yeast, salt and the softened onion. Gradually add the water and mix well to form a dough. Knead on a lightly floured surface for about 10 minutes. Form into a ball, cover with clingfilm (plastic wrap) and leave to rise in a warm place for 1 hour or until it has doubled in size.

Knead again for 5 minutes, then divide into 10 equal balls and gently press each with the palm of your hand to flatten slightly. Cover with a clean tea towel and leave to rise for 20 minutes.

Meanwhile, preheat the oven to 200°C/400°F/gas mark 6.

Decorate each bun with thin slices of red onion and a black olive, brush with olive oil and bake for 30 minutes, until golden brown. Leave to cool before serving.

Panini al rosmarino
Rosemary bread rolls

Lovely bread rolls enhanced by the addition of rosemary make a welcome appearance in any bread basket. Delicious served with an antipasto of cured meats and preserved vegetables or simply as a snack on their own or with some creamy ricotta cheese. If you prefer, the rosemary can be replaced with black olives or, for a more pungent flavour, anchovy fillets – or a combination of all three – but if using anchovies you won't need to add the coarse sea salt.

Makes 12 rolls

500g/1lb 2oz/4 cups '00' flour
1 x 7g sachet of dried yeast
7g salt
3 tbsp extra virgin olive oil, plus extra to rub
250ml/9fl oz/1 cup lukewarm water
needles from 4 sprigs of rosemary
a handful of coarse sea salt

In a large bowl, combine the flour, yeast and salt. Add the olive oil and gradually mix in the water to form a dough. Knead on a lightly floured surface for 10 minutes, cover with a clean tea towel and leave to rise in a warm place for 1 hour or until it has doubled in size.

Using your hands, roll the dough into a long sausage shape about 2cm/¾ inch thick – it may be easier to divide the dough in two or three pieces before rolling. Rub a little olive oil all over, sprinkle with rosemary and sea salt, slice into sausage shapes about 20cm/8 inches long and wrap round into a coil. Press lightly with the palm of your hand and place the rolls on a baking sheet, cover with a clean tea towel and leave to rise for 1 hour.

Preheat the oven to 200°C/400°F/gas mark 6. Bake for 15–20 minutes, until golden. Cool on a wire rack.

Girelle con melanzane
Aubergine bread rolls

These lovely rolls remind me of my early baking days when I would make bread rolls with whatever leftover vegetables I had around. The dough is rolled into a rectangular shape, topped with grilled aubergines (eggplants) and scamorza cheese, rolled up and cut into spiral rolls. It takes a little time to prepare but is really worth the effort. If you prefer, you can replace the aubergines with courgettes (zucchini) and the scamorza with mozzarella.

Makes about 15 rolls

12g/¼oz fresh yeast
1 tsp caster (superfine) sugar
3 tbsp lukewarm milk
300g/10½oz/ scant 2½ cups '00' flour
1 tsp salt
40g/1½oz/3 tbsp butter, melted
1 egg

for the filling
500g/1lb 2oz aubergines (eggplants)
2 tbsp extra virgin olive oil, plus extra
    to grease
salt and freshly ground black pepper
150g/5½oz scamorza cheese, thinly
    sliced
a few basil leaves, torn

Dissolve the yeast and sugar in the milk and leave for about 10 minutes. Put the flour and salt in a large bowl, add the yeast mixture, melted butter and egg and knead on a lightly floured surface for about 10 minutes, until you have a smooth dough. Cover with a clean tea towel and leave to rise in a warm place for 1 hour or until it has doubled in size.

Meanwhile, prepare the filling. Preheat a grill (broiler) or griddle pan. Thinly slice the aubergine lengthways and grill on both sides. Combine the olive oil, salt and pepper and brush over the grilled aubergine. Set aside.

Lightly grease a large baking sheet and line with baking parchment.

Lightly flour a work surface and roll out the dough into a roughly rectangular shape. Top with the scamorza, aubergine and torn basil leaves. Carefully roll up lengthways, taking care that the filling does not escape, and leave to rest for 10 minutes. Using a sharp knife, cut into slices about 4cm/1½ inches thick, place on the prepared baking sheet, cover and leave to rest for 1 hour.

Meanwhile, preheat the oven to 200°C/400°F/gas mark 6. Bake the rolls for 15 minutes, until golden. Leave to cool before serving.

Pizza ai funghi e speck
Wild mushroom and ham pizza

The secret to this pizza base is the sticky dough; it makes the resulting cooked pizza lovely and light. Don't worry about it being too sticky to handle, you don't have to knead it – if you prefer, wear some well-oiled latex gloves and you won't get the dough all over your hands. Make sure the top of the dough is well oiled before covering, otherwise the clingfilm (plastic wrap) will stick to it. Another tip when making this sticky dough is to use solid-based round or square baking sheets rather than the pizza trays with holes. In season, mixed wild mushrooms go really well with speck, a smoky cured ham from the Tyrolean region of northern Italy. If you can't find wild mushrooms, cultivated ones are delicious, too.

Makes 2 large pizzas

500g/1lb 2oz/4 cups strong (bread) flour
5g/1 tsp salt
10g/¼oz fresh yeast or 1 x 7g sachet of dried yeast
450ml/16fl oz/2 cups lukewarm water

for the topping
3 tbsp extra virgin olive oil, plus extra to grease and drizzle
1 garlic clove, finely chopped
½ red chilli, finely chopped
300g/10½oz mixed wild (or cultivated) mushrooms, cleaned and roughly chopped
salt and freshly ground black pepper
1 tbsp finely chopped fresh parsley
6 slices of speck (or other smoked ham), roughly torn
100g/3½oz Parmesan, grated

Put the flour and salt in a large bowl, crumble in the fresh yeast (or add dried) and gradually add the water to make a sticky dough. Cover the bowl with clingfilm (plastic wrap) and leave to rest in a warm place for about 30 minutes.

Generously grease two round baking sheets, about 33cm/13 inches in diameter, with olive oil.

Divide the dough in half and place each piece on a greased baking sheet, drizzle some olive oil over the dough, spread well, cover with clingfilm and leave to rest for at least 1 hour.

Meanwhile, make the topping. Heat the olive oil in a frying pan, add the garlic and chilli and sweat for a minute or so. Add the mushrooms, season with salt and pepper, and stir-fry for 4 minutes. Remove from the heat, stir in the parsley and set aside.

Preheat the oven to 230°C/450°F/gas mark 8.

Loosen the clingfilm over the pizza dough and use the clingfilm to spread the dough out on the baking sheet. Drizzle the dough with a little more olive oil, top with the mushrooms, ham and Parmesan. Bake the pizzas for about 7–8 minutes, slice and serve hot.

Pane dolce al cioccolato
Chocolate brioche

A perfect treat for breakfast or *merenda* (tea time) for the children. The 'slowness' of this recipe is in the proving, which you must do twice for at least 2 hours; this will ensure the lightness of the brioche. The mixture is quite sticky to work with, so don't worry, this is how it should be and the results will be worth it. You can make the mixture by hand, but a mixer will be quicker. I prefer to use dark chocolate, giving the brioche a slightly bittersweet taste, but if you are making this for children, use a good-quality milk chocolate.

Serves 8

250g/9oz/2 cups strong (bread) flour
4g (½ sachet) dried yeast
50g/1¾oz/¼ cup caster (superfine)
  sugar
a pinch of salt
1 tsp ground cinnamon
4 eggs, beaten
200g/7oz/generous ¾ cup butter,
  softened and cut into small chunks
85g/3oz dark or milk chocolate, broken
  into 8 pieces
1 egg yolk
2 tbsp milk

Line a 20cm/8-inch diameter round cake tin with greaseproof (waxed) paper.

Put the flour, yeast, sugar, salt, cinnamon and 4 eggs in a mixer and whizz for 10 minutes. With the mixer still on, gradually add the butter and continue to whizz for another 5 minutes. Switch the machine off, transfer the mixture into a bowl, cover with clingfilm (plastic wrap) and leave to rest in a warm place for 2 hours.

The mixture will be quite sticky; however, form it into 8 equal balls. Insert a piece of chocolate into the centre of each ball, making sure the chocolate is completely covered with dough. Place the balls in the prepared cake tin, cover with clingfilm and leave to rest for 2 hours.

Preheat the oven to 180°C/350°F/gas mark 4. Combine the egg yolk and milk and brush over the top of the brioche. Bake for about 25 minutes, until golden brown. Leave to cool in the tin for 5 minutes, then turn out and break off the pieces.

Cakes & desserts

———

The traditional Italian meal nearly always ends with fruit; a bowl of fresh, seasonal fruits placed in the centre of the table for everyone to help themselves, so when I think of dessert, I naturally think of fruit. A lot of Italian sweet treats like *crostate* (tarts and pies) and cakes include fruit and for me there is nothing nicer than a home-baked dessert oozing with sweetness from ripe, seasonal fruit. Slowly cooked apples or pears undergo an amazing transformation from when they are fresh, and turning fruit into wonderful desserts has always been a pleasure for me.

My mother, sisters and grandmother loved to make sweet treats, especially on Sundays or feast days, and I was always sent to get the fruit because I knew where the best was to be found. I was the first to climb the fig trees and pick the ripest – I knew when this was because I used to check each day. The same went for cherries, plums, peaches, apricots, pears, apples – and during spring I would come home with basketfuls of wild strawberries, which grew on the hillside. I remember my mum used to fill jars with morello cherries, sprinkle them with sugar and leave them out in the sun for days until the sugar had dissolved; the result was a sweet cherry syrup which was used to fill pies or make cherry ices or simply serve as an accompaniment to cakes. This was effortless slow cooking, as the warm sunshine did the work.

My sisters often made *crostate*, which were slowly baked when the wood-burning oven was still warm from the day's bread baking. The smell of this home cooking was amazing, filling the house as well as our nostrils, and I couldn't wait for the delicacy to come out of the oven, constantly checking, so I could secure the first slice.

A lot of traditional desserts and cakes were made during festivities, in large quantities, to share with friends and family. For instance, at Easter the *pastiera di grano* (wheat and ricotta pie) was a favourite and women would spend entire days making them – and many still do. I like to maintain this tradition and I reserve a day before Easter Sunday to make a batch to give away and, of course, one or two to keep for my family.

A lot of Italian cakes and desserts, including *babà all'arancia* (see page 154) and the Italians' favourite Christmas cake, *panettone* (see page 168), use yeast and require several slow risings; it is the slowness of the risings that give the desserts their lightness.

———

Meringa con zabaglione e fragole

Meringue with zabaglione and strawberries

Meringue is so simple to make at home; with an electric whisk the mixture takes just minutes to prepare. The addition of a little lemon juice helps to keep the meringue shiny. You then pop it in the oven on a low temperature for several hours and go and do something else while the meringue slowly cooks. This is a large meringue nest; if you prefer to make smaller nests, cooking time would be reduced by about half. It makes a delicious dessert topped with Italian zabaglione and some fresh strawberries.

Serves 4

3 egg whites
a pinch of salt
200g/7oz/1 cup caster (superfine)
  sugar
½ tsp lemon juice
10g/¼oz/1½ tbsp icing (confectioners')
  sugar, sifted
200g/7oz strawberries, hulled and
  quartered

for the zabaglione
4 egg yolks
100g/3½oz/½ cup caster (superfine)
  sugar
3 tbsp vin santo or Marsala wine

Preheat the oven to 75°C/165°F/gas mark ¼ or as low as it will go. Line a 24cm/9½-inch diameter round baking sheet with baking parchment.

Put the egg whites and salt in a bowl and whisk until stiff peaks form. Gradually add the caster sugar, whisking all the time. Add the lemon juice and whisk until the sugar has dissolved. Put the mixture into a piping bag (pastry bag) and pipe a large nest onto the baking parchment. Alternatively, if you don't have a piping bag, you can use a large spoon. Sprinkle with icing sugar and immediately place in the oven for 4 hours.

Remove from the oven and leave to cool slightly before carefully removing from the baking sheet. Leave to cool.

Meanwhile, make the zabaglione. In a small heatproof bowl, whisk together the egg yolks, sugar and vin santo. Place over a saucepan of gently simmering water, whisking all the time until the mixture begins to boil and thicken. Remove from the heat, whisk well to get rid of any lumps, and leave to cool.

Put the meringue on a serving plate, fill the middle with the zabaglione and decorate with strawberries.

Crostata di albicocche e nocciole
Apricot and hazelnut tart

If you like hazelnuts, you'll love this tart: ground hazelnuts are used in the pastry and the filling. It's simple to make but looks and tastes like a tart bought from a top pastry shop. Caramelizing the apricots gives extra flavour and colour. You can make the pastry a day or so in advance and store it in the fridge. The tart is delicious just as it is, or serve with mascarpone cream or good vanilla ice cream.

Serves 6

for the pastry
250g/9oz/2 cups plain (all-purpose) flour, sifted, plus extra to dust
a pinch of salt
125g/4½ oz/generous ½ cup cold butter cut into small pieces, plus extra to grease
100g/3½oz/½ cup caster (superfine) sugar
50g/1¾oz/⅔ cup ground hazelnuts
1 egg yolk

for the filling
450g/1lb apricots, halved or quartered
2 tbsp caster (superfine) sugar
100g/3½oz/7 tbsp butter, at room temperature
2 eggs
20g/¾oz/1½ tbsp plain (all-purpose) flour, sifted
100g/3½oz/1⅓ cups ground hazelnuts
100g/3½oz/¾ cup icing (confectioners') sugar

First make the pastry. Put the flour and salt in a large bowl and rub in the butter until the mixture resembles breadcrumbs. Mix in the sugar and hazelnuts. Add the egg yolk and 2 tablespoons cold water and work into a smooth dough. Form into a ball, wrap in clingfilm (plastic wrap) and leave to rest in the fridge for at least 20 minutes.

Preheat the grill (broiler). Put the apricots on a baking sheet, sprinkle with caster sugar and place under the hot grill for about 10 minutes, until caramelized. Set aside.

Preheat the oven to 170°C/325°F/gas mark 3. Grease a 24cm/9½-inch round tart tin and dust with flour.

To make the filling, put the butter in a bowl and beat until creamy. Whisk in the eggs one at a time, then whisk in the flour, hazelnuts and icing sugar until smooth and well combined.

Roll out the pastry on a lightly floured surface and line the prepared tin. Add the filling and top with the caramelized apricots. Bake for 45–50 minutes, until golden. Leave to rest for at least 10 minutes, then slice and serve.

Torta gelata alle ciliege

Cherry sponge dessert

This stunning dessert is halfway between a *semi-freddo* (ice cream) and a mousse and is perfect in spring/summer when cherries are plentiful. It's very simple to make and looks amazing. You make two plain sponge cakes and a cherry mousse-like filling, then assemble it – and the freezer does the rest. It can be made in advance and taken out of the freezer about 30–40 minutes before serving.

Serves 8

for the sponge cakes
3 eggs
150g/5½oz/¾ cup caster (superfine)
 sugar
1 vanilla pod, split lengthways and
 seeds scraped out
a pinch of salt
150g/5½oz/1¼ cups self-raising flour,
 sifted
butter, to grease
150ml/5fl oz/²/₃ cup maraschino
 liqueur

for the filling
2 gelatine leaves
750g/1lb 10oz ripe sweet cherries,
 pitted
3 tbsp white wine
grated zest of ½ lemon
85g/3oz/scant ½ cup caster (superfine)
 sugar
300ml/10fl oz/1¼ cups double (heavy)
 cream, whipped

for the topping
7 tbsp apricot jam
150g/5½oz cherries, pitted and sliced
 in half
a few small mint leaves

Preheat the oven to 180°C/350°F/gas mark 4. Lightly grease 2 x 20cm/8-inch diameter round shallow cake tins and line with baking parchment. Line the bottom of a 20cm/8-inch diameter, 10cm/4-inch tall, loose-bottomed cake tin with baking parchment. Put the gelatine in a bowl of cold water to soften.

To make the sponge, whisk the eggs and sugar together in a bowl until light and fluffy. Fold in the vanilla seeds, salt and flour. Pour into the prepared shallow cake tins and bake for 15–20 minutes, until springy to the touch. Turn out and leave to cool on a wire rack.

To make the filling, put the cherries in a saucepan with the wine, lemon zest and sugar and cook on a medium heat, stirring all the time, until the cherries are very soft and the liquid has evaporated. Remove from the heat and blend until smooth. Squeeze the excess water out of the gelatine leaves and stir them into the cherry mixture until dissolved. Leave until cold, then add the whipped cream.

Put one sponge in the tall cake tin, smooth side down, drizzle over half the maraschino and pour in the cherry filling. Put the second sponge on top, smooth side up, gently pressing down with your fingers, and drizzle with the remaining maraschino. Cover with clingfilm (plastic wrap) and leave in the freezer for at least 2 hours.

Carefully remove the cake from the tin and place on a serving plate. Sieve the apricot jam and heat gently to make a smooth glaze. Brush the glaze over the top of the cake and decorate with cherries and a few mint leaves. Serve immediately or store in the fridge.

Pere al forno con amaretti e mandorle

Baked pears with amaretti biscuits and almonds

Italians love pears and in the autumn they often slow-cook the fruit, either on the hob or in the oven. This recipe is very simple to prepare; as the pears bake, their juices mix with the wine, cloves and lemon to produce a really delicious 'sauce'. The addition of almonds and amaretti biscuits give a nice crunchy texture. Serve the pears just as they are or with mascarpone cream, whipped cream or good vanilla ice cream.

Serves 4

4 large pears, such as Williams or Conference
175ml/6fl oz/¾ cup white wine
2 cloves
50g/1¾oz/¼ cup caster (superfine) sugar
grated zest and juice of ½ unwaxed lemon
30g/1oz/¼ cup flaked (slivered) almonds, crushed
30g/1oz amaretti biscuits, crushed
½ tsp ground cinnamon
2 tbsp Marsala wine
30g/1oz/2 tbsp butter, divided into eight pieces

Preheat the oven to 180°C/350°F/gas mark 4.

Slice the pears in half lengthways and remove the pips, scooping out a little of the flesh. Set aside.

Combine the wine, cloves, sugar, lemon zest and juice in an ovenproof dish. Add the pear halves, cover with foil and bake for 1 hour, until the pears are cooked through.

Meanwhile, combine the crushed almonds, amaretti and cinnamon.

Remove the pears from the oven. Add the Marsala to the liquid. Fill the pears with the almond mixture, top each with a piece of butter, cover with foil and return to the oven. After 20 minutes, remove the foil and return to the oven for 10 minutes.

Leave to cool slightly before serving. Serve with the juice drizzled over the top and some mascarpone cream or ice cream if desired.

Cassata Siciliana al forno, di Elisabetta

Elisabetta's Sicilian baked cassata with ricotta

This recipe was given to me by my friend, Italian food blogger and exceptional pastry cook, Elisabetta Iudica. She just loves to bake and made this lovely Sicilian dessert for me. It is a lighter, less sweet variation of the traditional marzipan cassata; fresh ricotta and chocolate chips fill a delicate sweet pastry. Delicious as an after-dinner dessert or for afternoon tea, or, for me, with a freshly made espresso. Thank you, Elisabetta, for sharing your recipe and for keeping Italian cooking traditions alive and kicking in your food blog, La Mia Kitchenette.

Serves 8

for the pastry
300g/10½oz/scant 2½ cups '00' flour, sifted, plus extra to dust
½ tsp baking powder
a pinch of salt
150g/5½oz/generous ½ cup unsalted butter, cut into small cubes, plus extra to grease
150g/5½oz/¾ cup caster (superfine) sugar
1 egg
2 egg yolks
icing (confectioners') sugar, to dust

for the filling
500g/1lb 2oz/2 cups fresh ricotta, drained if necessary
200g/7oz/1 cup caster (superfine) sugar
30g/1oz dark chocolate chips

First make the pastry. Combine the flour, baking powder and salt in a bowl and rub in the butter until the mixture resembles breadcrumbs. Stir in the sugar, add the egg and yolks and work into a smooth dough. Alternatively, put all the ingredients in a food processor and whizz until they come together. Form the dough into a ball, wrap in clingfilm (plastic wrap) and leave in the fridge for a couple of hours.

Meanwhile, to make the filling, combine the ricotta, sugar and chocolate chips, but do not overmix. Cover with clingfilm and leave in the fridge until ready to use.

Preheat the oven to 170°C/325°F/gas mark 3. Lightly grease and flour a 20cm/8-inch round loose-bottomed cake tin.

Take about two-thirds of the pastry, roll out on a lightly floured surface and line the bottom and sides of the prepared tin. Using a fork, prick all over the pastry to prevent bubbles. Fill with the ricotta mixture, smoothing it over. Roll out the remaining pastry and cover the ricotta mixture, flattening it with your hand; seal around the edge with a fork, ensuring there are no gaps; the cake must be flat without a raised border.

Bake for 50–60 minutes, until golden all over. Leave to cool before removing from the tin and then leave for at least 2 hours before serving. Dust with icing sugar and serve.

Pampapato
Spiced chocolate treat

This nutty and spicy dense chocolate sweet treat originates from the province of Ferrara in Emilia-Romagna. The name *pampapato* means 'bread of the pope' because it was traditionally made in monasteries and convents and is shaped like the cap worn by the pope. Very simple to make, it is slow-baked at a low temperature. It is best made a couple of days before consuming. It is quite rich, so cut into thin slices when serving. Actually, it makes a nice energy snack when you're on the go and in need of a boost.

Serves 6

200g/7oz/generous 1½ cups plain (all-purpose) flour
100g/3½oz/⅔ cup whole almonds
100g/3½oz/generous 1 cup unsweetened cocoa powder
70g/2½oz/⅓ cup caster (superfine) sugar
50g/1¾oz/2½ tbsp runny honey
1 tsp mixed spice
20g/¾oz/2 tbsp raisins
125ml/4fl oz/½ cup milk
a little extra virgin olive oil, to rub
100g/3½oz dark chocolate

Preheat the oven to 150°C/300°F/gas mark 2. Line a baking sheet with greaseproof (waxed) paper.

Combine the flour, almonds, cocoa, sugar, honey, spice and raisins in a bowl. Gradually stir in the milk and mix well with your hands. Form into a domed shape about 12cm/5 inches in diameter, place on the prepared baking sheet, coat your hands with a little extra virgin olive oil and massage all over the *pampapato*. Bake for 1½ hours.

Remove from the oven and leave to cool completely.

Melt the chocolate in a heatproof bowl over a saucepan of gently simmering water and pour over the *pampapato*, spreading with a palette knife. Leave until set, and store in an airtight container until required.

Tiramisu al passito e arancia
Tiramisu with passito and orange

This popular dessert can be seen on menus of Italian restaurants all over the world. It is usually made with espresso coffee and sometimes double (heavy) cream is added, too. To make it less calorific I have simply used mascarpone, which in itself is rich, and to give it a bit of a twist I have used orange juice and a little *passito*, a Sicilian dessert wine, to soak the biscuits. If you don't have *passito* you can use another sweet wine, or if making this for children, omit the alcohol altogether. Make sure you use fresh orange juice, as the bought stuff can be sweet and sickly. Simple to prepare, with no cooking involved, it's not an 'instant' dessert because it is best made the day before and left to set in the fridge.

Serves 4

1 egg yolk
1 tbsp caster (superfine) sugar
½ vanilla pod, split lengthways and
    seeds scraped out
250g/9oz/generous 1 cup mascarpone
    cheese
175ml/6fl oz/¾ cup freshly squeezed
    orange juice
1 tbsp *passito*, or other sweet wine
12 savoiardi biscuits
cocoa powder, sifted, to dust
grated zest of ½ orange

Combine the egg yolk, sugar and vanilla seeds in a bowl and whisk until creamy. Add the mascarpone and continue to whisk until well mixed. Set aside.

Combine the orange juice and wine. Dip the biscuits quickly into this liquid, letting them absorb a little but not too much, otherwise they will fall apart. Line a large glass dish or four individual dishes with some of the biscuits, followed by a layer of the mascarpone mixture and, depending on the size of your dish, continue making layers like this, ending up with the mascarpone. Dust with cocoa powder and top with a little orange zest. Leave in the fridge for at least 6 hours or overnight.

Ciambella alle mandorle

Almond tea cake

This is similar to a tea loaf but round and plaited (braided) in traditional Italian *ciambella* style. Italian housewives often made a cake just like this one to use leftover bread dough. Not very sweet but with the subtle taste of almonds, this is a perfect tea time treat or delicious for breakfast with a cappuccino.

Serves 6-8

1 x 7g sachet of dried yeast
200ml/7fl oz/scant 1 cup lukewarm milk
600g/1lb 5oz/5 cups strong (bread) flour, plus extra to dust
½ vanilla pod, split lengthways and seeds scraped out
100g/3½oz/½ cup caster (superfine) sugar
100g/3½oz/1 cup ground almonds
100g/3½oz/¾ cup sultanas (golden raisins)
125g/4½oz/generous ½ cup butter, melted
60g/2¼oz/½ cup flaked (slivered) almonds
a little icing (confectioners') sugar, sifted, to dust

Check the instructions on the packet of yeast; if necessary, dissolve the yeast in the milk.

In a large bowl, combine the flour, vanilla seeds, sugar, ground almonds and sultanas. Make a well in the centre and gradually add the yeast and milk followed by 100g/3½oz/7 tbsp of the butter, mixing with your hands to form a dough. Knead on a lightly floured surface for about 5 minutes, cover with a clean tea towel and leave to rise in a warm place for 2 hours.

Divide the dough into three equal parts and roll each into a long sausage shape, roughly 55cm/22 inches in length. Plait the dough and join at the end to make a round cake. Line a baking sheet with baking parchment, put the ciambella on top, cover with a clean tea towel and leave to rise for 30 minutes.

Preheat the oven to 200°C/400°F/gas mark 6.

Bake the ciambella for 35 minutes. Remove from the oven, brush the top with the remaining melted butter, sprinkle with flaked almonds and return to the oven for 10 minutes. Leave on a wire rack to cool slightly and dust with icing sugar before serving.

Pastiera di grano
Springtime wheat and ricotta pie

It is believed that this dessert dates back to pagan times, when ancient Neapolitans in springtime offered all the fruits of their land to the mermaid Partenope: eggs for fertility, wheat from the land, ricotta from the shepherds, the aroma of orange flowers, vanilla to symbolize faraway countries and sugar in honour of the sweet mermaid. It is said the mermaid took all these ingredients, immersed herself in the sea of the Bay of Naples and gave back to the Neapolitans a dessert that symbolized fertility and rebirth. The recipe as we know it today was first made in Neapolitan convents; the nuns would make it for the local nobility. Today in the region of Campania, Easter would not be the same without this traditional dessert. It is found in pastry shops all over the region and also made at home, usually in large quantities, to be given away as gifts to family and friends. The pre-cooked wheat is sold in jars in good Italian delis. Alternatively, you can make it with pearl barley, cooked according to the instructions on the packet. The pies can be made a few days in advance and stored in the fridge until required.

Makes 2 x 18cm/7-inch round pies; about 8 servings

for the pastry

250g/9oz/2 cups plain (all-purpose) flour, plus extra to dust

100g/3½oz/7 tbsp cold butter, cut into small pieces

100g/3½oz/½ cup caster (superfine) sugar

grated zest of 1 orange

2 egg yolks

a little milk, to brush

a little icing (confectioners') sugar, to dust

First make the pastry. Sift the flour into a large bowl and rub in the butter until the mixture resembles breadcrumbs. Stir in the sugar and orange zest, add the egg yolks and mix to form a smooth dough. Form into a ball, wrap in clingfilm (plastic wrap) and leave in the fridge for at least 1 hour.

To make the filling, put the wheat, milk, butter and cinnamon in a small saucepan on a low heat and bring to the boil, stirring all the time, until the wheat has absorbed all the milk and the mixture is creamy. Leave to cool.

To make the crema pasticciera, put the milk in a small saucepan together with the vanilla pod and place on a medium–low heat until the milk reaches boiling point. Meanwhile, whisk the egg yolks and sugar together in a bowl until light and fluffy, add the cornflour and whisk until smooth. When the milk reaches boiling point, remove from the heat, discard the vanilla pod and gradually pour the milk into the egg mixture, whisking all the time to prevent lumps from forming. Once well combined, pour the mixture back into the saucepan on a medium heat and stir with a wooden spoon. As soon as it begins to boil, remove from the heat immediately and leave to cool.

for the filling

350g/12oz pre-cooked wheat or cooked
  pearl barley
150ml/5fl oz/⅔ cup full-fat milk
20g/¾oz/1½ tbsp butter
a pinch of ground cinnamon
350g/12oz/1½ cups ricotta
½ vanilla pod, split lengthways and
  seeds scraped out
250g/9oz/1¼ cups caster (superfine)
  sugar
grated zest of 1 orange
1 tbsp orange-flower water
3 eggs
2 egg yolks

for the crema pasticciera

200ml/7fl oz/scant 1 cup milk
¼ vanilla pod
2 egg yolks
85g/3oz/scant ½ cup caster (superfine)
  sugar
20g/¾oz/2½ tbsp cornflour
  (cornstarch)

Take the wheat mixture and whisk in the ricotta, vanilla seeds, sugar, orange zest and orange-flower water; gradually mix in the eggs and yolks. Add the crema pasticciera and combine well together. Set aside.

Preheat the oven to 180°C/350°F/gas mark 4.

Roll out the pastry on a lightly floured surface and line 2 x 18cm/7-inch diameter round loose-bottomed pie dishes or shallow cake tins, reserving the trimmings. Pour in the wheat and ricotta mixture. Roll out the pastry trimmings and cut out long strips about 2cm/¾ inch wide; arrange these criss-cross over the pies. Brush a little milk over the strips, then bake for 50 minutes, until golden brown.

Switch the oven off and leave the pies to set in the warm oven for about an hour. Remove and leave to cool completely. Sift over some icing sugar before serving.

Torrone
Italian nougat

Torrone is a nougat traditionally enjoyed at Christmas time in Italy; probably the most famous Italian torrone comes from Cremona in northern Italy, where legend has it that it was first made for an important wedding in the fifteenth century. Although torrone is normally bought from shops, you can make it at home. This recipe is a labour of love. Be prepared to spend a couple of hours stirring - ideally get someone to help you. You can flavour the torrone any way you wish - add candied fruit, orange zest, vanilla, cinnamon or coat it with melted chocolate. Slice in chunks, wrap in pretty tissue paper and ribbon and you have a lovely present.

Makes 500g/1lb 2oz

30g/1oz/3 tbsp shelled pistachio nuts
200g/7oz/1⅓ cups whole almonds, skinned
100g/3½oz/¾ cup whole hazelnuts, skinned
a sheet of rice paper
a little walnut oil, to grease 150g/5½oz/ scant ½ cup runny honey
150g/5½oz/¾ cup caster (superfine) sugar
2 egg whites
grated zest of 1 lemon (reserve the lemon)

Toasting nuts
Preheat the oven to 180°C/350°F/gas mark 4. Put the nuts on a baking sheet and toast for about 15 minutes, until light golden brown and crunchy. If you haven't been able to find skinned nuts, toasting will make it easy to rub off the skins. Set aside to cool.

First toast all the nuts (see tip). You will need a small loaf tin, about 19 x 8cm/7½ x 3¼ inches. Cut a piece of rice paper the same size as the bottom of the tin and another piece slightly larger and set aside. Lightly grease the sides of the tin with walnut oil and turn upside down so the oil doesn't run on the bottom of the tin.

Put the honey in a saucepan and cook over another pan of gently simmering water (or use a double-boiler), stirring all the time with a wooden spoon for 1½ hours.

About 20 minutes before the end of this time, put the sugar and 3 tablespoons water in a small saucepan on a low heat for 15–20 minutes, stirring until the sugar has dissolved and is syrupy. In a clean bowl, whisk the egg whites until stiff. Gradually fold the egg whites into the honey, still cooking over simmering water, and stir well for 5 minutes. Gradually stir in the syrup. Continue to stir for 30 minutes.

Stir the nuts and lemon zest into the honey mixture. Line the loaf tin with the smaller piece of rice paper and pour in the honey mixture, pressing well with a wet spatula, then press well again with half a lemon. Put the remaining piece of rice paper over the top, pressing well with your hands. Leave to rest for 2 hours in a cool place – but not in the fridge.

Tip the torrone out of the tin onto a board and slice with a sharp knife. If you want to give the torrone as a gift, wrap it in greaseproof (waxed) paper and store in an airtight container for up to 2 months.

Panettone

Traditional Italian Christmas cake

If you have ever wondered how to make your own panettone, and you enjoy a challenge as well as have a day to spare, this recipe is for you. The dough needs to rest at the end of each stage: this is what gives panettone its characteristic lightness. And of course you can get on with other things during these times. Ideally you will have a loose-bottomed panettone tin, 18cm/ 7 inches in diameter and 10cm/4 inches high – you could also use a slightly shallower and wider loose-bottomed cake tin.

There are many legends about how this cake originated and it appears that in ancient times the Romans sweetened a dough-like cake with honey; it is also said that poor people added a little dried fruit and sugar to bread dough as a Christmas treat. However, panettone as we know it today was created in Milan by two pastry chefs, Motta and Alemagna, in the early twentieth century. Its popularity spread over the years and it is produced industrially by many large companies, making it affordable for all Italians and becoming Italy's leading Christmas cake. In recent years it has evolved with flavourings such as chocolate, liqueur cream and others, but I find the original one with dried fruit and candied peel the best. In Italy panettone is traditionally served with a glass of *spumante* (light sparkling wine) at the end of the Christmas meal, but it is equally delicious with dessert wine or simply a nice cup of espresso or even tea.

Makes a 1.2kg/2lb 10oz cake

125g/4½oz/¾ cup sultanas (golden raisins)
1 tbsp rum
12g/¼oz fresh yeast
150g/5½oz/¾ cup caster (superfine) sugar, plus 1 tsp
4 tbsp lukewarm milk
500g/1lb 2oz/4 cups '00' flour
4 eggs, plus 3 egg yolks
150g/5½oz/generous ½ cup butter, softened at room temperature, plus a knob for the top
3g salt
40g/1½oz candied peel
grated zest of 1 lemon
1 vanilla pod, split lengthways and seeds scraped out

Step 1
Soak the sultanas with the rum and a little lukewarm water and set aside.

Dissolve 10g of the yeast together with 1 tsp sugar in the milk. Put 100g/3½oz/generous ¾ cup flour in a bowl, pour in the yeast mixture and work into a smooth dough. Form into a ball, cover the bowl with clingfilm (plastic wrap) and leave to rest in a warm place for about 1 hour, until it has doubled in size.

Step 2
Add 2 eggs to the bowl, crumble in the remaining yeast, add 175g/6oz/1½ cups flour and mix well. Add 60g/2¼oz sugar and 60g/2¼oz butter and use your hands to incorporate all the ingredients to form a sticky dough. Form into a ball, cover the bowl with clingfilm and leave to rest in a warm place for 2 hours, until it has doubled in size.

Step 3

Drain and squeeze the excess liquid out of the sultanas and set aside.

Add the remaining 2 eggs, 3 yolks and the remaining flour to the dough and work with your hands for 10 minutes – the dough will still be quite sticky. Mix in the remaining sugar and the salt. Mix in 50g/1¾oz butter until well amalgamated, then add the remaining butter. Add the candied peel, lemon zest, sultanas and vanilla seeds. Mix well, cover the bowl with clingfilm and leave in a warm place for at least 2 hours, until the mixture has doubled in size.

Step 4

Meanwhile, lightly grease a loose-bottomed panettone tin, 18cm/7 inches in diameter and 10cm/4 inches high (or other cake tin) and line with baking parchment.

Turn the dough mixture onto a lightly floured work surface and work for a minute, then place in the prepared tin, cover with clingfilm and leave to rest in a warm place for at least 2 hours, until it has doubled in size.

Preheat the oven to 200°C/400°F/gas mark 6.

Using a small sharp knife, make a cross on the top and place a knob of butter in the middle. Place on the bottom shelf of the oven and bake for 15 minutes. Reduce the oven to 190°C/375°F/gas mark 5 and continue to bake for 45 minutes. If you notice the top of the cake getting too dark too quickly, reduce the oven temperature to 180°C/350°F/gas mark 4.

Remove from the oven and leave to cool slightly in the tin. Remove from the tin and leave to cool on a wire rack.

Babà all'arancia
Orange-infused baba

Babà is a classic Neapolitan dessert which, according to legend, was introduced by the French and is usually made with rum. In my region, where lemons are plentiful, the pastry shops often make it with *limoncello* liqueur. For this recipe, I decided to give oranges a go, and they really work well. You need to make this at least one day before you intend to serve it because, once cooked, it needs to be 'dried out' overnight before being soaked in the syrup. This is the original large babà, made in a ring mould, rather than the small babàs sold in pastry shops.

Serves 8-10

450g/1lb/scant 4 cups '00' flour
50g/1¾oz/¼ cup caster (superfine) sugar
a pinch of salt
40g/1½oz fresh yeast, diluted in 2 tbsp lukewarm water
8 eggs
150g/5½oz/generous ½ cup butter, softened, plus extra to grease

for the syrup
2 large oranges
400g/14oz/2 cups granulated sugar
100ml/3½fl oz/scant ½ cup orange liqueur, or more if you prefer a stronger taste

Grease a 22cm/8½-inch fluted babà or savarin mould with butter.

Combine the flour, sugar, salt and yeast mixture in a large bowl. Whisk in the eggs and softened butter for about 10 minutes, until the mixture comes away from the sides of the bowl. Cover with a clean tea towel and leave to rise in a warm place for 30 minutes, until the mixture has doubled in size. Beat the mixture for a minute, then pour into the greased mould and leave to rise in a warm place for 20 minutes. Preheat the oven to 180°C/350°F/gas mark 4.

Bake the babà for 40 minutes, until well risen and golden brown. Leave to cool slightly in the mould, then turn out onto a wire rack and leave to dry out overnight.

Meanwhile, make the syrup. Using a vegetable peeler, peel the zest of the oranges in strips, taking care not to remove any of the white pith; set aside a few pieces and cut into thinner strips. Put the sugar in a saucepan and add 1.5 litres/2¾ pints/1½ quarts water and the orange zest, stir well until the sugar has dissolved, bring to the boil, reduce the heat and simmer very gently for 1 hour. Strain through a fine sieve and leave to cool. Add the orange liqueur and set aside.

Put the syrup in a container large enough to hold the babà. Very carefully place the babà inside and, using a ladle, drizzle the syrup all over the cake. When well soaked, carefully remove the babà, with the help of a fish slice, and place on a serving plate. Decorate with the reserved orange zest and serve.

Preserves

Preserving fruit and veg at the end of summer was a normal part of life when I was growing up. It was a way of keeping the scents and flavours of produce long after it was in season and was also a good reason to get together with friends and family – we celebrated the end of a bountiful season and went to work to preserve as much as we possibly could to see us through the winter. Bell peppers, aubergines (eggplants), courgettes (zucchini) and green beans were all preserved and we knew we would have to wait until the next summer before these vegetables reappeared in our gardens and market stalls. But also, in preserving, the taste changed, resulting in wonderful ingredients for antipasti or fillings for panini.

Our beloved tomato was the highlight of those late summer days – family and friends would gather together to bottle, sun-dry and make *concentrato* (tomato purée/paste) in the last of the hot summer sun. My job, as a boy, was to collect as many beer bottles as I could, in which to store a year-long supply of our local San Marzano tomatoes, grown around the Vesuvio area. Whole days would be spent carefully preserving tomatoes, and not just in our family: everyone in the village did the same – we even exchanged them as gifts to see whose tomatoes were nicer.

I still like to preserve as much as I can, and whenever I go on a mushroom hunt and strike lucky with basketfuls, I make sure they never go wasted and preserve them in oil to enjoy later in the year, usually at Christmas time. And when my friend Paolo has a glut of vegetables grown in his allotment, he shares them with me so they can be preserved. This year was it was beetroot and green beans. Markets are a great way of buying quantities of produce at good value, so if I see peppers or aubergines sold in bulk, as long as they are fresh, I buy them with preserving in mind.

Fruit, too, gets bottled; I love summer walks in the forest and fields and am always on the lookout for tiny damson plums, wild cherries and berries. Not only to be made into delicious jam but also to preserve in alcohol to liven up desserts.

Making preserves and bottling fruits and vegetables is a wonderful stress buster for me – not only do I enjoy foraging outdoors, I also love the ritual of preparing what I have collected, organizing the jars and putting them into my store cupboard. When the jars eventually get opened, each one has a story to tell – it may be where I picked that particular fruit or what sort of day it had been – and the taste of summer suddenly brightens up the dull of winter.

Zucchini crudi sott'olio
Preserved raw courgettes

Makes 1 x 500ml/18fl oz/2¼ cup jar

500g/1lb 2oz courgettes (zucchini),
  sliced into long, chunky matchsticks
2 garlic cloves, sliced
1 tsp dried oregano
1½ tsp salt
½ red chilli, finely sliced (optional)
  about 300ml/10fl oz/1¼ cups white
  wine vinegar
sunflower oil, to cover

Sterilize a 500ml/18fl oz/2¼ cup jar (see below).

Put the courgette matchsticks in a bowl with the garlic, oregano, salt, chilli (if using) and vinegar, making sure the vinegar completely covers the courgettes. Cover with a lid or greaseproof (waxed) paper, put a weight on top and leave to marinate for about 2 hours.

Drain off the liquid, reserving the garlic and chilli, and gently squeeze out the excess liquid from the courgettes. Place the courgettes together with the garlic and chilli in the sterilized jar and pour in the oil, making sure you completely cover the courgettes with oil. Secure with a lid, label and store in a cool, dark, dry place for at least 2 weeks before using. Once opened, store in the fridge.

Preserving basics
• Always use very fresh, good-quality vegetables and fruit.
• To sterilize jars, wash and thoroughly clean all the jars and lids you are going to use, then rinse the jars with a little white wine vinegar. Leave to drain, then dry well. Place the jars and lids in a large pan of boiling water and boil for a couple of minutes. Remove, drain and dry well.
• To pasteurize: once you have placed the preserves in jars, seal well, preferably using hermetically sealed lids. Wrap each jar in old kitchen cloths: this prevents it from breaking during boiling. Line a large pan with kitchen cloth. Place the wrapped jars in the pan and add enough cold water to cover them by 3cm/1 inch. Bring the water to the boil, then reduce the heat to medium and boil for the time stated in the recipe. Turn off the heat, but leave the jars in the water until it is cold. Remove the jars and unwrap, then dry with a clean tea towel, label and store in a cool, dark, dry cupboard.
• Before you store your preserves, remember to label them with their name and the date you made them.

Pomodori esiccati a casa

Home-dried tomatoes

In southern Italy, where the summers are hot, it is common to see trays and trays of tomatoes drying out on people's balconies and roof terraces. The taste is amazing, much nicer than industrially made sun-dried tomatoes, and I always try to bring some back with me. In England, where the summers are not so reliable, you can recreate this way of drying by using the oven on a very low heat. These are best made towards the end of August, when plum tomatoes are plentiful. It's worth making quite a lot seeing as the oven has to be on for such a long time. Very simple to prepare: you put them in the oven and forget about them – even if they go over the 6 hours' cooking time, no harm will come to them. Smaller tomatoes will probably need less time. Once dried out, you can use them immediately or preserve them in oil.

2kg/4lb 8oz ripe but firm plum
   tomatoes
salt

Preheat the oven to 100°C/210°F/gas mark ¼ or lower. Line a baking sheet with greaseproof (waxed) paper.

Slice the tomatoes in half lengthways, place on the baking sheet, skin side down, sprinkle with salt and place in the oven for about 6 hours. If after this time there is still liquid left, leave in the oven for a little longer to dry out completely; this will depend on the size of the tomatoes.

Remove from the oven and leave to cool.

Tips for using dried tomatoes
• Dress with extra virgin olive oil, garlic, fresh basil and dried oregano; add to a salad, top a bruschetta or pizza, or use in a pasta sauce.
• Preserve in sterilized jars (see page 172); make layers of dried tomatoes, basil leaves, a pinch of dried oregano and extra virgin olive oil, making sure you cover the tomatoes completely with the oil. Cover with a sterilized lid and store in a cool, dark, dry place.

Porcini sott'olio
Preserved porcini mushrooms

Porcino, cep or penny bun – the king of the forest during the autumn mushroom season. The succulent, delicate taste of this highly prized fungi is hard to beat and always a winner with hunters and restaurateurs. I love to search for them in the forests and when I spot the first one, I'm like a child, excited and eager to find more. If I find lots, I usually enjoy a plateful sautéed or with some pasta, but the rest I preserve so that I can enjoy them later in the year and give them away as presents to friends. Preserved porcini are delicious served as part of an antipasto of cured meats, alongside other preserved vegetables.

Makes 1kg/2lb 4oz

1kg/2lb 4oz fresh porcini mushrooms
300ml/10fl oz/1¼ cups white wine
   vinegar
2 tsp salt
8 black peppercorns
4 bay leaves
1 sprig of thyme
2 cloves
1-3 red chillies (optional)
   about 500ml/18fl oz/2¼ cups olive oil

Carefully clean the porcini, removing any earth and impurities with a small knife or brush, then go over them with a slightly damp cloth – don't wash the mushrooms or they will lose their lovely flavour. Trim the stems slightly; leave the smaller mushrooms whole and slice the larger ones.

Put the vinegar and 700ml/1¼ pints/2¾ cups water in a large pan together with the salt, peppercorns and bay leaves and bring to the boil. Add the porcini and boil for 4 minutes. Remove with a slotted spoon and leave to drain on a clean tea towel, cover with another clean tea towel and leave to dry out overnight.

Sterilize jars with a total volume of 1 litre/1¾ pints/ 4 cups (see page 172).

Put the mushrooms into the sterilized jars together with the thyme, cloves and a chilli (if using) and cover completely with olive oil. Secure with a lid and pasteurize for 30 minutes (see page 172). Label and store in a cool, dark, dry place for at least 1 month before using. Once opened, store in the fridge.

Barbabietole sott'aceto
Preserved beetroot in vinegar

Makes 1 x 1 litre/1¾ pint/4 cup jar

700g/1lb 9oz organic beetroot (beets)
a pinch of salt
450ml/16fl oz/2 cups white wine
  vinegar
½ celery stalk, finely sliced
15 juniper berries
5 black peppercorns
2 bay leaves

Sterilize a 1 litre/1¾ pint/4 cup jar (see page 172).

Wash the beetroot to remove all the dirt, place in a pan, cover with cold water, add some salt, bring to the boil and cook for 1½ hours, or until tender.

Drain and leave to cool. Carefully remove the skins, then slice the beetroot in halves or quarters and place them in the sterilized jar.

Put the vinegar and 3 tablespoons water in a small pan together with the celery, juniper berries, peppercorns and bay leaves. Bring to the boil, then boil for 3 minutes. Leave to cool, then pour over the beetroot in the jar. Secure with a lid and pasteurize for 20 minutes (see page 172). Label and store in a cool, dark, dry place for 2 weeks before using.

Peperonata sott'olio
Preserved peperonata

These tasty preserved peppers and tomatoes (photograph on page 182) are wonderful as part of a selection of mixed antipasto.

Makes 2 x 750ml/1¼ pint/3 cup jars

6 tbsp extra virgin olive oil
2 red onions, finely sliced
2 large garlic cloves, quartered
1 red chilli, finely sliced
1kg/2lb 4oz mixed (bell) peppers, sliced
  into thick strips
600g/1lb 5oz tomatoes, sliced
a handful of basil leaves
a pinch of salt
3 tsp capers
10 green olives
a pinch of dried oregano
about 400ml/14fl oz/1²/₃ cups sunflower
oil

Sterilize 2 x 750ml/1¼ pint/3 cup jars (see page 172).

Heat the olive oil in a saucepan, add the onions, garlic and chilli and sweat for a couple of minutes. Add the peppers, tomatoes, basil and salt, and gently stir. Cook on a medium heat for 5 minutes, then leave to cool.

Stir in the capers, olives and oregano. Fill the sterilized jars with the mixture and pour in enough sunflower oil to cover. Secure with lids and pasteurize for 25 minutes (see page 172). Label and store in a cool, dark, dry place. Once opened, store in the fridge.

Fagiolini della Regina Margherita
Preserved green beans

Makes 1 x 600ml/20fl oz/2½ cup jar

400g/14oz green beans, topped
  and tailed
salt
375ml/13fl oz/generous 1½ cups white
  wine vinegar
1 clove
2 basil leaves
small strip of lemon zest
6 tarragon leaves
1 small shallot, cut in half
6 black peppercorns
1 garlic clove, left whole
1 red chilli (optional)
about 4 tbsp sunflower oil

Sterilize a 600ml/20fl oz/2½ cup jar (see page 172).

Bring a pan of lightly salted water to the boil, add the beans and boil for 3 minutes. Drain and leave to cool.

Put the vinegar, clove, basil, lemon zest, tarragon, shallot, peppercorns and garlic in a small pan. Bring to the boil, then boil for 1 minute. Remove from the heat and leave to cool.

Fill the sterilized jar with the beans, pour over the vinegar mixture and top with a little oil. Secure with a lid and pasteurize for 20 minutes (see page 172). Label and store in a cool, dark, dry place.

Marmellata di limone
Lemon marmalade

I grew up with lemons – the best type, too, from Amalfi. We used them in a lot of our cooking, for medicinal purposes or just sliced and eaten on their own. Strangely, though, lemon marmalade was not made; it was not until I came to England that I discovered the delights of marmalade. In more recent years, oranges and lemons, which grow in abundance in southern Italy, have begun to appear in the form of jams and preserves. This lemon marmalade is really simple to make; the secret is to buy the best lemons you can find. It is not only good on toast, but is also delicious served with cheese. This recipe is very natural and a must for lemon lovers – if you prefer a less bitter taste, I suggest you boil the lemon peel another couple of times in addition to the one mentioned in this recipe.

Makes about 500ml/18fl oz/2 cups

1kg/2lb 4oz unwaxed organic lemons
500g/1lb 2oz/2½ cups granulated sugar

Wash and dry the lemons well, then peel and set the peel aside. Remove and discard the pith. Slice the lemons very finely, discarding any pips. Place in a non-metallic container. Add the sugar and mix well together, cover with clingfilm (plastic wrap) and leave to macerate for 12 hours.

Sterilize jars with a total volume of 500ml/18fl oz/ 2 cups (see page 172).

Finely chop the peel and place in a pan with water to cover, bring to the boil, then boil for 1 minute. Drain well.

Put the peel and sugary lemons in a saucepan and cook on a low heat for about 1 hour, until the marmalade begins to thicken. Remove from the heat, pour into sterilized jars, cover with lids, turn upside down and leave until cold. Label and store in your cupboard. Once opened, store in the fridge.

Lamponi e mirtilli sotto spirito
Raspberries and blueberries preserved in alcohol

I love to preserve summer fruit and enjoy it during the winter, when these fruits and the long sunny days are a distant memory. Soft fruit preserved in alcohol makes an extra special treat, especially at Christmas time, to serve as a dessert with some mascarpone or double (heavy) cream or as an accompaniment to chocolate cake or citrus tart. You can use the same method for cherries and tiny plums. You can also drink the fruit-infused alcohol, but please, be careful, not too much! You can buy pure alcohol from good Italian delis.

Makes 3

litres/5¼ cups/3 quarts
500g/1lb 2oz raspberries
500g/1lb 2oz blueberries
1 litre/1¾ pints/4 cups pure alcohol
800g/1lb 12oz/4 cups granulated sugar
zest of 1 orange, peeled in long strips
zest of 1 lemon, peeled in long strips

Put the berries in a large bowl, add the alcohol, cover with clingfilm (plastic wrap) and leave in a dry, dark place for 3 days.

Sterilize 3 x 1-litre/1¾-pint/4-cup jars (see page 172).

Put 1 litre/1¾ pints/4 cups water in a saucepan with the sugar, orange and lemon zests and place on a gentle heat, stirring until the sugar has dissolved. Leave to cool completely and then strain through a fine sieve.

Drain the fruit, reserving the alcohol. Combine the alcohol with the strained sugar syrup. Put the fruit in the sterilized jars to about one-third full, then add the liquid until the fruit is covered. Cover the jars with their lids and label. Leave for at least a month before using. Before serving, place in the fridge to enjoy cold.

Index

Dedication

To Jamie Oliver, who once learned from me and now I learn from him.

Acknowledgements

Thanks to: Liz Przybylski, for writing; Adriana Contaldo, for testing recipes; Laura Edwards for the photography; Tabitha Hawkins for prop styling; Lucy O'Reilly for cooking and styling at the photoshoots; Becca Spry, Maggie Ramsay and the team at Pavilion Books; Luigi Bonomi; Pat Herlihy at Russell Hume Butchers for excellent meat; Enzo Zaccarini at Vincenzo and Martin Levy at Fresh Direct for their lovely fruit & veg.

———

First published in the United Kingdom as
Gennaro Slow Cook Italian in 2015 by
Pavilion
43 Great Ormond Street
London WC1N 3HZ
This edition published in 2018

www.pavilionbooks.com

ISBN: 978-1-911624-49-3

A CIP catalogue record for this book is available from the British Library

10 9 8 7 6 5 4 3 2 1

Reproduction by Mission Productions Ltd., Hong Kong
Printed and bound by Times, Malaysia